John Watts

The massacres of St. Bartholomew, outside of Paris

24th Aug.-4th Sept., 1572

John Watts

**The massacres of St. Bartholomew, outside of Paris**
*24th Aug.-4th Sept., 1572*

ISBN/EAN: 9783743438170

Printed in Europe, USA, Canada, Australia, Japan

Cover: Foto ©ninafisch / pixelio.de

Manufactured and distributed by brebook publishing software (www.brebook.com)

John Watts

The massacres of St. Bartholomew, outside of Paris

The Massacre of St. Bartholomew,
⁂   outside of Paris.   ⁂
24th Aug.,—4th Sept., 1572.

Gypsies.
*Information Translated and Gathered from various sources.*
June, 1885. New York.

The Literature of the Thirty Years War.
*Army & Navy Quarterly. Vol. 1, No. 4 Oct. 1885.*

Torstenson · before · Vienna,
or the Swedes in Austria in 1645-1646,
with a Biographical Sketch of Field
Marshal, Generalissimus, Leonard
Torstenson.
November, 1885.

Francesca da Rimini,
*December, 1885.*

by ¹Watts de Peyster, Brevet Major-Gen. S.N.Y
Sole Honorary Member Third Corps (A. of the P.)
Gettysburgh Reunion Association; of the
Honorary Committee; and Associate
Member of the Military Service
Institution of the U. S.
&c., &c., &c.

# LIST OF PUBLICATIONS.

## J. Watts de Peyster:
### LL. D.

Master of Arts, Columbia College, of New York, 1872.—Hon. Mem. Clarendon Hist. Soc., Edinburgh, Scotland; of the New Brunswick Hist. Soc., St. John, Canada; of the Hist. Soc. of Minnesota, Montana, New Jersey, &c.; Life Mem. Royal Hist. Soc. of Great Britain, London, Eng.; Mem. Maatschappij Nederlandsche, Letterkunde, Leyden, Holland, &c., &c.—Colonel N. Y. S. I., 1846, assigned for "*meritorious conduct*" to command of 22d Regimental District, M. F. S. N. Y., 1849, Brigadier General for "*important service*" [first appointment—in N. Y. State—to that rank, hitherto elective], 1851, M. F. S. N. Y.—Adjutant General, S. N. Y., 1855.—Brevet Major-General, S. N. Y., for "*meritorious services*," by "Special Act" or "Concurrent Resolution," N. Y. State Legislature, April, 1866 [first and only General officer receiving such an honor (the highest) from S. N. Y., and the only officer * thus brevetted (Major-General) in the United States.]

### AUTHOR OF

REPORTS—1st. On the Organizations of the National Guards and Municipal Military Institutions of Europe, and the Artillery and Arms best adapted to the State Service, 1852. (Reprinted by order of the N. Y. State Legislature, Senate Documents, No. 74, March 26, 1853.) 2d. Organizations of the English and Swiss Militia, the French, Swiss, and Prussian Fire Departments. Suggestions for the Organization of the N. Y. Militia, &c. 1853.

Life of (the Swedish Field Marshal) Leonard Torstenson (rewarded with three splendid Silver Medals, &c., by H. R. M. Oscar I., King of Sweden). 1855.—Thirty Years War, and Military Services of Field-Marshal Generalissimo Leonard Torstenson (Series), N. Y. Weekly Mail, 1873; A Hero of the XVII. Century (Torstenson).—The Volunteer, Weekly Mag., Vol. I., No. I., 1869.—The Career of the celebrated Condottiere Fra Moreale, Weekly Mail, 1873.—Frederic the Great. (Series.) Weekly Mail, 1873.—Eulogy of Torstenson, 4to., 1872.

The Dutch at the North Pole, and the Dutch in Maine. 1857.

Appendix to the Dutch at the North Pole, &c. 1858.

Ho, for the North Pole! 1860.—"Littell's Living Age."—The Dutch Battle of the Baltic. 1858.

The Invincible Armada. (Series.) 1860.—Examples of Intrepidity, as illustrated by the Exploits and Deaths of the Dutch Admirals. (Series.) 1860-1. Military Gazette.

Gems from Dutch History. (Series.) 1855.—A Tale of Leipsic, Peabody's Parlor Mag., 1832.

Carausius, the Dutch Augustus, and Emperor of Britain and the Menapii. 1858.

The Ancient, Mediæval and Modern Netherlanders. 1859.

Address to the Officers of the New York State Troops. 1858.

Life of Lieut.-Gen. (famous "Dutch Vauban"—styled the "Prince of Engineers") Menno, Baron Cohorn. (Series.) 1860.—Military Lessons. (Series.) 1861-3.—Winter Campaigns. 1862.

Practical Strategy, as illustrated by the Life and Achievements of a Master of the Art, the Austrian Field-Marshal, Traun. 1863.—Personal and Military History of Major-General Philip Kearny, 512 pp., 8vo. 1869.—Secession in Switzerland and the United States compared; being the Annual Address, delivered 20th October, 1863, before the Vermont State Historical Society, in the Hall of Representatives, Capitol, Montpelier. 1864.

Incidents connected with the War in Italy. (Series.) 1859.

Mortality among Generals. (Series.) 1861.—The Battle of King's Mountain. (Series.) 1861-2, 1880. Oriskany, 1878—Monmouth, 1878—Rhode Island, 1878.

Facts or Ideas Indispensable to the Comprehension of War; Notions on Strategy and Tactics. (Series.) 1861 2. Eclaireur, Military Journal. (Edited.) 1854-8.—In Memoriam. (Edited.) 1st, 1857; 2d, 1862.

The Bible in Prison. 1853.—A Discourse on the Tendency of High Church Doctrines. 1855.

A Night with Charles XII. of Sweden. A Nice Young Man. Parlor Dramas. 1860-1.

Aculco, Oriskany, and Miscellaneous Poems. 1860.

Genealogical References of Old Colonial Families, &c. 1851.

Biographical Notices of the de Peyster Family, in connection with the Colonial History of New York. 1864.—Biographies of the Watts, de Peyster, Reade, and Leake Families, in connection with Trinity Churchyard. 1872.—Military (1776-1777) Transactions of Major, afterwards Colonel 8th or King's Foot, B. A., Arent Schuyler de Peyster and Narrative of the Maritime Discoveries of his namesake and nephew, Capt. Arent Schuyler de Peyster, N. Y., 1870.—Local Memorials relating to the de Peyster and Watts and affiliated families. 1881.—In Memoriam, Frederic de Peyster, Esq., LL.D., Prest. N. Y. Historical Society, St. Nicholas Society, St. Nicholas Club, &c., &c. 1882.

ARTICLES published in *United Service Magazine* (equal in matter to 12mo. volumes): Torstenson and the Battle of Janikau, July, 1879; Joshua and the Battle of Beth-horon—Did the Sun and Moon stand still? February, 1880; Hannibal, July, 1880; Gustavus Adolphus, Sept., 1880; Cavalry, I., Sept., 1880; Cavalry, II., Nov., 1880; Cavalry, III., Dec., 1880; Army Catastrophes—Destruction of Pharaoh and his host; how accomplished, &c., &c. February, 1881.—Hannibal's Army of Italy, Mar., 1881; Hannibal's Last Campaign, May, 1881; Infantry, I., June, 1881; Infantry, II., Aug., 1881; Battle of Eutaw Springs, 1781, Sept., 1881; Siege of Yorktown, 1781, Nov. 1881; Infantry, III, April, 1882; Waterloo, July, 1882; Vindication of James Hepburn, Earl of Bothwell, Sept., 1882, Oct., 1882; From the Rapidan to Appumattox Court House, July, 1883.—Burgoyne's Campaign, July-Oct., 1777, and Appendix, Oct., 1883.—Life and Achievements of Field-Marshal Generalissimo Suworrow, November-December, 1883.—Biographical Sketch of Maj.-Gen. Andrew Atkinson Humphreys, U. S. A., March 1884.—Address, Maj.-Gen. A. A. Humphreys, before the Third Army Corps Union, 5th May, 1884. Character and Services of Maj.-Gen. A. A. Humphreys, U. S. A., Manhattan, N. Y., Monthly Magazine, August, 1884.

Suggestions which laid the basis for the present admirable Paid Fire Department in the City of New York, in which, as well as in the Organization of the present Municipal Police of New York City, Gen. de Peyster was a co-laborer with the Hon. Jas. W. Gerard, and G. W. Matsell, for which latter Department he caused to be prepared and presented a Fire Escape, a model of simplicity and inestimable utility. Republished in the *New York Historical Magazine*. Supplement, Vol. IX, 1865. John G. Shea, Editor and Proprietor.

The Pearl of Pearls, or the "Wild Brunswicker" and his "Queen of Hearts;" a novel, founded on facts. 1865.—Mary Stuart: a Study. 1882; James Hepburn, Earl of Bothwell; a Vindication, 1882; Bothwell and Mary Stuart: an Enquiry and a Justification. 1883.—Bothwell, an Historical Drama, 1884.—The Life and Military Services of Sir John Johnson, Bart. 1882.—Notices and Correspondence of Col. A. S. de Peyster and Brig.-Gen. Sir John Johnson, Bart., during and after the American Revolution, 1776, &c. 1884.

State Sovereignty. 1861.—Life and Services of the great Russian Field-Marshal Suworrow. 1882.—La Royale, the Grand Hunt [or Last Campaign of the Army of the Potomac], Nos. I., II., III., IV., V., VI., 1872; VII., 1873; VIII., 1871.—Battles of Fredericksburg, Chancellorsville and Gettysburg in *Onward*, a monthly. 1869-70.—And Gettysburg and Williamsport, in the *Soldiers' Friend*, a weekly, 1870.—Col. J. Watts de Peyster, Jr., U. S. V., A Threnody. 1874.—Sir John Johnson, Bart.: An Address delivered before the N. Y. Historical Society, 6th Jan., 1880, with two voluminous Appendices of Authorities.

Centennial Sketches of the American Revolution, which appeared in the N. Y. *Times*, and especially in the N. Y. *Evening Mail*, and *Mail* and *Express*. 1776-82.—Decisive Conflicts of the late Civil War or " Slaveholders' Rebellion:" I. Shiloh, Antietam, &c., 1867; II. Murfreesboro to Chattanooga, &c., 1866; III. Gettysburg, 1867; IV. Nashville, 1876.—Biographical notices of Major-Generals Philip Schuyler—Address delivered before the N. Y. Historical Society, 2d Jan., 1877; Geo. H. Thomas, (likewise two Addresses delivered on the same subject before the N. Y. Historical Society, 5th Jan. 1875, and Jan. 1876); also, of Bancroft, Burnside, Crawford, Heintzleman, Hooker, Humphreys, McAllister, Mahone, Meade, Edwards Pierrepont, Pleasanton, Sickles, Tremaine, &c., &c.

The Battles of Monmouth and Capture of Stony Point: a series of voluminous and exhaustive articles published in the *Monmouth Enquirer*, N. J., 1879.—Eclaireur (The), A Military Journal, Vols. II. and III., edited 1854-5.

History of the Third Corps, Army of the Potomac. 1861-65. This title, although not technically, is virtually correct, for in a series of elaborate articles in dailies, weeklies, monthlies, monographs, addresses, &c., everything relating to this Corps, even to smallest details, from 1861 to 1865, was prepared with care, and put in print. These articles appeared in the *Citizen*, and the *Citizen and Round Table;* in *Foley's Volunteer*, and *Soldiers' and Sailors' Half-Dime Tales of the late Rebellion;* in Mayne Reid's magazine *Onward;* in Chaplain Bourne's *Soldiers' Friend;* in "*La Royale or Grand Hunt* [of the Last Campaign] *of the Army of the Potomac*, from Petersburg to Appumattox Court House, April 2-9, 1865," illustrated with engraved likenesses of several of the prominent Generals belonging to the corps, and careful maps and plans ; in the life of Major-General Philip Kearny; in the "Third Corps at Gettysburg; General Sickles Vindicated" * * Vol. I., Nos. xi., xii., xiii. *The Volunteer;* in a Speech delivered before the Third Army Corps Union, 5th May, 1875, profusely illustrated with portraits of Generals who commanded, or belonged to that organization, &c. These arranged and condensed would constitute a work of five or six volumes 8vo., such as those prepared by Prof. John W. Draper, entitled the "Civil War in America," but were never given as bound volumes to the public, because the expense was so great that the author, who merely writes for credit and amusement, was unwilling to assume the larger outlay, in addition to what he had already expended on the purchase of authorities, clerk-hire, printing, &c., &c.

and publicly professed the reformed (Protestant or Huguenot) doctrines, and gathered around him a number of distinguished theologians who shared his views. Among these were Jacques Lefevre and William Farel, subsequently distinguished as Protestant divines.

Briconnet, however, was less of a zealous propagandist than an ambitious courtier. Accordingly, by an astounding change of front, he deserted his party, and, to win his pardon from the court for what he styled his errors, he became the most pitiless persecutor of the religion for which he had previously shown the most lively devotion. His abandonment of his friends was the cause and the prelude of bloody collisions. As soon as the plan of extermination had been definitely resolved upon by the Secret Council, and the hour of execution determined, a messenger was despatched to Meaux. He was accompanied by Lefroid, a ferocious member of the Romanist League, and was accredited to Louis Cosset, the Royal Procurator, or attorney. This Cosset at once assembled all the robbers and murderers who had rendered themselves conspicuous by their fanaticism and their ferocity since the commencement of the French civil wars. He fixed a place for their assembling the very same day, at 7 P. M. All were to be armed and ready to fall upon the Protestants. At the same hour the gates of the city were shut. Cosset chose for associates to engineer the execution, Denis Roland, an usher or tipstaff, "*a man worthy of a thousand gallows for his robberies and his exactions;*" Pigeon, a bargeman; and some priests. They divided their followers into bands, who commenced by seizing and imprisoning the Protestants and then pillaging their dwellings. The massacres did not occur until the morrow, but continued for three days. The women and girls were violated and then murdered. The Protestants who were in the country about, and those who sought a refuge there, escaped neither pillage nor death.

TROYES, CAPITAL OF CHAMPAGNE, 90 MILES E. S. E. OF PARIS.

The news of the massacres in the royal city arrived in Troyes on the 26th of August. The Romanists at once fell upon the Protestants and the pillaging, the murders, continued for nine days (4th September.) The victims who sought asylums in the houses were followed thither without pity, tracked like wild beasts and massacred.

ORLEANS, 58 MILES S. S. W. OF PARIS.

The announcement of the murderous decree reached this city on the 26th of August and at once the imprisonments and the robberies began. The number of Protestants murdered is set down at 1,200. This does not comprise fifty women and many little children. The massacres and the havoc lasted three days. Some Protestants escaped from the city. Certain of the magistrates, accomplices of the assassins and robbers, devised an expedient, which, in a measure, enticed the fugitives back into Orleans. They caused an amnesty, entire and without restriction, to be made public, in favor of all those who would return to the (Roman) church. Some unfortunates, in the hope of saving their lives and their properties, resolved to abjure their faith to a Cordelier (Fransciscan friar) designated by the proclamations to receive them. These unhappy men were none the less robbed and murdered. "These '*Little Massacres,*'" says a contemporary historian, " lasted fifteen days."

BOURGES, 123 MILES S. OF PARIS.

In this city, as in almost every locality where the Leaguers were masters, massacres were executed with the same circumstances; closure of the gates of the city; imprisonment of the Protestants; pillage of their property. The blood continued to flow for many days. The bands of assassins were led by Boirat, captain of the Burgher militia, his brother, an Echevin (somewhat like an assistant alderman), a member of the municipal government and other fanatics belonging to the same family: Montjan —sword cutler, Ambroise—shoemaker, Yves Camaille—butcher. All the Protestants imprisoned in the course of the 26th and 27th of August were pitilessly massacred.

LA CHARITÉ, N. E. OF BOURGES ON THE LOIRE.

The company of the Duke of Nevers, composed of Italians, marched into this city the very day of Saint Bartholomew, 24th of August, and halted there under pretext of being reviewed. The officers had received secret orders from the Duke of Nevers. Soon afterwards these foreign soldiers united with the Leaguers, attacked and pillaged the houses of the Protestants. The rich of this party were subjected to heavy ransom. On the 3d of September massacres began and continued for many days.

SANCERRE, N. E. OF BOURGES, IN THE DIRECTION OF LA CHARITÉ.

The Protestants who had escaped from the massacre in Orleans, in Bourges, and in La Charité—a sad misnomer for a place destitute of brotherly love—took refuge at Sancerre, whose population was almost entirely Protestant, and combined with them for their common defense. Their calm and determined attitude surprised and frightened the Romanists, so that the latter did not dare to attack them. The Protestants, although most numerous, did not take advantage of their superiority. They would not permit any reprisals, thus to deprive their persecutors of every pretext for summoning to their assistance the troops of the Duke de la Chatres, who had received orders to repair to Sancerre. They always showed themselves in public in large numbers and perfectly organized, but without ostensible weapons; so as not to violate the last Royal edict, which prohibited carrying arms; which edict was intended to deprive the Protestants of the means of defending themselves.

Almost all the towns of Brittany, west-north-west province of France; of the Anjoumois, capital Angers, to the south-east of this; and of Saintonge, more southerly again, were theatres of the most frightful disasters.

Lyons, the second city of France, was, after Paris, the most unfortunate of municipalities. Mandelot, the governor, who was a partisan of the Guises, had orders to accomplish the extermination of all the Protestants, without distinction of age or sex. At first he hesitated to execute this infernal order with all its intended rigor.

He confined himself to ordering the gates of the city to be closed, and imprisoning the Protestants under pretext, thus, of placing them under the protection of the magistrates and of the public force (police) and thereby saving them from the popular fury. This, however, amounted to nothing, since he charged the Burgher militia with the arrest of the intended victims. This citizen organization summoned to its aid all the Romanist Leaguers of the country, and these escorts, assigned under the pretence of safeguards, led their prisoners into by-streets, murdered them there and then cast their corpses into the Rhone. The bands of cut-throats were under the direction of one Boidon, an assassin and robber by profession—a wretch who subsequently terminated his horrible career on the scaffold, at Clermont, in Auvergne. These pillages and massacres had already lasted three days, when, on the 29th of September, arrived from Paris de Perat, decorated with the Royal Order of Saint Michael and bearer of letters from Queen Catharine. With him was associated one de Rubis, and several Echevins (assistant aldermen?) of Lyon, who had been sojourning some time at Paris, attending to the interests of the Lyonese merchants. The letters confided to de Perat announced in effect, that the King desired that Lyon should imitate the capital; that all the Protestants should be exterminated. The governor, Mandelot, alleged that he was every hour expecting direct orders from the king. At the same time, however, he published a notice that all those who professed the Reformed religion must repair without delay to the government hall. These unhappy people thereupon hastened to place themselves under the safeguard of the military authority. La Pierre d' Auxerre, Advocate Royal, declared that the King and the Queen Mother ordered the extermination of all the Protestants, not only those already in prison, but all those who could be arrested. For this he produced no written authority. Nevertheless Mandelot yielded to his arguments and soon after Bordon, Mornieu and Le Clou, companions in the debaucheries, and comrades in the crimes of La Pierre, proposed to the public executioner to associate himself in their enterprise. This grim functionary, however, had more humanity than his superiors. He boldly told them "that he performed his functions simply in executing the sentences of the magistrates and that he would not sully his office by the massacre of innocent people." The soldiers in the citadel made a like reply to a similar proposition from La Pierre and his fellow-villains: "What you demand is against honor. We are not assassins. What evil have these unfortunates done, that you wish us to slaughter them?" The murderers were thus compelled to purchase the services of some bandits and the

Guards of the City Hall (composed of 800 Burgher militia). These they divided into bands and by them, all the Protestants, confined in the convents of the Franciscan and Celestine monks, were murdered.

The principal merchants who professed the Reformed religion, had been shut up in the palace of the Archbishop. The Leaguers first imposed heavy ransoms upon them, and, notwithstanding, killed them afterwards. Mandelot and Saluces hurried to the palace of the Archbishop to stop the slaughter, but they were too late. Mandelot, in order to evade the terrible responsibility of this massacre, hastened to prepare an accusation setting forth the facts, directed against the actual authors of this crime. He promised a hundred crowns of gold to whoever would produce proofs of their guilt. This ostentatious demonstration of indictment and of reward made no impression on the criminals. They were sure of impunity. Their fury redoubled, and on the evening of the very same day that these official documents appeared, they repaired to the prison of Roanne, crowded with Protestants, fastened cords to the necks of these, dragged them to the Rhone and threw them into the river. The courts of the arch-episcopal palace were filled with corpses. Mandelot had them conveyed to the opposite side of the river, in order that they might be interred in the Cemetery of the Abbey d'Aulnay, but the monks set their faces against it, under the pretext that these heretics were unworthy of burial. Then the members of the League, at a concerted signal, themselves removed the heaps of dead and cast them into the Rhone. "The bodies of the fattest were given over to the apothecaries." The number of victims exceeded 800. The lives of two ministers and some Protestant laymen were saved by Saluces, commandant of the citadel.

The Rhone cast ashore the corpses thrown into it. These encumbered the environs of Tournon, Valence, Bourg, Vienne, Le Pont de St. Esprit, Avignon, Arles, &c., towns along its course to the sea. The authorities were obliged to compel the boatmen with their boat-hooks to shove back the dead bodies into the Rhone, and for a long time the riparian populations would neither eat of the fish of the river, nor make any use of its waters.

VALENCE, on the left bank of the Rhone, and ROMANS, 10 miles to the north-east, on the right bank of the Isere. In both these towns some Protestants were murdered; but their fellow-worshippers were saved by the courageous firmness of Simiane de Cordes.

Claude of Savoy, of Tende, who commanded in DAUPHINY, refused to execute the orders of the Secret Council which were brought to him by Boniface de la Motte. To this court emissary, he made this noble reply: "It is impossible that such orders could have originated with his Majesty. They must have been conceived by enemies to the throne and public tranquility; by people who prostitute the name of the King in order to gratify their passions." This generous refusal cost him his life. He died of poison administered to him at Avignon, a city belonging to the Pope.

BAYONNE, EXTREME S. W. OF FRANCE.

The Viscount d'Orte, governor of this city, took the wisest and most energetic measures to restrain the Romanist Leaguers. No Protestant was attacked. To the orders of the King he likewise made a memorable answer: "Sire, I have communicated the commands of your Majesty to your faithful citizens and men-at-arms constituting the garrison. Among them I have found none others but good citizens and brave soldiers, and not a single executioner. For this reason both they and myself very humbly supplicate Your Majesty to be pleased to employ our arms and our lives in things which are possible, however dangerous they may be. For such we place ourselves at your disposal, even to the last drop of our blood." This refusal to obey unjust and sanguinary orders likewise cost his life to this brave citizen. He died poisoned a short time afterwards; and the government of Bayonne was given to the Count de Retz, a creature of the Secret Council.

AUVERGNE.

The Protestants of this province escaped extermination solely through the devotion of Saint-Heran, its governor, who had the courage to imitate the generous refusals which the Count of Tende and the Viscount d'Orte opposed to the royal command.

DIJON had only reason to deplore a single victim, Clermont de Traves, brother-in-law of the Count of Grammont. Advantage was taken of the absence of Charny, who commanded in this city, to kill this Protestant gentleman.

MACON.—The Protestants were almost all put in prison. The governor, Philibert de la Guiche, adopted this measure to save them and it was successful. The prison served as a veritable and secure refuge for the unfortunates destined to the knife; and this brave governor was able to make their enemies respect his determination.

NISMES, in Languedoc, afterwards, in 1815, like Avignon and other towns in the south of France, the scene of bloodthirsty bigotry, won, on the other hand, in 1572, an honorable record. Its Romanist inhabitants did not share the atrocious frenzy of the Leaguers, and themselves rallied to the defence of the Protestants. They united with the latter for the common maintenance of order in the city and, therein, the orders of the Secret Council were not executed.

ROUEN, NORMANDY, 68 MILES N. W. OF PARIS, ON THE SEINE.

Tannequi-le-Veneur, the governor of this city, at first resisted, not only the instigations, but the menaces of the Leaguers. Very soon, however, his authority ceased to be recognized. The numerous Protestants who inhabited this vast and populous city were shut up in prisons on the 17th of September, 1572. The cut-throats assembled in arms before the prison, forced their victims to come forth, one after another, and murdered them. The number of victims ranged between 800 and 900. All their houses were pillaged. As for the corpses, they were first stripped of their clothing; this, by an affectation of piety, was bestowed upon the poor. Then the bodies were thrown into large holes dug for the purpose, outside the gate de Caux. The provincial parliament promulgated a sentence against the robbers and assassins. But this decree was nothing but a cruel and scandalous piece of deceit. These murders of the Protestants at Rouen, in 1572, were a perfect type of the massacres of Paris by the Jacobins in 1791. In both cases the victims belonged to the best classes of society and the cut-throats to the worst.

TOULOUSE, Languedoc.—Infamous in 1762 for the judicial murder of the Protestant Calas, which roused the indignation of Europe, this city was the stage of the last act of the long tragedy of desolation and of crime. The massacre of the Protestants of this city closed the lists of the crimes of Saint Bartholomew. Duranti, Advocate General, was accused of having given a frightful signal for the murder of his fellow-citizens. He was afterwards promoted to be First President of the same provincial parliament to which he had been attorney-general. Subsequently, when desirous of opposing new aggressions of the very Leaguers of whom he had been the accomplice, he perished, together with Dassis, his brother-in-law, assassinated by them in 1589. His corpse was wrapped up in the canvas of a grand picture representing Henry III., who had incurred the hatred of members of the League in consequence of his alliance with the Protestant Henry of Navarre, afterwards Henry IV.

Michelet mentions selling the bodies of fat Protestants to apothecaries.

History has consecrated the names of the magistrates, of the governors, of the military commandants, of the citizens, who glorified themselves by their heroic resistance to the orders of the Secret Council—good men, who here and there in different cities and some of the provinces, saved a portion of the population, their innocent fellow-citizens, so unjustly proscribed.

Truth and justice requires the mention of the following noble men, in addition to those already cited as exceptions to the general list of ferocious instruments of royal and priestly infamy: M. M. Sonagues at Dieppe (North); the Count of Garces in Provence (S. E.); the First President of the Parliament of Grenoble (E.); President Jeannin, at Dijon; Villars, at Nismes; the Marshal de Matignon, at Alencon; de Rieux, at Narbonne; Curzas, at Angers; Bouillé, in Brittany; Hennyer, Bishop of Liseux; all the Montmorencies throughout their vast domains, and in the towns and cities wherever they held commands.

Salignac-Fenelon, then French ambassador at London, received orders to justify these massacres to Queen Elizabeth. His bold and honorable answer to his king, Charles IX., came near costing him dear. He was threatened with a severe punishment for making it. "Sire," were his words, "I should render myself an accomplice of this terrible deed, if I attempted to excuse it. Your Majesty must address yourself to those who counseled the execution."

Even the massacre of St. Bartholomew has found apologists; moreover, refutations have not been wanting. Such discussions or excuses simply imply a total ignorance of the epoch. Opinion is now definitely fixed in regard to this capital crime, its origin, instigators, motives, method and iniquity.

A French officer justly characterized it as worse than a crime. It was a blunder; followed up by worse blunders, if less meanly sanguinary crimes. The Revocation of the Edict of Nantes and its consequences completed the list. These deviltries of bigotry continued for over 200 years and were most disastrous to France. In driving out the Huguenots, they drove out industry, economy, knowledge, honesty and thought—the origin and stimulant of progress. The revulsion of the Revolution was the necessary consequence of the centuries of such crimes. The rulers set the example and demoralized the people. In like manner the utter depravity of the imperial rule of Louis Napoleon generated the excesses of the Commune. The pendulum never ceases to vibrate, nor the application of the law of of compensation, even in this world. The cruelty towards the Huguenots and their expulsion was the source of the calamities of France in 1870.

The Huguenots furnished nerve and brain to Prussia. Frederic the Great was their pupil in all that made him truly glorious. When Prussia succumbed, in 1806, it was Huguenot blood which mitigated the fall. The first Prussian general who fell on French soil in 1870, bore a Huguenot name. It is claimed that when the victorious Germans rode into Paris in 1871, eighty descendants of Huguenots rode in the staff of the triumphant Emperor who had so much to avenge and avenged it. The same race inspirited the United States of Holland; gave snap to the early manhood of this city; helped William the Third to the crown of Great Britain and performed leader's and yeoman's work in his military successes. What is more, the greatest French admiral who ever shed glory on the Bourbon flag, Duquesne, was a Huguenot. No title, no honor, no reward would have been considered sufficient to buy his perversion. He resisted every temptation, and although France could not dispense with his services, it was mean enough to refuse him a grave in consecrated ground. And his indignant sons bore forth with them into exile the heart which only beat for the service of his ungrateful country.

Viennet, a member of the French Academy, terminates his biography with these words: "He who alone had raised the French marine to the first rank among the navies of the world, could not obtain even a mausoleum in his native country."

Woe to those empires in which priests direct public affairs!

J. WATTS DE PEYSTER.

# GYPSIES.

Information Translated and Gathered
from Various Sources.

BY

★ J. WATTS de PEYSTER. ★

JUNE, 1885.

NEW YORK:
CHAS. H. LUDWIG, PRINTER, 10 & 12 READE STREET.
1885.

# GYPSIES.

## SOME CURIOUS INVESTIGATIONS, COLLECTED FROM VARIOUS SOURCES, RESPECTING THIS RACE OF MYSTERIOUS ORIGIN.

"His captain's heart * * * reneges all temper ;
And is become the bellows and the fan
To cool a gipsy's lust."

"O this false soul of Egypt! this grave charm,
Like a right gipsy, hath, at fast and loose,
Beguiled me to the very heart of loss."
                                    SHAKSPEARE. 1608.

"The companion of his [the Tinker's] travels is some foul, sunburnt quean, that since the TERRIBLE STATUTE [against Gipsies and the like], recanted *gypsiisme*, and turned pedlaress."
    SIR THOMAS OVERBURY'S " *Characters*." Sig. I. Circa, 1614.

"Outlandish persons calling themselves *Egyptians*, or *Gypsies*, are another object of the severity of some of our unrepealed statutes."
    BLACKSTONE, " *Commentaries*." B. IV., c. 13. Circa, 1765.

— •◆• —

GIPSIES.—Translated from "*Zedler's Grosses Universal Lexicon aller Wissenschaften und Künste welche, etc.*" Leipzig and Halle, 1749.

Gipsies—*Ger.* Ziegeuner, Zigeuner, Zigeiner, Zigainer, Zügeuner ; *Lat.* Cingari or Zingari. A wandering and trooped-together mob, which has stolen in over almost all Christendom, and are variously designated, for, besides the names given above, they are called Attingani, Cigani, Cingai, Cyani, Cigari, Cyngai, Zigeuni, Zigeneri, all, however, words of the same stem. Even the word Attingani, which is the name given them by the Greeks, appears to be one with the others, if the syllable "At" be thrown off and the "t" changed into C or Z. They are called also Taten or Tattarn, or Heyden, also Saracenen, Saráceni and Agareni, or (corrupted), Zagareni, especially, too, Egyptians (Ægyptiani), from which it is supposable that the name Cyani or Zingani comes. Since our forefathers, the Germans, were accustomed to shorten names, they may have thrown away the two first syllables of Ægyptiani and left only Ciani remaining. See Jacob Thomasius' " Dissertation on the Cingari," Leipsic, 1652, § 4, and so on. In France they are called "Bohemians." They are also called by some learned men Nubians.

Some derive the name Zigeuner (Gipsy) from the German as meaning "Zieht-einher" (Come-in), because these people had no fixed dwelling-place but wandered about hither and thither (*Zeiler's Sendschreib. Epist.* 71) a derivation which is further confirmed by the circumstance that the common people gave the name Zihegan to land-tramps before Gipsies were heard of (*Zeiler's Sendschreib: Letter* 276.)

As regards the origin of the Gipsies, no agreement has, as yet, been arrived at. It is, however, certain and proved, that they were first seen in Germany in the fifteenth century, under the Emperor Sigismund.

Zeiler writes, they first appeared in Hesse, in the year 1414, but almost all historians put their first appearance in Germany in 1418. Jacob Thomasius, in his "*Dissert. de Cingaris,*" §§ 16, 17, prefers this latter date. Counting from this date they passed through all Germany in two years and afterwards turned into Italy, France and Spain. The first bands that came into Germany consisted of 14,000, including men, women and children, and were split up into various small tribes, of which some wandered hither, some thither.

They had with them horses, mules and asses and were under the command of a king or colonel (obrist) named Michael. Aventinus, however, says the colonel whom they had in 1639, when they were in Bavaria, was called Zindelo, or Zandadel. Stumpfius tells us, in his "KajserChronic," that at their first appearance they paid for the necessaries of life they wanted with hard money and that they possessed much gold and silver, although they wore poor and ragged clothes. The Emperor Sigismund, it is said, gave them, on account of their good behavior, a free pass and safe conduct (Thomasius, *loco. cit.,*). Otherwise the gipsies were of a dark complexion and not over cleanly in their clothing and general way of life. They said they were Christians and that they were from Lower Egypt (Klein-Egypten). On this account they were called, in the emperor's free pass, Egyptians. This is also corroborated by three gravestone inscriptions over their colonels, which Mart Crusius cites in his "Swabian Annals." The *first* runs thus, " Counting from the birth of Christ our Saviour, in the year 1445, on St. Sebastian's Eve, died the noble-born Lord Panuel, Duke of Lower Egypt and Lord of Hirschhorn in the same country." The *second*, "Anne Domini 1453 Obüt nobilis comes Petrus de Minore Ægypto in die Philippi et Jacobi Apostolorum." The *third*, "In the year 1498, on Monday after the Festival of St. Urban, died the well-born Lord John, Frey Graf of Lower Egypt. May God be gracious and pitiful to his soul." As to the cause of their wandering, the people gave out that they had denied Christianity and for seven years became heathen, and this sin they desired to atone for by seven years of pilgrimage. They mixed the Pope in with it as having laid on them the penance of seven years wandering for having forsaken Christianity (" *Zeiler's Sendschreiben, Epist.* 71). Others say that their pretext was that by their wanderings they were doing penance for the sins of their forefathers, who had refused hospitality to the Virgin Mary and the Jesus-child at the time of the flight into Egypt. Others pretended that the gipsies had previousiy lived in Singara, a city of Mesopotamia, and since they were driven thence by Julian the Apostate had never been able to regain their country, and for this reason they wandered about the world. Others seek their origin in Assyria, others in Cilicia, others in the Caucasus, many in Tartary, others in the province of Zeugitana in Africa, others in Nubia and Abyssinia. So some derive the name from the Zechis, Zichis, Zinchis, who had their dwellings by the Don on the Palus Mœotis and came from Asiatic Sarmatia (Abel's "German and Saxon Antiquities," P. II. p. 329, &c.) Indeed, some would make the gipsies the descendants of Cain, who, like their ancestor, are fugitives and vagabonds, and must wander over the face of the earth (Thomasius, *loc. cit.*, § 54). But these do not know what they are talking about since the whole race of Cain perished [?] in the flood. If some wish to make them out the descendants of Ham this might be, but there is no apparent cause why they should, on this account, be tramps and vagrants, since others of Ham's race have settled habitations.

The gipsies' own account of the cause of their wandering was only a fiction by means of which they wished to make people willing to tolerate them. This at first succeeded. People pitied them and felt scrupulous about injuring them. It was also supposed that on the ending of their seven years of pilgrimage they would return home. This did not take place, and when called to account for it they replied that the way home was barred to them, that they were not able to return to their country, or that they were obliged to begin another seven years of pilgrimage, and if they did not do so they would be visited with failure of crops and other national visitations. Stumpfius, indeed, says that the *original* gipsies returned to their country on the ending of the seven years. This cannot be so, since as vagrants they had no home and no proper country. They may have wandered into other Christian countries, but there were always many of them remaining in Germany and we have records that since that time there have always been more or less there. Some are disposed to consider the gipsies who were still to be found in Germany as only a crowd of thieves, murderers, knaves and other riff-raff, who, after the departure of the *gipsies* proper, collected together and wished to pass for those people. And it cannot be denied that all sorts of loose characters may have joined them, whom they also willingly received and whom they knew how to stain of a dark color by various inventions so that they could not be recognized. It is even related of a Spanish nobleman that he fell in love with a gipsy girl and was thus induced to join their company (Thomasius, §62). In any case it is beyond doubt that many original gipsies remained in the country, to whom all sorts of reckless people joined themselves.

That the original gipsies were more honest than their successors cannot be certainly asserted although Thomasius maintains that it was so. They were, in any case, deceivers who attempted to profit by all kinds of falsehoods as to their own history and circumstances. Yet their successors may have become worse and worse, as is usually the case with such vagabonds. They were shameless beggars who possessed themselves of what they could not obtain fairly by trickery and violence, as also they were excellently trained by all manner of arts and deception for getting people's money away from them. For this purpose they addicted themselves to all sorts of fortune-telling and conjuring, also they pretended to many medicinal secrets, which were, however, nothing but simple nonsense and deception. When cunning did not answer, they resorted to violence, with robbery, murder and plundering. They are even accused of being spies for the Turks, and betrayed to the latter the plans and projects of the Christians. For this reason, ☞ since the year 1500, severe orders and ordinances were issued against them in almost every Christian country in which they were found.⚐

They indeed gave themselves out to be Christians and had their children baptized, but this was only with the expectation of receiving the usual godparents' presents. Otherwise they were but poor Christians, since they availed themselves neither of hearing the Divine words nor of partaking of the Holy Communion.

If it be asked to what nation did the gipsies belong and whence they came, such a question it is difficult to answer. They gave themselves out, as has been said, for Egyptians; but this is not in accordance with truth, for Belonius declares that he had seen the gipsies in Egypt in great numbers under the palm trees on the river Nile and that they were there as much strangers as they were everywhere else (*Zeiler, Epist.* 532). D. Wagenseil, of Altdorf, has here and again maintained in his writings that the gipsies sprang originally from the Jews, who, in the 13th and 14th centuries, suffered dreadful persecutions in Germany and other countries, so that those who escaped fire and the sword betook themselves to the forests and there lived for a time, as much as possible, concealed. Finally they came out with a changed language and disguised as to clothing, and gave themselves out as Egyptians. Afterwards all kinds of loose vagabonds associated themselves to them for the purpose of enjoying a free, disorderly life. (See S. Huebner's *Staats-Zeitung*, and Conversations Lexicon, Article "Zigeuner.")

This idea is contradicted by the circumstance that it is difficult to conceive how such a multitude of men—14,000—could remain so long concealed in the forests. The black color of the gipsies, too, opposes itself as not being that which we find in the Jews. Those seem to hit the mark more nearly who say that they first came into Germany from Turkey and the Turkish-Hungarian frontier, for here they are, to the present day, frequently met with. About Gross-Waradein in Hungary there are many gipsies, some having houses, who maintain themselves partly as horse dealers, partly as smiths and partly by stealing. They also sometimes act as hangmen or executioners in Hungary and Transylvania. Some of them pick up exhausted cattle and tan their skins. In Transylvania some of them wash out gold from the sand of rivers and brooks and are obliged to deliver such sand-gold to the imperial treasury at a certain price. They generally go naked and eat the carrion of dead horses, cattle and sheep thrown into the flayer's-field. They get from the inhabitants the diseased and dead cattle, whose flesh they smoke in their huts or dry in the sun and eat as a great delicacy, but generally raw and uncooked. Of fortune-telling they understand nothing nor do they attempt it as an occupation. In the year 1676 the gipsies plundered the Hungarian miner town of Potack and set fire to it, as well as to the church. Among these gipsies was found a French engineer, Pierre Durois, who had been with them some eight years, and meantime drawn large bills of exchange on France. He was captured by the Imperialists and on him were found plans of almost all the Imperial cities, and the cities of Upper Hungary. It is said that the gipsies of Wallachia furnish musicians, although their music sounds miserably enough. [Of late years gypsy bands and gypsy peculiar music have been in great repute in Eastern Europe.] [1794.] (Mark Zeiler's description of the Kingdom of Hungary, pp. 29, 748, 1017.) The gipsies came first into Germany and thence wandered into other European countries, therefore it is quite supposable that they came from Hungary and the Slavonic countries about it. Thomas Brown says, in Pseudodox. Epidem., L. VI. C., 13, that the gipsy language is Slavonic, which is a further argument for the above-given view, since that language is very common in Hungary and Turkey and even at the Turkish court.

Nevertheless, although they may have come thence into Germany, Hungary cannot be their original country and the question remains, where is this to be sought? But where can such be found, since the gipsies are a vagrant people, and at home nowhere? The opinion which we find in Salmon's "Present History of Persia," Chap. ix., p. 247, may, perhaps, be the best. He says, "The Fackirs in Mahommedan, the Kalenters in Heathen, and the Gipsies in Christian lands, are as like as one egg is to another, and they are without doubt one race. The Kalanders or Kalenters are essentially heathen begging-monks and the Fackirs Mahommedan ones. These latter so often go into India, because there are, in that country, as many Mohammedans as heathen, and both orders of devotees (the Kalenters and Fakirs) think as much of one religion as of another, that is, they hold to none. So they form light companies and are now in Persia, now in India, now in Egypt, now in Europe, in which last we call them (*Gipsies*) Zigeuner, Heathen or Tartars. I consider all three sorts, altogether one and the same people, whether they be in Asia or in Europe, only that, according to the people with whom they are, they assume a somewhat altered appearance and name. With the heathens and Mahommedans they pass for a sort of monks who deny themselves in everything, therefore it would not answer for them to take females, generally and openly, with them. Nevertheless, it occurs. When it is necessary, they take them secretly with them on their journeys in Christian lands. When they find in Catholic ones bands of pilgrims, in Protestant ones, again, beggar bands, consisting of one or more whole families, the gipsies put themselves on a like footing, often join with them, as in Asia with the Fakirs and Kalenters, in one troop, according as they are at one place or another. That they are one people, however, sometimes in Europe, sometimes in Asia, can be seen in Duke Henry of Saxony's "Travels in the Promised Land," which in 1498, according to the custom of his time, he made there. The author of the biography of this prince relates the following, "He (the Duke) spoke but seldom of this journey, as it was now almost forgotten, unless indeed some particular inducement or occasion for it presented itself, such as the mention of the Gigeunter or Zigeuner (Gipsies, as they are called). Against them he was fierce, calling them traitors or spies in the land, because they had recognized him and told who he was, in Syria, in consequence of which he encountered much anxiety and danger. On this account he would not suffer them in his territory, so that during the whole time that I was at the court of Freiberg and otherwise in his Grace's cities and employment, I never saw a gipsy, although they were in the country nevertheless." (See "An Introduction to the History of the Electorate of Saxony.")

But now-a-days it is only too well known that these gipsies are nothing else than a congregated troop of bad characters, who have no willingness to work, but choose to make a profession of idleness, stealing, fornication, gluttony, drunkenness, gambling and the like. One finds among them discharged and deserting soldiers, dissolute servants and apprentices who do not wish to profit their masters, degenerate sons who have run away from home, female beggars who have received a public whipping and who, besides, can no longer earn anything as procuresses or prostitutes. They stain their faces with green nutshells, in order to increase their ugliness and that they may more easily induce the inexperienced to believe that they come from the hot oriental countries. They form for themselves a peculiar language and separate dialect [Argot], in order thus to appear more foreign and that they may communicate with each other concerning their plans without being understood by other people. The real gipsy-troops elect a chief from among themselves, who commands them all and to whom, in general, they yield obedience. The females wear long mantles under which they may the better conceal the stolen clothes and other goods. They have with them horses, pistols and all sorts of arms for use when occasion offers. They especially wish to appear very well versed in calculating nativities, in cheiromancy and in fortune-telling and they prophesy to people, mostly to the vulgar and for a fee, those things that their dupes wish to hear. They take pains to inform themselves of events in the lives of certain persons, so that they may be ready to relate to them past circumstances and thus create in them and others the impression that they can, with equal skill, foretell the future. They pretend to be able to promise fires and to set them agoing in the most dangerous place, where, nevertheless, they do no damage. Of this we have examples in that they sometimes make fires in barns and the building does not catch. They prefer encamping on the frontier, so that in case they are sought for and pursued they may easily pass into a foreign territory. They also commonly live in the forests. They are accustomed at particular times to have their children baptized, and on such occasions to choose rich and prominent persons for Godparents, in order that they may have the better time in revelling and rioting on the christening gifts received from the sponsors.

It is, besides, certain that the gipsies of every period have been Godless, bad people, who were persecuted most justly. Mr. Hom [Horn?] has given in his unpresuming "Thoughts on City and Country Beggars" the following description of the gipsies as they were to be found in the Coburg territories, according to their most recent condition and mode of living. He says: "They confess and avow that they are divided into several bands or troops, which are made up of some six hundred, which are under one captain, of the name of Reichert, and that they assembled every year at a rendezvous. The bands are twenty, thirty, forty, or, at different times, more or less strong. Generally they have no arms, but they have some horses, by means of which they can more easily transport and save their baggage and booty. In the day they send their women and children into the neighboring villages to steal, which they know how to accomplish in a most masterly and handy manner, under the pretext of begging and telling fortunes, while they abstract clothing, goods and small utensils from the houses of the peasants, catch up chickens and geese or whatever they can find to pilfer. To the inhabitants of the places where they find their lodgment and night-quarters they do no injury, but buy their own food or feed on what they stole elsewhere, so that such hosts shall not betray them and when they return may be ready to harbor them again. They put out sentinels to guard against an unforseen attack and are so swift and nimble that, especially in the woods, they can hardly be overtaken. Their women commonly carry very long and straight knives concealed on their persons, with which they, in case of necessity, defend themselves, and are able the more promptly to kill and more easily carry off the stolen poultry. When asked how they make a living they answer, partly by horse-dealing, partly by begging, partly also from their pay which they get in bills of exchange sent out of Little Egypt by the emperor of Turkey over the Red Sea to the Roman emperor, and by the latter commonly transmitted by the Messrs. Fugger, of Augsburg. ☞ Since now these gipsy people, as has been said, do much mischief, it is a just and equitable punishment for them, that it is, almost everywhere in Germany, the law that they be sought out by armed pursuit wherever they may be, in towns, villages, hamlets, underbrush or woods, and forcibly expelled from the country. On any marked resistance they may be shot dead. When they are captured they are to be executed without any grace or indulgence and without any further legal proceedings, simply and alone on account of their forbidden way of life and manifest disobedience. The women and children, for their part, are to be condemned for life to the houses of correction and work. The best way for discovering the gipsies is that the mounted road police should fully do their duty and patrol zealously, likewise that the gamekeepers and foresters should always immediately report what they may meet in the way of such bands of thieves and loose characters and not allow themselves to be diverted from this duty by either gifts or threats."

In the same way, even now-a-days, the gipsies are looked upon as mischievous bad characters, indeed, as spies, foreign scouts and traitors in Christendom. In this view they have been frequently banished from Germany as well as from other countries. Indeed, by a decree of the Kammer Gericht at Speyer they were deprived of all legal protection and declared outlaws (Jablonski Lex. Becmann).

In this connection the first, not unreasonable, question is, are these so-called gipsies to be tolerated in any well-constituted commonwealth, or may it be said of them with justice that they form of themselves a kind of separate commonwealth? [as the Romanists, who are only really true to the Pope, do in every country]. The first question is fairly answered in the negative, in view of the manifold crimes committed by them, this particularly by *Besold* de Trib. Domest. Societ. Spec. c. 4, n. 4. and by *Klock* de Aerario, Lib. II., c. 102, n. 28, &c. The second question, however, in view of their continual vagabondism and other evils occasioned in the commonwealths and states, in which they at any time have attempted to settle down. Of the first, *Besold* gives instances in his Tractat. de Princ. et Fin. Polit., c. 8, n. 8, and many others agree with these ideas. Thus one finds, not alone in these imperial decrees, various ordinances against the gipsies, but whole " circles " in Germany, as well as single departments, have, from time to time, and when this otherwise useless mob has somewhat increased, were themselves compelled not only to repeat such imperial decrees in their countries, but in some measure to sharpen them. As regards the imperial statutes, we find in the final decrees of the Diet at Augsburg, of the year 1500, Title Zigeunern; at Speyer, 1544, "Aber der jenigen Zigeuner halber, &c;" at Augsburg, or in the re-formation of a good police, of 1548, Title, von Zigeunern; at Augsburg, 1551, § " Nachdem uns auch angezeigt, &c.," and in the next following § " Damit nun in dem, &c." As also in the police regulations at Frankfort, of 1577, Title 28, " Of *gipsies*, in relation to those who call themselves gipsies and wander about the country, it is strictly forbidden to all Electoral princes, Princes and governments, on the allegiance which they bear to the Holy Empire, that, as regards these *gipsies*, when credible proof exists that they are scouts, traitors, spies, and explore Christian countries for the benefit of the Turks and of other enemies of Christendom ——— (strictly forbidden) to allow them to travel in or through their states, to traffick, to give them safe conducts, escorts, or passports and, since the gipsies have obtained some passports, or may obtain them hereafter, such passports are, by virtue of this decree broken, nullified and abolished. The gipsies must immediately get themselves out of all German countries, keep out of them, and not let themselves be found in them, for when they, nevertheless, hereafter enter them, and if any one does them violence or injures, them, that person shall not be considered as having committed a crime, or having done anything wrong."

Subsequently, it being found that the above-mentioned laws, contained in imperial statutes, did not suffice to drive off this vagrant mob from German lands, not only whole circles, but also separate imperial states have been forced, not only to repeat these laws in their lands, but also, according to the circumstances and exigencies, to make them more severe in one or another point.

Here belongs, first of all, the imperial decree for the rooting out of the gipsies wandering hither and thither about the country, and of other collections of thieves, robbers and murderers, as also regarding those who harbor them : " We, Charles VI., &c., to all and each of our subordinate spiritual and secular land or town rulers, and to all our lieges, subjects and vassals, of whatever rank or dignity, who inhabit our archduchy of Austria (Lower and Upper Ems), our gracious good wishes; and we graciously give you to understand, that although very appropriate mandates have been issued on repeated occasions by our forefathers formerly reigning as lords and as the secular princes of our archduchy of Austria, having for object the complete banishment of the gipsies wandering about the country along with their wives and children and the other rabble of thieves, robbers and murderers who have joined themselves to them ; and despite of our own gracious orders and especially of the general public decree issued on the 1st of July, 1720, for the general quiet and security of the country, in which we announced to all, the bann and the death punishment issued against these people; for all this, it appears, to our great displeasure, that these wholesome ordinances and the efforts for carrying them out have not accomplished their desired object and full effect, and that meantime certain of our subjects have had the audacity to give the forbidden lodgments and shelter to this gipsy rabble, pests of the country, both within and after the most carefully arranged time allotted for their departure.

When now our own most highly honored lord and father Roman emperor and prince of this country, of most Christian memory, most righteously ordained, as early as the 22d of November, 1689, in a general decree of that date, against harbourers and all those who, in what manner soever, give illegal aid and shelter to this wicked rabble, the incommutable punishment of death, and, inasmuch as by long lapse of time, this decree seems to have become almost forgotten, we now renew, confirm and publish it in the form following, that although we retain the punishment of death, as in the former, against the gipsies wandering hither and thither in the country, as well as against the mob of thieves, robbers and murderers who have joined them, we also ordain, that their harbourers and all those who, by day or by night, secretly or openly, within or beyond the time allowed for their quitting the country, give forbidden shelter, &c., to the so often denounced mischievous gipsies and robber-mobs be imprisoned and beheaded, whether such have been sharers of the property robbed and stolen or not, whether they have done so with the hope of gain or not, if they have given them illegal occupation of their houses, barns, grounds, or other place fitted for concealment; consequently in whatever way the forbidden harbouring may have been accomplished, that such harbourer shall be arrested, imprisoned and there [at once, without trial] beheaded, literally with a stroke of the sword sent from life into death.

We command, therefore, to you, who are the first-named, but especially to the local magistrates, most graciously, but at the same time in the greatest earnest, that for contributing to the greater abhorrence and destruction of the gipsies and land-wasting robber mobs, they renew the placards which, by our order of the 1st July, 1720, were to be posted at the principal road-crossings of every district : to the effect that any individual of the beforenamed gipsy and robber bands, who resists arrest with the use of arms, may be killed; and also we command that these magistrates add in these placards, with great distinctness of expression, that any person who voluntarily provides these people with a resting place, shelter, by whatever name it may be called, shall be visited with the like death punishment. And finally, in order

that this wholesome law and regulation may remain fresh in the memories of our subjects, and that none of them may shield himself under plea of ignorance or any other subterfuge, we also request and order you, state officials and village magistrates in general, as also you, village magistrates, separately, that you read in public to our subjects in the common assembly (Panchadung) every year this renewed definite statute, and that you at the same time earnestly admonish them to heed it, so that every one may know how to conduct himself and keep out of trouble.
Given at our capital and residence, the city of Vienna, August 18th, 1722."

The above statute is to be found, word for word, as we have given it, in Faber's "*Europäisch. Staats-Cantzley*," Part XLI., p. 724 and so on; also in Anton Balthasar Walther's "*Silesiæ Diplomaticæ*," T. II., part 1st, Part Generalia, pp. 236, 237, 239, and many following. In the same way, in the Duchy of Silesia, when it was still under the dominion of Austria, there were issued many imperial superior-official decrees against the gipsies, aiming at their extirpation, particularly among these one dated Bernstadt, ☞ 5th Sept., 1618, in which former orders are confirmed; with the addition that, if they are not out of the country within fourteen days, and they attempt violence or other dangerous proceedings, they are to be arrested and punished with death; further, under date of Brieg, 21st March, 1619, it is ordered that the gipsies be driven out, arrested, and, according to circumstances, put to death or banished. This by the country police itself, or, if necessary, with the conjoined force of the country and cities. In the same tenor of the 12th of February, 1683; of the 4th December, 1685; of the 28th of April, 1688; of the 3d of June, 1689; of the 13th of August, 1695; and of the 8th of August, 1703, and its renewal of the 27th of September, 1703, and of the 3d of February, 1706, that the gipsies must be driven back, that the militia must be used for this purpose and if ☞ the gipsies resist they are to be put to death. And not less the same of the 19th April, 1708, that for keeping back the gipsy rabble there are to be set up in all places near the frontiers placards on posts on which their punishment is to be described (*abgemahlet*.) In the same way, an order of the 26th July, 1715, regarding the extirpation of the gipsy mob declared outlaws; again, of the 23d June, 1721, and of the 25th March, 1726, regarding extirpation and punishment of gipsies.

As regards the Electorate Saxon countries, there likewise has been no failure in this respect. From time to time the sharpest and most emphatic decrees against such licentious and land-destroying rabble have been made public. Especially the *gipsies*, who, besides, are outlawed completely throughout the Holy Roman Empire, are not to be suffered in any corporation under penalty of 100 Rhinegold florins, to be paid by such corporation, or the forfeiture of its charter ("Entziehung der Gerichte"). Police ordinances of 1617, n. 19, and of 1661, Title II.; also as a consequence of the mandate of 1709, § 12, their children must not be baptized at any other place than that in which they were born and when this has been ascertained with certainty.—Police ordinances of 1661, Tit. II., § 4. Compare also the general law, Art. 6. And in general they are not to be tolerated on the main roads, housed, sheltered or entertained, as may be seen in many supplementary mandates to the same effect, of the years 1579, 1590, 1621, 1652, 1670, 1684-'6, 1689, 1703, 1713, 1720, and 1722; as also in the official circulars concerning them of the years 1590, 1652, 1665, 1689 and 1696, and elsewhere. To further illustrate the subject we will, here, add the already mentioned most gracious mandate of his royal majesty of Poland and Serene Elector of Saxony, 4th April, 1722, as the last and newest of the kind, against the strong bands of gipsies recently forcibly driven out of Hesse and the bordering states, who then moved into the Thuringian forest and have been seen on the frontiers of Saxony. They are to be banished, the land being found necessary:

"We, Frederick Augustus, by the grace of God, King, Elector, &c., command to all and each, &c., our Greetings, Grace and Kind Will, that they should bear in mind what we and our forefathers, resting in God, have issued through this country in the way of sharp and earnest mandates, both in the year 1689 and subsequently at different periods up to the present time, against the robber gipsy rabble, for the purpose of hunting out and exterminating them, and that they should attend to their contents under the head of gipsies, as respects the pestiferous thief-robber bands, who have reappered in our lands.

Since then, however, up to the present time, the fatherly objects intended for the best good of our subjects cannot be attained and we now receive the most trustworthy information that the gipsy bands, not long ago forcibly driven out of Hesse and other neighboring countries and which are said to consist of some 1500 persons, have moved into the Thuringian forest and that already some of this miserable mob have been seen in one and another village on the frontiers. If so, being that necessity unavoidably requires us to control this people, in good time, and with all possible energy, lest they should in our country, as it has already happened in neighboring parts, collect themselves together and here likewise be able to commit murders, robberies and plunderings, we have found it necessary for turning off this evil, not only to repeat and renew the mandates and orders first mentioned, past and present ; but also, by virtue of this, our now given mandate, to sharpen the others in respect to their object and again to order, as we have already done by our general field marshal and directing cabinet minister, Count von Fleming, to our militia, also now to all our vassals, officials, corporations and all subordinate magistrates of the country, that as respects themselves and those under their control, they shall, without delay, make sufficient dispositions for the purpose; and that, when eight days have elapsed from the publication of this our mandate, which shall be posted up everywhere in the corporations, on the pillars along the roads and frontiers, and in other public places, if any gipsies are found and caught in the towns, market-places, villages, woods and fields of our electorate and its appertaining lands, even if they present open passports or other certificates, that such gipsies are not only given up for confiscation and execution as outlaws, as it was directed in the above-quoted mandate of 1689, but it is permitted and worthy of reward that they be at once shot down or otherwise killed, on the spot, and their property taken from them, and that no one who in this way does anything against them shall be held as having committed any wrong or crime, or be made answerable for what he has done. The women and children, however, so taken and caught, are to be delivered over to the next office or court, and either confined and kept at work in the place where they were taken, or if there be there no provision for so doing, be taken thence to the poor and correction house near Waldheimb, or to other poor and correction houses, according to opportunity and circumstances. In addition, for the quicker expulsion of this hurtful race, and the more thorough searching for them, according to the precepts of our mandate, issued in the year 1710 against the thief and robber hordes; on occasion of the gipsies being sighted or pursued, the alarm bells are to be rung, or some other signal given, in order that in conjunction with the inhabitants and subjects, at the same time the militia also and gamekeepers, which last are included in the same orders, shall assemble in as strong force as quickly as possible, when called out, so that the whole may act against the oft-mentioned gipsies in the way prescribed, or as the necessity of the circumstances may require, and thus our intentions for the safety of the country and of our loyal subjects may be the more appropriately and certainly carried out. To the same end our upper circle chiefs and officials and other judicial magistrates, upon and near the frontiers, are not the less to communicate diligently and properly with the neighboring proprietors and officials, and arrange for a mutual understanding how the hunting up and expulsion and following up of this frequently-mentioned gipsy rabble is to be accomplished in the most effectual, easiest and quickest way.

Accordingly now, the, at the commencement mentioned, our vassals, officials, and all and each our judicial authorities and subordinate magistrates, as well as all subjects, will and must know how to properly and exactly observe this decree and to arrange what will be sufficient for carrying out and enforcing it.

In more emphatic witness whereof we have with our own hands signed this mandate and ordered our privy seal to be impressed on it. Done and given at Dresden, on the 4th of April, in the year 1722.

AUGUSTUS REX. [L. S.]
Henry von Bunua.
Jno. Christopher Gunther. S[ec'y]."

See the "Annals of Christopher Ernst Siculs," Leipzig, Sect. xvii., p. 166, &c., and by virtue of an official circular dated from the Electoral Saxon castle at Budissin, 18th October, 1652, there also exists a "most gracious order," in the margraviate of Upper Lausitz, along with that of his Electoral Serenity of Saxo y, in his police order issued at Dresden, on the 23d of April, 1612, referring to his already issued statute concerning gipsies, thus, to-wit: " In virtue of the there drawn-up imperial decree and electoral transcript, and in virtue of the superior magisterial instructions in the margraviate of Ober-Lausitz, drawn up in conformity therewith, the already-named *gypsies*, who are accustomed to move up and down the country and to plague and overpower its inhabitants with robberies, thefts and all sorts of chicanery, are not to be suffered in the country, much less to be allowed to live and trade therein, or to have security and protection given to them, but they are to be hunted out of the land. In case, however, that they show themselves contumacious, the authorities of the place where they attempt to encamp themselves are allowed to seize all their property and to throw them into prison and without delay to refer to their superior officials for further orders. Also no one will be held to account in any way who does any violence to them, who, as is said in the letter of the high imperial decree and its electoral transcript, are outlaws in property, estates and body. In order that this transcript and circular, intended and adapted for preserving the safety of the country, avoidance of threatened danger and furthering of the common good, may come to the knowledge of everyone, it is not only to be posted at the usual places, but to be read from the pulpit. In other respects the superintendence of the gipsy bands in Electoral Saxony belongs to the most praiseworthy (hoch-lobliche) country government, as is shown by Wabst in his historical account of the present land-judiciary of Electoral Saxony and its appertaining lands, Sect. II., c. 1., §12, n. 1."

In the Royal Prussian and Electoral Brandenburg lands, they were likewise set, most earnestly, and by all serviceable means and ways, upon driving out and extirpating the gipsy land-tramps who, by means of fortune-telling, prophecies, root-medicines, lying and deceit, robbery and stealing and the like other offences and wickedness, exceedingly mislead simple and inquisitive people and get their property, yes, often in one day and night make more evil and mischief where they are quartered than the preachers can root out, so as to put things right, by many sermons. To this end it is not only as already ordered in the church-visitation of the Insterburg, and other Lutheran offices of Prussia, in the year 1638, to the effect that gipsies are not to be received and sheltered in the towns, suburbs, and villages, but to be turned into the fields and not suffered in the country; and that those who contravene this order and for some supposed slight gain receive and house such bad and harmful people, are liable to a fine to their landlord of 20 Polish florins; but it is also by various recent royal orders, as that dated Marienwerder, 29th October, 1709; Königsberg, 21st May, 1710; Köln on the Spree, 24th Nov. p. 73, 1710; it has been most strictly commanded that no gipsy shall be tolerated in the royal Prussian dominions. (See William Henry Beckher's short extracts from the principal royal Prussian edicts and decrees, under the word "Zigeuner"—gipsy). And likewise Gruben's Corp. Constit. Prutea, p. 1, N. 5., p. 73 and P. III. N. 373, 374 and 375, p. 507, &c. See another edict, dated Berlin, 26th July, 1715. His royal Prussian Majesty Frederick William, of most glorious memory, thus complains:

"His majesty understands to his great displeasure that despite the previously so frequently issued edicts against gipsies, land-tramps, impudent beggars and the like thievish rabble, nevertheless once again large bands of such vagabonds, worthless fellows and village thieves are to be found in his royal-electoral and other possessions, and that, already, many have been arrested and imprisoned. From a fatherly care for his land, for the safety of travellers and general intercourse and commerce, and that everyone may enjoy the royal protection, these people should, on the one hand, be kept away from the frontiers of his provinces, and, on the other hand, that quick judgment should be passed on them when taken, and thus the land be cleared of such dregs of people: he decides on this account hereby to order and decree:

1. That henceforth no traveller, male or female, whose rank and condition is made doubtful from his outward appearance or any other reason, shall be allowed to enter his majesty's frontiers or passes, fortresses or towns, unless he present, in addition to his travelling pass, a passport from the government or magistrates of the place whence he comes, describing the place where he belongs, his profession and purpose, and thus legitimizing his person. For this purpose, and that it may be the more exactly executed and all evasion of it prevented, for such towns, market places, and the like, where the gates are not guarded, and for their suburbs, there, the innkeepers, publicans and tapsters are made responsible for demanding the aforesaid pass and attestation from every stranger and traveller who enters their house, to look it through, and in case they observe anything suspicious in the papers or in the behaviour of the stranger—for immediately informing the authorities of the place. This they shall not omit under a heavy money penalty, and in case they may be detected in any collusion with such stranger or traveller, or with the worthless fellows before mentioned, they shall, without fail, be visited with bodily punishment.

2. Since, also, experience has taught that such rabble are wont to disguise themselves under the names of lottery dealers, thimble-riggers, jugglers and "fast-and-loose" players, and with the occasion to ply their thieveries, such people are henceforth not to be suffered in his majesty's towns, market places or villages, either at yearly or weekly fairs or [fairs held at] church-ales, unless they have a special royal permit: this under penalty of the confiscation of their booths or under that of personal arrest, but against all such persons the frontiers of his majesty's dominions shall be entirely closed and barred off from the exercise of their in any case suspicious trades.

3. Should it be that, in spite of the earnest royal ordinance, a worthless fellow, pickpocket or cutpurse crosses the frontier and practices his wickedness and he be taken in the act, then, in order to spare the treasury the expense of his maintenance and of other judicial costs, but at the same time to deprive these thieves of the hope that under prolonged arrest they may by force or cunning get away and escape punishment, the following short judicial proceedings will be applied to the case:

'When such thieves are caught in the act of real stealing and one may be sure of it, they should at once be brought before the magistrates of the place, who must, particularly at the times of public yearly markets and church-ales, be present and assembled in their office or other headquarters, and the crime with its chief circumstances shall be presented to them in a short written statement. Should it happen that the delinquent, notwithstanding, shamelessly denies the fact, the witnesses present are to be sworn in presence of the delinquent, and then on the sum of their testimony, there always being at least two witnesses, the delinquen- shall at once, without reference to the value of the stolen property, or whether the theft was fully accomplished or not, and without further appeal to the King's majesty or to his government, be flogged and, for all time, banished the country.'

4. Should it, however, happen that any of this thievish mob commit such an act of theft as is by common law a capital crime, then the regular process of inquiry, "*servato Juris ordine*," is to be instituted against these misdoers. The magistracy of the place, however, shall see to it that the trial be, as far as possible, hastened and finished.

In regard to this it is commanded to the supreme court at Berlin; to all the royal departments, high or low ; to the spiritual and secular officers; to magistrates in the towns and country; and to the royal treasury officials, respectfully to obey and in their respective places give effect to this gracious expression of the royal wishes. In order that this royal edict may be universally known, it is to be affixed to and posted upon the gates and in the inns and tapsters' houses." See Fassman's " Life and Acts of Frederick William, King of Prussia," part II., p. 40, &c.

Soon after, there was issued, because the discharged and invalided soldiers, as well as others. partly poor, partly loose and bad people, did not choose to be constrained from begging or from exercising forbidden traffic and unallowed business, another royal edict, under date of 1st March. 1717, in which it was ordered that all such hucksters and beggars, whether they were invalids and other natives, or strangers, or gipsies, should, with all their baggage, their wives and children, immediately on being taken up, be carried to the nearest military post, and thence to the nearest fortress, there to be confined, to be kept at work and on bread and water, and further directions concerning them to be then asked for. *Ibid. p.*, 47.

A renewed and exceedingly sharpened edict against robberies and thefts appeared, dated Berlin, 24th November, 1724, according to which ten dollars was to be paid every time to the detecter of a gipsy or thief company, ☞ the gipsies or thieves caught at their work to be hanged without further inquiry, and those who resisted to be shot on the spot. *Ibid, p.* 693.

Further a new and very much sharper edict against the gipsies, tramps and foreign beggars wandering about the country, under date, Berlin, 30th November, 1739, was as follows:

"We, Frederick William, by the Grace of God, King of Prussia, &c., &c., declare and publish: Inasmuch as, to our great displeasure, it has been abundantly proved that our, at various times issued wholesome ordinances against the *gipsies*, wandering beggars, and vagabonds, who so often show themselves, have been but loosely observed, indeed almost entirely put out of sight, and we desire to have everywhere complete compliance with these circulars tending to the good of the commonwealth.

Thus we renew and confirm all edicts published to this effect, especially the one of the 20th December, 1727, as earnestly as impressively issued, that all foreign beggars and land-hurtful loose rabble shall entirely leave the country, and as regards the natives of that sort, that they shall retire to the places of their birth or to those where they have hitherto for some years lived and maintained themselves. This done, all those who may be anywhere found and taken up shall be immediately carried to the fortresses, where they must be at once received according to the directions of our circular-orders of the 25th April, 1728, to all commanders of such. In the same way we renew the printed instructions of the 20th November, 1730, as to what is to be done in regard to getting rid of *gipsies* and other vagrants, and what for the purpose of keeping the country clear of such dissolute people. Such are to be seized on the frontiers at the first village they enter and at once carried off.

We, however, sharpen and extend the working of the above, so that from now on, any district magistrate who knowingly accords to such *gipsies*, vagrants and wandering beggars a residence or even shelter and a night's lodging on his property, and such people are not immediately, or as soon as may be, in conformity with our orders, at once arrested and carried off, shall be visited with the loss of his magistracy and with a thousand dollars fine in money. The bailiffs and communities, on the other hand, who are neglectful, or do not give to the above-mentioned magistrates proper assistance, are to be punished with severe and certain bodily punishment and according to the circumstances even confinement in a fortress.

So soon as such a one, gipsy or vagrant beggar or land-tramp, may be caught and it appears from his examination that he, by clear daylight, has gone through this or that village and at all begged therein, or otherwise acted suspiciously and was seen by people, but not arrested, an official account must at once be sent in to the government (office?) and this must at once have the case investigated by a treasury employé (ex-officio) and cause the guilty persons to be punished in conformity with this edict. In virtue of which it is enjoined upon all our governments, war and domain-departments, colleges of justice, general treasury officers and treasury employes, officials, district magistrates and commanders, to act energetically in respect of this, as well as of all other orders issued regarding *gipsies*, country-beggars and vagrants, and that no one may excuse himself under plea of ignorance they are to have this edict read every year from the pulpit.

Officially issued with our genuine autographical signature and stamped with our royal signet [apparently more emphatic than the privy seal] Berlin, November 30th, 1739.

Fr. Wilhelm.

S. v. Cocceji.

[Contrast this rude justice of a rough old temporal king with the merciless judicial edicts, following, of a spiritual Romanist Prince and Priest Ruler.]

See Ludwig's "Literary Analecta." Part II., p. 1075, A.

Beside this there is no deficiency in pretty sharp ordinances of other German imperial princes and states against the gipsies. Thus, as an example of the like sharpened ordinance, his electoral princely grace at Mayence, in concert with the four associated Circles issued such in 1714 against the *gipsies*, foreign beggars and other dissolute rabble owning no allegiance, by virtue of which he extends the punishment ☞ of DEATH without any formalities to gipsies and notorious pickpockets, simply and alone on account of their forbidden manner of life and on account of their proved disobedience, their wives and children are to be beaten with rods and branded. Land-tramps, vagrants, beggars, wounded soldiers, foreign Jews and other rabble having no domicile, whether provided with passes and discharges or not, are to be hunted up and forcibly ejected across the frontiers, and in case of any showed resistance, they are to be knocked down and even shot dead. This is the amount of the ordinance as found in the *Electis Juris Publici* of Mayence, Vol., VI., Part VIII., p. 656, &c. In its full composition it runs as follows:

"First. It has been again most humbly represented to the most high worthy prince and lord, the Lord Lothaire Francis, Arch-Bishop of Mayence of the Holy See, Arch-Chancellor and Elector of the Holy Roman Empire throughout Germany, Bishop of Bamberg, &c., and he has learned with great dissatisfaction that as regards the stringent orders, both Imperial and of the Circle, often published and made known, against the still hither and thither vagabonds, reckless to the common weal, more hurtful *gipsies*, pickpockets, Jew-beggars and other masterless thief-rabble who often also bring with them commonly all sorts of contagious diseases; these orders seem no longer to be sufficient. In addition it also appears that there is often a want of proper execution and carrying out of the so wholesomely conceived arrangements of the empire, circle, and other governments, and their proposed object has, up to this time, not been attained.

Second. It has been obvious that in our Circles themselves, and in one and another of the high and respectable departments, they have given free domicile to such reckless and thievish rabble, and thus with knowledge of it, whether from fear or other pretext; beside not applying the rigour of punishment directed in the before-mentioned ordinances and not going hand in hand for properly supporting each other. Therefore, at the last assembly of the associated worthy Upper Imperial Circles, it has again been held necessary on this occasion, not only to repeat and confirm the already-taken resolutions and the circulars containing them in their full contents; but also to, at the same time, freshly and most stringently ordain that, when discovered, all *gipsies*, notorious pickpockets, ☞ without any grace or indulgence, *sine strepitu judicii*, (without any judicial fuss), and without any further proceeding, simply and only by reason of their forbidden manner of life and proved disobedience, shall be executed with, or, if necessary, by some more severe manner of capital punishment. ☞ Their wives and grown children, however, when they are not at the same time convicted of a theft, shall be flogged, branded and for ever banished from the land, or condemned to perpetual confinement in the correctional workhouses; and because this loose, wicked and irresponsible rabble begin to move about in places where, on account of the forest, they think to find more concealment and security, and their number visibly increases, even so that, in spite of the guards posted here and there, indeed even in villages so guarded, one still hears, almost daily, of breaking into houses, of robberies, and also despoiling of travellers, this protection notwithstanding. Their daring impertinence is growing to such a degree that they do not hesitate at threatening the countryman who refuses them a night's lodging, with murder and the torch; that already various sheds, together with the grain in them, have been consumed, having, it is supposable, been fired by these wretches. Thus the country people are withheld by fear from carrying out with the necessary energy and vigour the wholesome regulations decreed by the Circle. It has been further unanimously resolved and ordered to be published everywhere, to-wit: That from the publication of this order all land-tramps, vagrant-beggars, wounded soldiers, foreign Jews, *gipsies* and other irresponsible rabble who are not born in the country or in some other way its subjects-whether having passes and discharges or not, are, without excep, tion, at once to quit the whole territory and to bestow themselves elsewhere, or should they remain the most severe and effective punishment will be inflicted on them. ☞ That they be hunted up by armed force everywhere, whether in towns, market-places, villages, copses or woods, and forcibly driven out, also that in case of their offering resistance they are at once to be knocked down or shot dead on the spot. ☜ In order to prevent those in such cases often occurring collisions as to jurisdiction, through which, according to daily experience, many wholesome laws and regulations are rendered unfruitful and remain in the lurch, it has been most definitely determined and approved among the electoral princes and the various governments, that when one or another of the like foreign land-tramps, beggars, soldiers, foreign Jews, vagrants, irresponsible rabble—or, also, others, in a certain measure subjects of the most worthy Circle governments or persons belonging to them—are captured or brought in by scouting parties, patrols, or other arrangements such as it may have been thought well to make, then any one has the power and authority, and indeed is under obligation, as concerns the one or the others of these classes, to give safe convoy for delivering the strangers and foreigners from out their governments and districts, by the most advisable way (and so as to prevent their escape or the like) to the nearest garrison next some fortified place without regard to local intermediate jurisdiction of any species being opposed or unopposed to it. The fortress is also at once to pass them on to another, and so on, until the frontiers of the circle are reached. For so acting there is to be no possibility of anything being quoted as, or of itself, tending to the legal prejudice or to the legal privilege or advantage, or by whatever name any consequence may be called, for the present or in the future, against any one so acting. And since it has further been discovered that some shameless and audacious persons conceal themselves in the garb of clergymen or other religious professionals, it is in the same way decreed that such strangers, and especially religious persons who say that they are returning from Italy or any other place of pilgrimage, be closely watched, and that, when they are not fully provided with sufficient passes and testimonials, they be detained on their entering the territories of the associated Circles, carried from place to place up to the proper Ordinary, by him examined, and, according to circumstances, handed further on or discharged. Since also, finally, it has been found that the mischievous poachers or venison-thieves creep into the forbidden proprietary forests and that they therein, with the, by the highest authority forbidden, rifle, not only cause great damage, but are audacious enough to murderously attack and fell keepers on guard against them, lest they be recognized, brought in and put in arrest by them, and since consequently they take up and carry on the same capitally punished sort of life as the herein so often mentioned mischievous pickpockets and *gipsey* rabble with whom they now and then associate themselves. On this account it is therefore decreed, that, first of all, each one of the high and most worthy Diets provide in their forests for the necessary arrangements and watch that these may be cleared of the deer-stealers and these last arrested and subjected to the punishment due them, and also that they give to each other on proper pointing out and description of the delinquents, all help necessary for taking and delivering them up and that they do not knowingly give to any reputed poacher forbidden concealment or shelter under penalty of like punishment. It is still, as aforesaid, more than ever to be observed, so far as circumstances will permit, that even when the crime is committed in the forest of others, nevertheless, the criminals are to be arrested and they are to be treated with the same penal rigour. In order now that no one may excuse himself by pleading ignorance of the decree now issued, this circular, like the preceding ones, is, by the gracious special order of the Prince Elector to be repeatedly read out and announced in the districts and to be affixed at the open gipsy resorts, signboard posts, as well as to the church doors, and like the previous ones, especially the last of the 2d May, 1711, publicly printed and published, to be most literally complied with. According to which every one will know how to judge and how to prevent injury to himself.

*Signed* under the most venerated prince-electoral grace and hereto impressed the office seal, Mayence, 22d March, 1714.

[L. S.]

In like manner, quite lately, at the consultations of the Circle of Suabia, held for a time at Ulm, the security of the main roads within its territory was a prominent subject, as is evident from the following circular:

"Since repeated proof is made to the now, here present, general assembly of this Circle, that, despite the manifold and also recently published circulars, and the capital punishment therein declared, the gipsy, pickpockets and other irresponsible rabble so excessively hurtful to the public are once more wandering about hither and thither in this worthy Suabian Circle and have become so bold as, on the 22d of last month, to again attack the Imperial and German post-messenger, and so to misuse him that had he not saved himself by flight, the letter bag with all its contents would have been taken from him. And now it is an unavoidable necessity, in order to oppose such wickedness and at once to preserve from danger the correspondence so important for the public, and the safety of the letter post, from all such commencements of outrage. Thus we wish properly to admonish through this circular all the high and respectable communities to keep a watchful eye in this regard in their lands, territories and governments. For this purpose they are at once, not only to renew and repeat the often recited district punishments, but also, on any request or intimation, to afford speedy assistance to the postmasters, and this with regular soldiers or in the absence of such, with a trustworthy [armed] and sufficient force and day or night to give this assistance, so that the conveyance of letters, on which so much depends, shall not be hindered and shall be put in safety against the like wicked and highway robber crew. And when such malefactor in this way shall be detected in the act and caught, then, without formalities, his trial shall be had, according to the present Circle orders, and it is allowable without mercy to inflict upon him the extremest capital punishment, if necessary to break him on the wheel, as a warning and example to others. To the various documents to the same purpose the present circular is affixed and published, under the common official seal of the five princely benches.

Signed at Ulm, 19th May, 1749. *The Councillors, the Envoys and the Ambassadors of the Princes and States of the worthy Suabian Circle present at the now assembled General Convention.*

According to the High-princely Saxe-Gotha territorial order, P. II., c. 4., tit. 23, in regard to the gipsies, their possessions and belongings shall, according to the complete prohibition of their travelling in German countries contained in the imperial statutes, be taken from all such gipsies as venture to enter the lands of the princedom of Saxe-Gotha, and they, with their wives and children, shall be driven out of it. And in virtue of the circular issued in the same country, of the 29th January, 1664, in respect to the watch association, the gipsies are summarily to be driven off from the frontiers. For this purpose the officers appointed for the defence of the country are to aid the courts of justice in all localities. And to this end the troops of every district, with their arms and the necessary powder and shot, are to be kept ready, exercised and provided, as also to the end of pursuit from one district or government to another, as is allowed and to be done by virtue of the imperial ordinances.

In the duchy of Würtemberg the *gipsies* were not tolerated, more specially for the reason that they have several times ventured to betray the Duke of Würtemberg, Eberhard, to the Sultan of Egypt, as is shown in *Crusii*. Annal. Suev., *Lindenspür* ad. Ordinat. Wurtemb., p. 120, n. 2.

Now it cannot be denied that the just now enumerated ordinances and the punishment contained in them may, at first sight, appear to many to be altogether too severe. But just as it is the common good which requires any punishment, so these wholesome laws were required by imperious necessity to make this punishment severe. On this ground the severity of military discipline which often punishes a soldier who, in spite of orders, has stolen a single fowl, with death, is justified, although as an abstract proposition there is no proportion between a fowl and the life of a man. If, however, one fully considers the circumstances which give rise to such severity, the doubt concerning it will soon disappear. Thus writes a certain Politicus (statesman?) : " The punishment of the least fault is made very severe that the greater crimes may be avoided the more easily, on account of the momentous results which come from the least point of neglected military discipline. It would be right if, in the proper manner, this severe law were published, ' Any soldier who steals even a fowl shall be punished by the " froice," since he has preferred the pleasures of stealing before the sanctity of the laws and the public security, and thus he would seem to consent to what he knew would be the punishment of his act.'"

If now there be a justification of the severe punishments of soldiers, then the severity of the punishments in regard to gipsies and the like rabble are much more justifiable, for they are, according to the extent above shown,—which has been above shown under imperial outlawry—and thus their havings and belongings, their bodies and lives, notwithstanding one or more public passports may be exhibited, since these were by the imperial ordinances completely revoked, broken and annihilated.

Preiss, as also especially in the Electis Juris Publici, T. VI., in the Eighth Part, p. 654, &c., has expressed himself decidedly. Still more concerning this gipsy rabble is to be found in the treatise on the subject, by Ahasuerus Fritschen, "*de Origine, Patria and Moribus Zingarorum;*" as also in Johannes Lunnæu's "de Jur. Publ. Lib." IX., c. I., n. 161, &c.; in Camerarius' "Hor. Subcif." Cent. I., c. 17.; Cent. II., c. 38 and 75, and Cent. III., c. 75; in Schonborner's "Polit." III., c. 26; in Flemming's "*Deutschen Jäger,*" Theil II., p. 44, &c.; in Ludolph's "*Schau-Buhne,*" Theil I., p. 400; in Zubner's "*Natur- Kunst- Berg-Gewerck- und Handlungs-Lex.*;" Arnctiel's "*Mitternächtische Völker*" (Northern Peoples), Th. III., p. 45, &c.; in Falckenstein's "*Nordgauisches Alterthum*" (Antiquity of Northern Countries), Th. I. p. 125, lit. 11; in Jacob Thomasius' "*Disp. de Cingaris ;*" in the "*Allgemein. Chronik,*" (Universal Chronicle), VI. Band, p. 66; in Micaelius' "*Histor. Eccles.*" (Ecclesiastical History), T. I., p. 887 ; in Wegener's "*Einleit. zu den Welt und Staats-Gesch.*" (Introduction to the History of the World, States, &c.), p 422; in Bresslauis; *Samml.* XXXIII., Versuch (Essay), p. 69; in Tharsander's "*Schau-Platz,*" Th. III., p. 331, &c.; in Nerret's "*Heiden Tempel,*" p. 1097; in Aventi's "*Annal.*" p. 835; in Aligem's "*Histor. Lex.*" T. IV., p. 973; in Bodin "*de Republ.*" Tit. V.; in Paulus' "*Zeit und Lust,*" T. I., N. 198, p. 690; in Voetius' "*Sips.*" T. II., p. 654; in Camer's "*Dor Subsis.*" Cent I., p. 195, &c. See also, in addition, the Article, "*Zeugitane,*" a country in "Africa proper," on the Mediteranean See, in the same (Zedler's) Universal Lexicon : &c., &c., therein.

GIPSIES, a word corrupted from Egyptians, is the name given in England to a wandering race of people who are [now] found scattered over many countries of Europe, whither they migrated from the East about the beginning of the fifteenth century. Pasquier, in his "Recherches Historiques," says that they first appeared at Paris in the character of Penitents or Pilgrims, in August, 1427, in a troop of more than 100, under some chiefs who styled themselves *Counts*, and that they represented themselves as Christians driven out of Egypt by the Mussulmans. They obtained permission to remain in the kingdom; other troops [bands] followed, and they wandered about in all directions, unmolested for many years, committing petty depredations, and their women assuming the calling of fortune-tellers. In 1560 an Ordonnance of the States of Orleans enjoined all imposters and vagabonds styled "Bohemians," or "Egyptians," to quit the kingdom under pain of the galleys. *The name of Bohemians, given to them by the French, may be owing to the circumstance of some of them having come to France from Bohemia*, for they are mentioned as having appeared in various parts of Germany previous to their entering France; others derive the word from

"*Boëm*," an old French word signifying a Sorcerer. (Moreri, Art. *Bohemiens;* and Ducange's "Glossary," Art. *Ægyptiaci*.) The *Germans* gave them the name of "*Zigeuner*," or Wanderers; the Dutch called them "Heiden," or Heathens; the Danes and Swedes "*Tartars*." In Italy they are called "*Zingari ;*" in Turkey and the Levant "*Tchingenes ;*" in Spain they are called "*Gitanos ;*" in Hungary and Transylvania, where they are very numerous, they are called "*Pharaoh Nepeti*" or "*Pharaoh's people*." The notion of their being Egyptians is probably derived from the circumstance that many of them came immediately from Egypt into Europe, but it seems proved that they are not originally from that country, their appearance, manners, and language being totally different from those of either the Copts or Fellahs. There are many gipsies now in Egypt, but they are looked upon as *strangers*, as indeed they are everywhere else.

It is now generally believed that the gipsies migrated originally from India at the time of the great Mohammedan invasion of TIMUR BEG; that in their own country they belonged to one of the lowest castes, which resemble them in their appearance, habits, and especially in their fondness for carrion and other unclean food. Pottinger, in his 'Travels,' saw some tribes resembling them in Beloochistan. There is a tribe near the mouths of the Indus called *Tchinganes* [somewhat similar to their Italian and Spanish, and almost identical with their Turkish and Levantine appellation].

The gipsies, in their language, call themselves *Sind ;* and their language has been found to resemble some of the dialects of India (*Bombay Transactions*, 1820). They have no traditions or records concerning their origin; no religion of their own, but they adopt the outward forms of the people among whom they live, whether Christians or Mussulmans. Everywhere they exhibit the same roving habits, a dislike to a fixed settlement and to the arts of husbandry, uncleanness in their food, licentiousness, ignorance and intellectual apathy, a disposition to pilfer and to impose on the credulity of others. They seldom commit violent robbery or other heinous crimes, being fearful of punishment. Maria Theresa ordered those in her states to be instructed in agriculture, with a view to their permanent settlement; but her endeavors were not very successful. In Hungary and Transylvania, however, many of them follow some regular trade and have fixed habitations; they wash gold from the sand of the rivers, and they work iron or copper; some are carpenters and turners, others are horse-dealers, and even keep wine shops or public houses. They abound in Wallachia, Moldavia, and Bessarabia, and they are found in Russia as far as Tobolsk. Grellman, in his '*Versuch über die Ziegeuner*,' Gottingen, 1787, conjectures that there are between 700,000 and 800,000 in Europe, of whom 40,000 are in Spain, chiefly in the southern provinces. In England they have much diminished of late years, in consequence of the inclosure of land and the laws against vagrants. J. Hoyland has collected the most accurate information that could be procured concerning this strange race, in his "*Historical Survey of the Customs, Habits, and Present State of the Gipsies ; designed to develop the Origin of this Singular People, and to promote the Amelioration of their Condition.*" 8vo., York, 1816. He has largely made use of the work of Grellman, "The Penny Cyclopædia of the Society for the Diffusion of Useful Knowledge." London, 1838, vol. xi., GIPSIES, p. 225.

Die || Zigeuner || in || Europa und Asien || (The Gipsies in Europe and Asia) : Ethnographisch-linguistische Untersuchung || vornehmlich || ihrer Herkunft und Sprache,|| nach gedruckten und ungedruckten Quellen. || von || Dr. A. F. POTT,|| ord. Prof. der allgem. Sprachwissenschaft an der königl. Preuss. Universität || Halle-Wittenberg.|| Erster Theil.|| Einleitung und Grammatik.|| Halle, 1844.|| Druck und Verlag von Ed. Heynemann || London, bei Williams & Nordgate.

This is said to be the best and most exhaustive authority on the origin and language of the Gipsies and was imported for examination and citation in the pamphlet on that subject now passing through the press. Too late for the original purpose its facts will be used in a larger work, for which all these studies in relation to the Gipsies were prosecuted with diligence and care.

A GUY D'AGDE, in the "*Dictionnaire de la Conversation*," article "*Bohemiens*" (Gipsies), has not a single good word for these people, charging upon them that they are not capable of any crime which indicates the possession of energy and courage, in a word, of manhood; but only those which awaken sentiments of contempt and disgust.

In the *Supplement* to this great work, this utterly degrading character is somewhat relieved of such blasting stigma by the statement that in the XVth and XVIth centuries they were noted as military artificers among the Poles and Turks, and that subsequently they became distinguished as musicians. In Russia the gipsies were not considered either as *Outlaws* or utter *Outcasts*, or even vagabonds. In Germany, two centuries since, they were looked upon as *Spies* in the interests of the Turks and penalties fearfully severe were from time to time promulgated against them. In case they did not obey the laws for their expulsion they were to be flogged until they bled, then to have their nostrils slit, their heads and beards shaved close, and, finally, to be transported out of the country. Any violence committed against them was not culpable.

In Hungary the judicial oath administered to them is curious "As God drowned King Pharaoh in the Red Sea, even so may the Tsigane be buried in the bowels of the earth, and may he be accursed if he does not speak the truth. May nothing honorable or dishonorable succeed with him. At the first trot may his horse be miraculously changed into a donkey and himself hung on the gallows by the executioner if he testify falsely."

The gipsies have little or no, if any, religion. According to M. Poissonier, Moldavia and Wallachia were inundated by the gipsies. In the latter principality the proverb runs: "Prayer never passes the lips of the Tsiganes and and their church was constructed of curds or lard and the dogs ate it." This same is also said of them by Velasquez, in Spain. In Harper's exhaustive "Cyclopædia of Biblical, Theological and Ecclesiastical Literature," Gipsies are carefully treated:

"They bear different names in different countries. In France they are *Bohemiens* (because they first came thither from Bohemia, or from *Boem*. an old French word meaning " sorcerer," because of their practicing on the credulity of the vulgar; in Spain, *Gitanos* or *Zincali ;* in Germany, *Zigeuner ;* in Italy, *Zingari ;* in Holland, *Heydenen* (Heathens); in Sweden and Denmark, *Tartars*; in Sclavic countries, *Tsigani ;* in Hungary, *Cziganjok*; in Turkey, *Tshengenler*; in Persia, *Sisech*; in Arabia, *Harami*. Various nicknames are also applied to them, as *Cagoux* and *Gueux* in France; *Zieh-Gauner* (Wandering Rogues) in Germany; and *Tinklers* in Scotland. They call themselves ROM (men, or husbands; comp. Coptic *Rem*), CALO (black), or SINTE (from Ind; hence Zincali, or black men from Ind.)

Some writers have connected them with the Σιγύνναι, mentioned by Herodotus (V., 9), as a people of Median extraction dwelling beyond the Lower Danube, and the Σιγυννοι, described by Strabo (§ 520), as living near Mount Caucasus, and practising Persian customs. Others have referred them variously to Tartary, Nubia, Mesopotamia, Assyria, Ethiopia, Morocco, &c.; but the account which the Gipsies, at their appearance in Western Europe gave of themselves, claimed " Little Egypt " as the original home of the race, whence they were driven in consequence of the Moslem conquests. * * The results of the investigations made within the last hundred years in the fields of comparative philology and ethnology prove beyond reasonable grounds of doubt that the theories above named are erroneous and that we must look to India, "the nursing home of nations," *(tellus gentium nutrix)*, as also the fatherland of the gipsies. It is now the almost, if not entirely, universally received opinion, that they came to Europe from Hindustan, either impelled by the ravages of Tamerlane, or, more probably, at an earlier date, in quest of fresh fields for the enjoyment of their vagabond life, and the exercise of their propensity for theft and deception. This view of their origin rests upon their physiological affinities with Asiatic types of men, as well as on the striking resemblances between the Gipsy language and Hindustanee, and the similarity of their habits and modes of life to those of many roving tribes of India, especially of the NUTS or *Bazegurs*, who are styled the Gipsies of India, and are counterparts of those in Europe, both in other respects and also in having no peculiar religion, since they have never adopted the worship of Brahma. The NUTS are thought by some to be an *aboriginal race*, prior even to the Hindus. Another theory, which seeks to reconcile the Gipsy statement of an Egyptian origin with the clear evidences of a Hindu one, would find their ancestors in the mixed multitude that went out from Egypt with Moses (see *Exod.* xii., 38; *Num.* xi., 4; *Neh.* viii., 3), and who, according to this view, passed onward to India and settled there, and from their descendants subsequently bands of Gipsies migrated to Europe, probably at different times and by different routes (see Simson). . . . The Gipsies call *their language* "ROMMANY," and modern philological researches prove that it belongs to the Sanscrit family. It has doubtless received additions and modifications from the languages of the countries in which the race has sojourned, yet it is still so nearly the same with modern Hindustanee that a Gipsy can readily understand a person speaking in that dialect—a fact which tends to verify the statements made as to the zealous care with which the Gipsies have cherished their ancestral tongue.

# ARMY AND NAVY QUARTERLY.

## AN ECLECTIC MAGAZINE.

VOL. I.—OCTOBER, 1885.—NO. 4.

### CONTENTS.

|     |     | PAGE |
| --- | --- | --- |
| I. | Electricity as applied to Naval Purposes. By Lieutenant W. A. CHISHOLM-BATTEN, R.N. (From the *Journal of the Royal United Service Institution*.) | 385 |
| II. | The Functions of Cavalry in Modern War (concluded). By Major GRAVES, Twentieth Hussars. (From the *Journal of the Royal United Service Institution*.) | 405 |
| III. | The Literature of the Thirty Years' War. By J. WATTS DE PEYSTER, Brevet Major-General S.N.Y. | 422 |
| IV. | The Actual and Ostensible Condition of the Russian Cavalry. By H. VON DEWALL. (Translated from the *Jahrbücher für die Deutsche Armee und Marine* by STANISLAUS REMAK, late First Lieutenant Fifth U. S. Artillery.) | 460 |
| V. | A Russian Criticism upon "The Actual and Ostensible Condition of the Russian Cavalry." (Translated from the *Jahrbücher für die Deutsche Armee und Marine* by STANISLAUS REMAK, late First Lieutenant Fifth U. S. Artillery.) | 484 |
| VI. | The Moral Element in Military Discipline. By Lieutenant Field-Marshal the ARCHDUKE JOHN. (From the *Journal of the Royal United Service Institution*.) | 493 |

PHILADELPHIA:

L. R. HAMERSLY & CO.,

1510 CHESTNUT STREET.

BOSTON: NEW ENGLAND NEWS COMPANY.  
WASHINGTON: A. BRENTANO & Co., 1015 Pennsylvania Ave.  
LONDON: B. F. STEVENS, 4 Trafalgar Square.

LONDON: SIMPKIN, MARSHALL & Co.  
YOKOHAMA: KELLY & Co.  
BERLIN: EUGENE DZONDI, Behren-Strasse 67.

PARIS: GROVES & BLACKBURNE, 1 Rue Scribe.

*Price, 50 Cents.*     $2.00 *per Annum.*

Copyright, 1885, by L. R. HAMERSLY & Co.

Entered at the Post-Office at Philadelphia, and admitted for transmission through the mails at second-class rates.

# COLDEN'S Liquid Beef Tonic.

Established 15 Years.
OBSERVE the NAME
Beware of Imitations.

ORIGINAL LABEL:
"Colden's Liebig's Liquid Extract of Beef and Tonic Invigorator."
(Originated and first Prepared by the Liebig Meat Extract Co. London, Eng.)

### An Invaluable Aid in Medical Practice.
### Differs Essentially from all other Beef Tonics.

**COLDEN'S Liquid Beef Tonic** is endorsed by scores of physicians, who are growing to realize more and more its importance in repairing, in accordance with the principles of dietetics, the **waste which disease entails.** It consists of the extract of Beef (by Baron Liebig's process) spirit rendered non-injurious to the most delicate stomach by extraction of the Fusel Oil, soluble Citrate of Iron, Cinchona, Gentian and other bitter tonics. An official analysis of this preparation by the eminent Chemist, ARTHUR HILL HASSALL, M. D., F. R. S., and an endorsement by the late SIR ERASMUS WILSON, F. R. S., is printed on the label of each bottle

As a **nutrient**, and a **reliable tonic** in all cases of debility and weakness, Malarial Fever, Anæmia, Chlorosis, Incipient Consumption, etc., it is the best preparation ever used. It acts directly on the sentient Gastric Nerves, stimulating the follicles to secretion, and gives to weakened individuals that first prerequisite to improvement—an appetite. It strengthens the nervous system when unstrung by disease, and has been employed with remarkable success as a remedy for Drunkenness and the Opium Habit.

### Its Range of Action Embraces all Cases of Debility.

In order that physicians may form some idea of the nature of its ingredients, I will upon application in person, or by letter (enclosing a card), send a sample bottle of COLDEN'S LIQUID BEEF TONIC to any physician in regular standing, in the United States. Please ask your Dispensing Druggist (if he has not already a supply) to order it. In prescribing this preparation, physicians should be particular to mention "COLDEN'S"—*viz.*: " *Ext. carnis, fl. comp. (Colden's.)*" It is put up in pint bottles, and can be had of Wholesale and Retail Druggists generally throughout the United States.

**C. N. CRITTENTON, Sole Agent, 115 Fulton St. New-York.**

## GLENN'S
# Sulphur Soap.

ALL physicians know that *skin diseases* are more or less constitutional, or dependent upon some specific poison in the blood, which if eradicated by internal treatment needs something to remove its appearance from the surface. Experience has proved that the best possible aid in the accomplishment of this end is obtained by the use of *Sulphur in soap*. GLENN'S SULPHUR SOAP is the best combination of its kind, and the one now generally used. It is for sale by all Druggists, at **25** cents a cake, or 3 cakes for **60** cents.

## CONSTANTINE'S
# PINE TAR SOAP

Has been on trial among physicians for very many years as a toilet Soap and Healing Agent, and its superior virtues have been unanimously conceded in all cases where the use of tar is indicated. Unsolicited expressions of its excellence have been received from the Medical Faculty generally. IT IS THE BEST TAR SOAP MADE. None genuine unless stamped "A. Constantine's Persian Healing Pine-Tar Soap." For sale by all Druggists.

Either of the above-named Soaps will be mailed to any address on receipt of price and three cents extra per cake for postage.
**Depot: C. N. CRITTENTON, 115 Fulton Street, New York.**

# SCOTT'S EMULSION
## OF PURE COD LIVER OIL
### AND HYPOPHOSPHITES OF LIME AND SODA.

The Standard Emulsion of Cod Liver Oil.

ALMOST AS PALATABLE AS MILK.

*The only preparation of its class that will not separate nor grow rancid in any climate.*

*It contains more strengthening and fat producing qualities than any other preparation in the world.*

*It is indorsed by the medical profession universally.*

*And in consumption, wasting disorders of children, scrofulous conditions, and general debility, it is most marvellous in its healing and strengthening powers.*

**SCOTT & BOWNE,**

**NEW YORK.**

Sold by Druggists Generally.

# VANITY FAIR
### Flake Cut Smoking Tobacco,
#### IN TINS, FOR ARMY AND NAVY USE.

This popular brand is prepared in a condition to keep in any climate, and, by an ingenious arrangement of a sponge in the cover of every box, consumers can dampen to suit their convenience.

Requisitions for this Smoking Tobacco can be filled on application to proper department. If your commissary does not keep this brand in stock, and is unwilling to order it, we will supply direct, at factory prices, by registered mail or express.

### FRAGRANT VANITY FAIR AND CLOTH OF GOLD CIGARETTES,
#### 13 First Prize Medals Awarded.

**WM. S. KIMBALL & CO.,** - - - - **Rochester, N. Y.**

## EAST FLORIDA SEMINARY,
### GAINESVILLE, FLORIDA.

Located at the most healthful point in the State. Admirably adapted to the requirements of delicate lads who cannot endure the cold weather or heated school-rooms of the North. Complete English, Classical, Scientific, and Business Courses. Military Department under charge of an officer of the Regular Army. For descriptive catalogue of the Seminary, apply to   Col. E. P. CATER, Gainesville, Fla.

## THE NEW YORK TRIBUNE.
### FALL OF 1885.

ANIMATED, READABLE, THOROUGHLY AMERICAN, WHOLESOME.
THE SUNDAY ISSUE A BRILLIANT PAPER.

Two Thousand Dollars' Worth of News, Sketches, and Stories for a Few Cents.

THE TRIBUNE contains more items of news—telegraphic, local, social, athletic, sporting, etc.—than any other New York paper.

Its Sunday collection of notable articles by distinguished writers at home and abroad, who write over their own signatures, is without a parallel in New York. Read the lively review of all manly sports in the Sunday paper.

Geo. W. Smalley's letters from London give a clearer idea of English affairs and politics than the London papers themselves. This is admitted.

THE TRIBUNE represents the great business interests of the country, and the prosperity of our own people, in the controversies now going on relative to the tariff. In the discussions relative to Army and Navy, THE TRIBUNE favors putting the country into a state of good defence.

THE TRIBUNE, Daily and Sunday, $8.50 per year; Daily only, $7.00; Semi-Weekly, $2.50 per year; Weekly, $1.25.
   Address   **THE TRIBUNE, New York.**

(Trade-Mark.)      (Trade-Mark.)

We have solved the problem at last—producing a **Smoking Tobacco** equal in delicacy of flavor to the choicest of the fancy brands, and at the same time have been able to put it at the popular price of

**5 CENTS a package, neatly put up in Tin Foil Wrapper.** VICTORY! It is manufactured from the finest Golden Leaf grown in the most famous fields of North Carolina and Virginia. It is the only Tobacco in the country which has received testimonials from gentlemen known to every veteran soldier in the United States.

### Read what "Old Rosy,"

The Hero of Corinth and Stone's River, says: *"It is delightful for smokers." Yours respectfully,"*

Gen. Paul Van Der Voort, late Commander-in-Chief of the Grand Army, sends the following: *"Your Victory Smoking Tobacco is delightful ammunition for the Meerschaum. I like it very much."*

Gen. Geo. S. Merrill, ex-Commander-in-Chief of the Grand Army, says: *Your Victory is well named. For delicacy of flavor it can't well be surpassed, and it is laden with contentment when put into a pipe. Yours very truly,"*

**Greatest in Quantity!**

**Finest in Quality!**

**Cheapest in Price!**

☞The **Victory Smoking Tobacco** should be found at all tobacconists. If you cannot find it send to us direct, inclosing **SEVEN CENTS** in stamps, and we will mail you a sample package. In such a case you will do us a favor also to send us the name of the leading Tobacco Dealer or Grocer in your town, in order that we may take steps to place it where you can procure it conveniently in future.

Have you tried the Celebrated **GOLD COIN CHEWING TOBACCO?** The best and purest. Popular price, **FIVE** cents. By mail, same as "**Victory.**" Address

### D. BUCHNER & CO., New York City.

Mention "Army and Navy Quarterly."

# COMPARATIVE WORTH OF BAKING POWDERS.

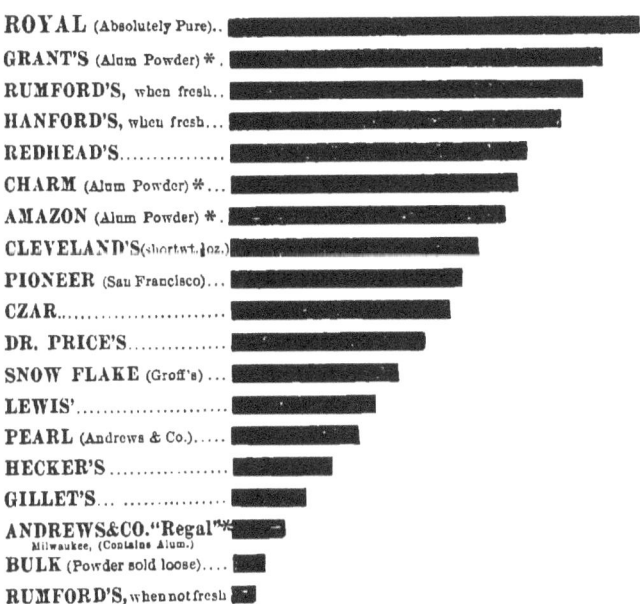

ROYAL (Absolutely Pure)..
GRANT'S (Alum Powder) *.
RUMFORD'S, when fresh..
HANFORD'S, when fresh...
REDHEAD'S...............
CHARM (Alum Powder) *...
AMAZON (Alum Powder) *.
CLEVELAND'S(shortwt. 1 oz.)
PIONEER (San Francisco)...
CZAR.........................
DR. PRICE'S...............
SNOW FLAKE (Groff's)...
LEWIS'......................
PEARL (Andrews & Co.).....
HECKER'S..................
GILLET'S... ................
ANDREWS&CO."Regal"*
Milwaukee, (Contains Alum.)
BULK (Powder sold loose)....
RUMFORD'S, when not fresh

## REPORTS OF GOVERNMENT CHEMISTS

As to Purity and Wholesomeness of the Royal Baking Powder.

"I have tested a package of Royal Baking Powder, which I purchased in the open market, and find it composed of pure and wholesome ingredients. It is a cream of tartar powder of a high degree of merit, and does not contain either alum or phosphates, or other injurious substances. E. G. LOVE, Ph.D."

"It is a scientific fact that the Royal Baking Powder is absolutely pure.
"H. A. MOTT, Ph.D."

"I have examined a package of Royal Baking Powder, purchased by myself in the market. I find it entirely free from alum, terra alba, or any other injurious substance. HENRY MORTON, Ph.D., President of Stevens Institute of Technology."

"I have analyzed a package of Royal Baking Powder. The materials of which it is composed are pure and wholesome. S. DANA HAYES, State Assayer, Mass."

The Royal Baking Powder received the highest award over all competitors at the Vienna World's Exposition, 1873; at the Centennial, Philadelphia, 1876; at the American Institute, New York, and at State Fairs throughout the country.

No other article of human food has ever received such high, emphatic, and universal endorsement from eminent chemists, physicians, scientists, and Boards of Health all over the world.

NOTE—The above DIAGRAM illustrates the comparative worth of various Baking Powders, as shown by Chemical Analysis and experiments made by Prof. Schedler. A pound can of each powder was taken, the total leavening power or volume in each can calculated, the result being as indicated. This practical test for worth by Prof. Schedler only proves what every observant consumer of the Royal Baking Powder knows by practical experience, that, while it costs a few cents per pound more than ordinary kinds, it is far more economical, and, besides, affords the advantage of better work. A single trial of the Royal Baking Powder will convince any fair-minded person of these facts.

* While the diagram shows some of the alum powders to be of a higher degree of strength than other powders ranked below them, it is not to be taken as indicating that they have any value. All alum powders, no matter how high their strength, are to be avoided as dangerous.

# THE
# ARMY AND NAVY QUARTERLY.

VOL. I.          OCTOBER, 1885.          No. 4.

## ELECTRICITY AS APPLIED TO NAVAL PURPOSES.[1]

BY LIEUTENANT W. A. CHISHOLM-BATTEN, R.N.

I. Application for General Purposes.
II. Application for War Purposes.

THESE are in some cases mixed, and there is no sharply-defined line between them,—take electric lighting as an instance. The ordinary internal lighting of a ship is quite distinct in itself from search-lighting, though produced by much the same means. They have both grown independently; but in a ship of war, the great object should be to combine the two.

Electricity is a great power in skilled hands, and can be used with safety and certainty even by slightly trained men, if only enough care and thought be taken in designing electrical appliances to make their use easy and abuse difficult.

The applications of electricity on board ship are various, and differ greatly. Sometimes it is necessary to use the electric force in such a way that it has power to melt any metal, to produce an intense light rivaling that of the sun, to propel a vessel, or to give severe and even fatal shocks to those handling its mechanism. At other times it is so gently applied that although it acts through the human body, it cannot be felt by the most tender child; and at others, it is so exquisitely sensitive that it will carry faithfully the distinct tone of a

---
[1] Read before the Royal United Service Institution.

certain voice, and indicate a change in its neighborhood so slight as the movement by inches of an ounce of lead.

The two properties of the electric current which are generally made use of are, first, that of causing heat when a comparatively great resistance is placed in the circuit; and, secondly, that of giving magnetic properties to any conductor through which it passes.

An apology is due for going into matters so simple, but in case there may be some who may not be familiar with these points, they will be briefly explained.

Electricity for naval purposes is produced by what may be termed a generator, which is generally either a machine deriving its power from the burning of coal, or a battery deriving its power from the slow burning of zinc.

The next part of any electric appliance to be considered is the circuit, that is to say, a conductor, generally metal, which allows the current to circulate from the generator to the place of application, and back again. This is generally formed of copper or iron wire.

The part of the conductor or lead which goes from the generator to the place of application may be called the main, and the part which comes back may be called the return.

When the result desired is the developing of heat or light, a high resistance, that is a small conductor, or one of a comparatively badly conducting substance, is introduced in the circuit at the desired place.

For instance, if the electricity originally obtained by the burning of coal, and then carried in an accumulator, be allowed to pass by a main wire which must touch the accumulator, to an incandescent or glow-lamp and back by a return wire, heat and light are produced in the thread of carbon in the lamp, which has a high resistance.

Or again, if the electricity produced by the burning of zinc in a battery be allowed to pass through the main to a small wire and back again, sufficient heat is produced to fire a charge of gunpowder.

When the result required is an exertion of magnetic force, the simplest, or at any rate the most familiar, form is the electric bell. In a circuit from a battery which slowly burns zinc, a current passes round a coil of wire, causing it to act as a magnet and to attract a piece of iron which makes the clapper strike the bell.

Or again, if the current, originally obtained from the burning of coal, be allowed to pass by the main to a magnetic arrangement and back by the return, the result is magnetic action which causes motion, and is sufficient to drive a boat or any useful machine.

Thus much of the simple principles of electricity.

*Electric Lighting.*

The most important application of electricity for naval purposes is, perhaps, the lighting of ships.

Electric lighting is almost entirely carried out by an extension of the simple appliances which have been described. The current passes from the electric machine or generator along the main to the lamps and back by the return; that is to say, the illumination in a ship of war is carried out by a large number of glow-lamps—usually about three hundred—of about twenty candle-power, that is, twenty wax candles, eight to the pound. The electric machine is usually driven by a steam-engine.

The advantages claimed for the use of electric lighting on board ship are many of them applicable, as you will notice, to its use on shore.

1. It is cheaper than oil,—at any rate than the oils allowed to be used on board men-of-war, and still more so than candles, which have hitherto been the general illuminants.

2. There is far greater safety from fire, as there is no occasion for carrying matches about or lighted candles, which in spite of rigid rules are often used naked. This is hardly surprising when one hears of the trouble which has to be taken to avoid naked lights being used in mines; the use of electric lighting also does away with that incubator of fires,—the lamp-room.

3. It hardly heats the air, and does not foul it at all.

Many merchant steamers and some ships in the navy are thus lighted, the principal reason against its extended use in the latter being the fact that men-of-war pass much of their time without getting up steam, but in troop-ships it has been almost universally introduced.

Andrews & Co., of Glasgow, have just completed on board the "Etruria" a large installation which, in its proportions, surpasses anything that has hitherto been attempted in the application of electric light to steam-ships. The "Etruria" carries about eight hundred and fifty lights, and a brief description will no doubt be interesting. Swan glow-lamps are used, and of these ninety are distributed in the engine-room, stoke-holes, etc. One hundred and three lights altogether are used for lighting the main dining-saloon, eighty-four of which are suspended over the tables in three-light electroliers hanging from the ceiling. The remainder of the lamps are in small brackets and pendants so as to give light over the side seats. Above the saloon is the music-room, having seventeen lights round the walls and over the piano and organ. The smoking-room has also seventeen lamps. The remainder of the lamps are distributed about the ship, one hundred and seventy-two being in the state-rooms.

Besides the actual internal lighting of ships, electricity is used for the bow and mast-head lights. I understand that the Board of Trade does not object to the use of the electric light for ships' side lights, but it requires oil-lamps to be kept in reserve in case of failure. With regard to mast-head lights, however, the Board discourages the use of electricity, partly on the ground of its liability to get out of order in consequence of vibration, and partly in consequence of the brilliancy of the light tending to interfere with shore lights, and cause confusion. It is in fact not used for mast-head lights, and only in a few cases for side lights, and it has not been thought necessary to issue any general instructions, though the Board of Trade is now in communication with the Admiralty on the subject.

On this point there has been some discussion. The first lights used were very much brighter than the oil-lamps which they replaced, and caused mistakes from their being taken for light-houses, or from the distance of the ship using them being misjudged. There is, however, great advantage in their use, from such use securing certain knowledge that the lights are all right. This is effected by the current passing to the lamp through an indicator on the bridge, in view of the officer of the watch.

The ordinary lights carried by ships-of-war when cruising in company are now in some cases electric, and the electric light has been ingeniously adapted to signaling purposes.

One of the most complete arrangements got out by the well-known firm of Sautter Lemonier is as follows:

Two groups, of five glow-lamps each, are suspended at a certain distance above each other, and the current is allowed to pass to one or more of them by a key-board in the deck-house. In order to prevent mistakes, the signal is set before the current is allowed to pass to the required lamps, and this setting lights up a corresponding signal in front of the operator, thus: He wishes to show four lights, and puts four lamps in connection with a main switch. In doing so, he uncovers four little illuminated windows in front of him. Satisfied by the appearance of this signal, he switches on the current from the generator, confident that his signal will be correct. A switch is merely a means of connecting or disconnecting one conductor from another, as is also a firing key, which will be mentioned later on. Or the signaling may be done by hoisting the light and signaling with the key; or again by dipping the light in a bucket. There is also an application of the glow or incandescent lamp for the purpose of coaling or doing other work at night. In this case a group of about a dozen lamps are placed under a reflector which is triced up to the yard-arm, so as to light up the deck of the ship and the coal wharf or vessel alongside.

The glow-lamp is also useful for the diver, either in thick water or at night; but special precautions have to be taken to prevent the globe being broken by pressure, and for this purpose it is inclosed in a second thick glass globe.

The electricity for the lamp is either derived from above water through wires kept carefully dry, and not touching any metal, or it is in some cases provided by a battery carried by the diver with the lamp.

Messrs. Siebe & Gorman's lamp is of the latter kind. The lamp is mounted in a parabolic reflector fixed to the side of the battery-box. The battery will keep a constant light going for four to five hours.

We now come to a different form of illumination, called the arc light. In this arrangement, a suitable current of electricity is allowed to pass through two carbon rods in contact, and then they are slightly separated. The effect of this resistance or space introduced into the circuit by separating, is to produce a very brilliant light, proceeding partly from the heated carbon rods, and partly from a luminous arc between them.

This light is very intense, too much so for many purposes. The carbons burn away, so that some arrangement is necessary for bringing them within the proper distance for the arc, and for replacing them when entirely consumed.

This arc light has been used for internal lighting, mast-head lights, and coaling lights, but the necessity of having some apparatus for feeding the carbons and other causes have forced it to give way generally, for these purposes, to the simpler glow light.

For the search light, however, used for discovering torpedo-boats approaching a ship, bombarding forts, and so on, the arc light is a necessity, as great intensity is required. The search light is a warlike appliance, but had better be considered in connection with other uses of electric lighting. It is very useful for other purposes, such as clearing the anchor at night, and such peaceful, or at any rate unwarlike operations. When the arc is used for a search light, its rays are all collected by means of lenses or mirrors, and projected in one beam, so as to get the strongest possible light.

The difference in power is immense between the glow and arc lights in ordinary use at sea; the glow-lamp representing only a few candles, seldom more than twenty, but the arc as now used about twenty-five thousand, and a far more intense arc light has been produced on shore. A boat can be discovered by it at a great distance.

In the West Indies, in a fine clear atmosphere, a building has been picked out clearly enough to be aimed at with a gun, at a distance of two and a half miles, the light used being about eight thousand candles; but great difficulty was experienced in keeping the beam on the object, as one could not see any distance unless standing away from the light.

To obviate this, means have been devised for directing the beam by an observer at some distance from the lamp.

The search lights in general use are worked by a man who screws the carbons together as they burn away; this method, undoubtedly crude, has been adopted chiefly for simplicity's sake, but it is high time that a suitable automatic lamp—that is, one which is self-feeding—should be introduced, and that the direction of the beam should be in the hands of the observer, although he is necessarily at some distance from the light.

The electric lights belonging to the ships have been considerably used during the operations in Egypt; one was landed, generator and all, at Alexandria, and another at Suakim. The light was also much used at the latter place from on board, for discovering the approach of the enemy at night.

For signaling, the arc light has been used for many years, the process being to flash the beam up in the sky in longs and shorts, using the Morse or some similar code.

To show what may be done in this way, it may be mentioned that during some of the electric light night exercises carried out at Portsmouth from the Torpedo School, the flashes of a light of about twenty thousand candles were distinctly seen thirty-one miles from the ship, a low range of hills intervening; and a similar light was reported to be seen still farther when shown from a tower of the Philadelphia Exhibition last year.

Again, some ships being anchored in Ragusa and others in Gravesa, signaled to each other in spite of the hills between, by flashing an arc light up in the sky.

There is no difficulty in lighting up a building at two miles' distance with a twenty thousand candle light.

*Electric Communications.*

From signaling by the light at a distance, one passes naturally to other means of communication for which purpose electricity is more universally used than for any other.

Telegraphy, in the nature of things, is not in use much outside the ship, from the difficulties of bringing in the wires with a ship swinging round her anchor; but means have been devised for this useful object which are especially applicable to light-ships: telephones, and so on, can of course be used from a ship moored head and stern,—in fact, light is sometimes supplied in this way.

As regards electricity within the ship herself, the uses are manifold.

The ordinary electric bell I need hardly dwell upon, but the two appliances most especially required in men-of-war are first, a means of knowing the speed of the vessel at any time, and secondly, of telegraphing distances of the enemy ascertained in the tops, to the captain and gun-batteries.

I am not aware of any method, which is in very general use, for obtaining the first result. But there are numerous approaches to it.

There are many instruments which give the speed of the ship or engines for a greater or less period of time, but what is required in a man-of-war is to know the speed at any instant.

Various electric logs do the first; that is to say, the space passed over can be noted during any period, but the speed at a given instant is not shown. Even an instrument which showed at any instant the speed of the engines would be a useful improvement.

The principle of most electric logs is that the revolutions of the fan periodically close a circuit. When this is done, a dial hand moves on one division, usually a tenth of a mile. If, then, the electric log be joined up to a recorder in the captain's cabin, and another in the chart-house, and set at noon, both the captain and the officer of the watch can see at any time how far the ship has run since then, or since the last time the instrument was looked at.

The difficulties of a joint which shall connect two conductors, and yet be able to stand continually being revolved, appear to have been dealt with in an original manner in the "Dollond" log; the principle is protected by patent, and is applicable to the attachment of wires for signaling to light-ships or other vessels swinging round their anchors.

This log will be sufficient to give an idea of these instruments.

The log used in the navy for recording the distance passed over by a ship consists in a fan which is towed on the quarter of the ship, and which, as it revolves, shows the number of miles passed over on a dial plate attached. The disadvantage is that it has to be got on board in order to see how much distance has been run.

Other logs which are much used in mail steamers have a fan towing, but the recorder is on the taffrail, and is turned by the towing line.

The disadvantage is that the recorder can be in one place only, and only one recorder can be used.

It is claimed for the electric log that it is more trustworthy than the taffrail log, and more useful than either, in so far as one or more recorders can be placed in any required position. The advantage is obvious in any ship in cruising time; but in a ship of war in action its value is enormously increased, for it is easy to place telephones in connection at any required point in the pilot towers, at the Whitehead directors, gun directors, and gun-deck, for in firing a gun it is necessary to know speed, and still more necessary when firing a torpedo.

It indicates at once any mishap to the log, by fouling or carrying away.

It saves the labor, loss of time, and error of registration involved in hauling in the log, which can remain in the water, unless fouled, until entering port.

The instantaneous registration of the distance run between two bearings enables navigators to calculate with accuracy their position in reference to a light, headland, or other fixed object.

The indicator can be reset on board at any moment.

The addition of a small self-contained apparatus and a bell, which can be placed with the indicator or in any other part of the vessel, communicates by sound the regular working of the log, and enables the officer on watch to detect any irregularity and to take instantaneous bearings at given distances, without referring to the indicator or the log.

A distance indicator devised by Lieutenants Jackson and Anson, of the "Vernon," has undergone already a trial in the "Excellent" and "Vernon," and has been favorably reported on. The indicating hand is rotated in either direction, one step at a time. A spring brake prevents it from being thrown out of adjustment by the concussion of firing heavy guns. A bell is fitted in the receiver which rings each time a signal is completed. In the transmitter, a red disc shows when the circuit is completed, and the battery running on circuit. The instruments are carefully protected from wet; they will work in any position, and are entirely unaffected by damp and gun-fire; two wires are used with each circuit for connecting transmitter with receiver. The commutator, however, is of delicate construction, and the springs on the armatures require careful adjustment for efficient working with low battery power.

The great defect seems that there is no method of telling whether the two instruments, transmitter and receiver, are indicating the same signal, and if the battery be left on circuit for long it may fail to work the instrument.

The telephone is used from ship to shore, when ships are moored. In the "Vernon" one was used to the captain's house and found most useful. Through this telephone, some eight years ago, an officer recognized Professor Bell's voice, which he only knew from having heard him lecture in London, and he did not know the professor was in Portsmouth.

The application of the telephone to diving is most valuable, and in my experience was perhaps the means of saving a man's life. He was just able to say, "Pull me up," and was found quite insensible. It is strange to be capable of hearing a man below water, a mile away, as well as if he was at your side. Some difficulties were experienced at first, but have now been completely overcome. The same apparatus can be adapted for use on shore.

Telegraphy for parties landed, though not a usual equipment, is very useful, and I have seen shipmates with a small field telegraph consisting of a couple of sounders and reels of wire carried by men.

For automatic indicators, electricity may be used to indicate too great a rise of temperature in any compartment, to indicate if the ship is off her course—this is similar to an arrangement which will be described for steering a torpedo—or to indicate if the barometer falls beyond a certain point.

The application of electricity to testing the lightning conductors of ships is so simple that any trained seaman can obtain the resistance, without delicate instruments, with fair accuracy.

The propulsion and steering of boats by electricity is a subject which almost requires a separate paper to itself, and although sometimes used for war and sometimes for peace, the appliance is naturally similar whether a boat be carrying a torpedo or a policeman. Some particulars of two boats which could carry either may be interesting.

The "Electricity," which was fitted by the Electrical Power Storage Company two years ago, and which has run successfully many hundreds of miles, is twenty-five feet long.

The "Australia," built by the order of Messrs. Stephens, Smith & Company, is of the same length; batteries or boxes of stored electricity in the boat, work a screw propeller. The cost of the "Australia" is about one hundred and eighty pounds complete.

Each boat carries eight besides the coxswain. Speed about seven or eight knots.

The advantages of electric propulsion are,—

(1) Entire absence of noise in the boat; in fact, the only noise is that caused by the plash of the water against the boat's bows.

(2) No smoke to interfere with the man steering.

(3) No "flare up," which is practically impossible to prevent in very fast boats from the great draught up the funnel.

(4) No heat, which tells so much on the stokers in a torpedo-boat.

(5) Not so large a number of men required as in a steamboat.

The disadvantage of this form of motive power is of course the necessity of having means to recharge the cells again after use; but should this prove a successful experiment, regular charging stations could easily be provided for a boat to go alongside and have her cells charged, as, for instance, night patrol-boats could be charged alongside a jetty during the day for use at night. From the absence of heat this form of motive power would be most valuable in very hot climates.

The various appliances in a submarine cable-ship are special in their character, and are hardly to be considered generally naval.

One of these is a cable creeper which has a push in angle of the creep, so that if it catches a cable it rings a bell.

Now in the descriptions about to be given, reference will be often made to "testing." This testing is for the purpose of seeing whether the circuit, including the actual place of application, is in good order. The principal test is to see that the conductor and appliance have a complete circuit. To do this, a small current is allowed to pass round the circuit, too small to cause any appreciable heat, or to work the magnet, but large enough to affect an indicator or ring a bell, which only require a small current, thus showing all is correct. Should there be any break in the circuit, the little current cannot pass, and so cannot ring the bell or affect the indicator.

The current is supplied by a battery. A simple test-battery and indicator will easily show whether there is any break or not in a coil of wire, or any electric circuit.

ELECTRICITY APPLIED TO WAR PURPOSES.

*Firing Guns.*

We will now consider the applications of electricity to war purposes afloat, the first, the one considered most important, being firing guns.

The method of firing guns by electricity is simple.

The method of heating a wire by passing electricity through it has already been explained.

To fire a gun, the electric current is allowed to pass through a piece of fine wire surrounded by powder, and placed in the vent of the gun.

A firing key is used to allow the current to pass from the battery through the main wire to the little tube of powder in the gun, and then back by the return. If a very small current be sent through the circuit, it will not heat the resistance; and if it be made to ring a bell in the pilot-tower, the officer in charge knows that the circuit is all right.

Some of the advantages of firing guns by electricity are as follows:

When firing a broadside of guns together, if electricity be used, it is fired much more simultaneously than when using hand firing; and when firing single guns, the action is more instantaneous. This may be illustrated by a well-known machine. Any man trying to fire a gun at a certain time, or when certain objects are in a line, is only more or less successful in doing so,—generally less.

Another very important advantage of firing guns by electricity is that they can all be fired by an observer clear of the smoke of the gun-deck.

Again, the guns can be fired from a bullet-proof pilot-tower as the ship passes close by the enemy by any one person or the captain himself, the crew lying down or being placed out of the way. This is especially advantageous in ships which have their guns on the upper deck exposed to machine-gun fire.

Again, there are cases where the object cannot be seen from the gun, and electric firing provides an easy means of firing from aloft on the mast. Thus a ship in the Suez Canal fired at a train in motion, which was only visible from aloft, and hit it.

Again, the gun can be aimed at a fixed floating plank, and be arranged so as to fire when the plank is touched. In fact, it acts as a spring gun against torpedo-boats.

Electric firing for a single gun was recommended by the Chilian officers after the action in which the " Huascar" was taken, as the most likely to be effective.

It must be allowed that there is the disadvantage with electricity of the chance of damage being done to the circuit, but this would be shown by the bell in the pilot-tower. On the other hand, the advantage is that its use simply alters a heavy pull-off to a light one,—in fact, it may be called a hair-trigger.

*Automatic Firing.*—This is an arrangement for firing when the ship is rolling; for instance, the gun is required to be fired when the ship is upright, the circuit passes through a balance so arranged as only to connect the two parts of the circuit, that from the generator and that to the gun, when the ship is upright; so that directly the ship is in that position the guns are fired.

The method is claimed to have been brought to great perfection, but is not so simple as it looks.

Electricity may be used to light up the foresight at night. An appliance for this purpose has been invented by Captain McEvoy, the well-known torpedoist. It consists of a little battery and glow-lamp, which is screened except in the direction of the foresight. The electricity has to pass through a similar arrangement to that mentioned above for automatic firing, so that the lamp is only lit when required.

It is capable of a much more practical application than automatic firing, as a wide margin can be allowed to cover any error from the rolling of the ship.

It seems specially useful for resisting night torpedo attacks.

And now for torpedoes, which come next, at least, in importance.

Electricity is used for firing, propelling, and discharging torpedoes.

Just a word as to what torpedoes are. They are movable submarine charges of explosives, used offensively.

The name "torpedo" is, oddly enough, derived from the electric fish, but I do not suppose he who first applied the word ever thought that electricity would be so much used for firing these charges.

### Firing Spar Torpedoes.

The spar torpedo is the simplest form, consisting of a charge at the end of a pole, which is put under an enemy's ship, and exploded.

For this form of torpedo electricity is now exclusively used, and the arrangement is usually as follows: To the battery a firing-key is attached by a wire. This key is joined to the main, so that on pressing the key the circuit is complete through a fuse which is similar in principle to the glow-lamp and which is in the torpedo, then back by the return to the battery,—an exactly similar plan to switching on lamps or firing guns.

There is also an arrangement by which the battery is joined to the main direct, and the main goes to an automatic firing-key in the head of the torpedo, which acts on striking, then by the fuse and return wire back to the battery.

A combination of these methods is generally used, though probably a separation of them would be better. The spar torpedo, though so simple, has at present the greatest score—at least half a dozen ships—against traveling torpedoes, one; and towing torpedoes none. The cases occurred in the American civil war, Russo-Turkish, and Franco-Chinese wars.

As in the case of the gun, a small current can be sent through the fuse, and can ring a bell or work an indicator so as to show the circuit is correct.

### Firing Towing Torpedoes.

The next torpedo, which to a great extent owed its want of favor in our service to being introduced without electrical means of ignition, is the towing torpedo. This is, I believe, always fired by contact with the enemy's ship. When electricity is used, the circuit is from the battery to a contact piece in the torpedo, then to the fuse, and back by the return to the battery.

Though we are only concerned with electric firing, it should be explained that if any other method of exploding a torpedo is used, it is, after once being made dangerous, equally so to friend or foe.

With all electrical appliances the removal of the wires from connection with the battery renders the torpedo as harmless as a box of explosives can be.

Batteries are the usual generators for firing torpedoes. Sometimes, however, an exploder is used in which the power is derived from a man's muscular action.

### Firing, Propelling, and Steering Fish Torpedoes.

Fish torpedoes claim our attention next, and there are many kinds of them; but those with which electricity is used are few; in them the force developed in some part of the circuit is made use of to produce motion or put the rudder one way or the other, or simply to fire.

When electricity is used for igniting the charge, all torpedoes are fired in a similar way to one of those described for the spar and towing torpedoes, namely, at will or by contact.

1. There are torpedoes which are propelled from, and controlled from their base, as the Sims, named "controlled torpedoes."

2. There are torpedoes which contain their own propelling power and are uncontrolled and unconnected with the position from which they are started; for instance, Paulson's. They have been called "auto-mobile" torpedoes.

3. There are others which contain their own propelling power but are connected with and controlled from their "base"; for instance, the Lay. They have been called locomotive.

First, those *driven* by electricity.

This is done either by electricity stored in accumulators and put in the torpedo, or through wires bringing the electricity from the base of operations.

In addition to fixed submarine mines, it has been considered necessary, in some cases, for coast defense to make use of a controlled motive torpedo, principally for attacking ships which attempt to clear a passage through the submarine defenses.

For this purpose a torpedo is required having the following properties:

1. Long range.
2. Handiness with the helm.
3. A heavy charge, so as to be dangerous even if stopped by a ship's net defense.
4. Security from enemy's fire.
5. Power of passing floating obstructions.
6. Not easily seen or stopped by enemy.
7. A motive power always ready, and not dangerous.
8. Constant speed to end of run.
9. Charge exploded at proper depth, for a charge on the surface is comparatively harmless.

The torpedoes of Ericsson, Lay, Howell, Whitehead, etc., are not considered by some good judges to fulfill these requirements as completely as that of Sims.

Common defects are, great complication, difficulty of preparing and keeping the torpedo ready, danger of explosion from the substance which drives it, great exposure to fire of enemy, want of speed, charge at the surface, etc.

The Whitehead is considered unsuitable on account of its comparatively short range, because it cannot be steered, and for other reasons.

The Sims torpedo is of the ordinary cigar or fish shape, and is driven by a current of electricity from a generator on shore, which passes through a wire laid out by the torpedo as it goes, and works a screw propeller. The torpedo can be steered and fired by electricity from the shore through the same cable. The torpedo is suspended a few feet below the surface from a float which is just awash. There are two different sizes,—the larger carrying two miles of wire and a charge of four hundred pounds of dynamite.

The two-mile torpedo is of copper so as not to rust, and is about twenty-eight feet long. The cable, which will just sink, is carried in a chamber to which the water is freely admitted, so that the buoyancy of the torpedo is but little increased as the cable is paid out. The charge is in the head. The wire chamber, which has a short tube underneath leading aft, through which the wire is paid out, is in the centre, and the driving and steering gear are in the after part of the torpedo. The steering is done by a separate current from a battery; the helm can only be put hard over either way, and when released is brought amidships by the action of the water.

The torpedo is suspended by strong steel frames about four feet under a boat-shaped copper float of about the same length as the torpedo, but whose bow is a few feet farther aft. A steel cutwater connects the bows, and, as it slopes downward and forward from the float, tends to force the torpedo under any boom or floating obstruction it may meet with.

The float is built in water-tight compartments, and filled with some buoyant substance, so that it is difficult to sink it. It carries the usual two upright rods,—one with a white, the other a red ball in the daytime and lamps at night. The rods are pivoted with counterweights so as to give and lie flat when passing under an obstruction, and to rise again when clear. The speed is said to be twelve knots.

The cable is of copper wire, and a small insulated wire in the heart of the main cable is used for steering.

The torpedo may of course easily be arranged to fire on contact if required. When it was tried by running at a spar, a spectator who was in a boat near did not see it, although watching for it, until it was within five hundred yards. The torpedo hit the spar in two successive trials within four feet of the point aimed at, and the marks on the spar were one and a half feet from each other.

The float has been riddled by bullets, and yet remained serviceable.

The great disadvantage of the torpedo is its want of speed. Some less clumsy method of maintaining it at its proper depth would, doubtless, very much increase the speed.

There is no doubt an advantage in controlled torpedoes which have their motive power on shore, and therefore have to carry less weight, but they can be only used from a special base.

Then those *steered* by electricity, though with some other driving power.

*The Paulson Torpedo.*—In this fish torpedo the steering is electrical. The motive power is supplied by liquefied carbonic acid. This torpedo is automatically steered in a direct or straight course by means of a mariner's compass, the needle of which, on any deviation of the torpedo from its course, makes contact with one or other of two insulated studs situated on either side of one end of the needle, and completes an electric circuit; a lever then causes one propeller to revolve at a quicker speed than the other, and thus steer the torpedo and bring it back to its set course. Supposing the torpedo to be approaching an ironclad, the mass of iron would cause the needle to make contact with one of the studs and the torpedo to be steered directly away from the ironclad, unless its path were due north and south (magnetic), and, to prevent this, a needle of a second compass in the head of the torpedo is arranged to short circuit the battery when attracted to one side or the other by the mass of iron.

The shell of the torpedo is made of compressed waterproof paper pulp, which is light and strong, has no effect on the compass-needles, and is not easily affected itself.

In order to render the weapon more effective, it may be controlled over part of its course by means of an electric cable paid out from the torpedo as it progresses, and by which the current from a battery on any shore or on a ship is conveyed to the two magnets so as to steer it on a desired course. When the whole of the cable is paid out, it is automatically detached, and the self-steering apparatus comes into operation.

*The Lay Torpedo.*—This well-known weapon is another example of the application of electricity to steering a torpedo. It is driven by other means, but lays out an insulated cable as it runs, and through this it is steered. It carries a very heavy charge, and it is usually run just on the surface. It has not made such rapid improvements as the Whitehead in point of speed. The usual rods or lights are used for directing the torpedo, and very good practice is said to have been made by it.

It has not been fortunate in war, for although there was a rumor that during the late war in South America a Chilian vessel was blown up by the Lay, I do not think that was the fact. There was an attempt to use it from a ship in the same war, but that method could hardly be expected to be successful.

## Discharging Fish Torpedoes.

The simplest form is to ring an electric gong as a signal for the man standing by the torpedo to start it, for it must be understood that it is usually started from somewhere down below in a ship, and therefore it is necessary to have somebody up above to decide when it is to be sent on its journey. An improvement is, at the order " Ready," to full cock the discharging arrangement, the same movement connecting up an electric circuit which has only a break on deck, and which, when traversed by a current, puts in motion the machinery for discharging the torpedo.

Another and greater improvement is the torpedo tube, being fitted on the inside with a cartridge, which, when ignited, projects the torpedo.

The clutch, which keeps the torpedo in the tube, is arranged in such a way that when withdrawn it makes electric contact with an otherwise insulated binding screw on the right of the gun.

The torpedoes are arranged to be discharged by an officer who is in the pilot-tower. In this case the firing key is in the pilot-tower, between the battery and the place of application, and there is a break at the tube, so that there are two breaks in the circuit; when very nearly at the moment for firing, the word is passed down, when the lever is pulled by hand, freeing the torpedo and making contact at the gun. The torpedo is then fired by pressing the key in the chart-house.

The torpedo battery, which may be considered as a part of a defense system, has been devised to defend any channel left in mines for the passage of friendly ships.

It consists of a submarine framework, in which are fixed torpedo tubes, each holding a fish torpedo.

The observing station, which may be distant and quite invisible to an enemy, is connected to the battery by a wire which goes to an electric fuse.

A weight released by the explosion opens the valve of the engines and frees the torpedo from the tube.

*Firing Submarine Mines.*

Submarine mines are used by ships for the purpose of defending themselves, or any harbor in which they may be lying, or for the security of which they may be responsible, or for dropping behind them when retreating. They are charges of explosive, defensive and fixed, fired under water.

The difference between torpedoes and mines is this: If you want to be blown up, you must go to the mine; but if you don't want to be blown up, you must stop the torpedo coming to you.

The electrical methods of firing them are two: (1) firing at will; (2) firing by contact.

The observation method of firing at will may be briefly described as firing a submarine mine when the enemy is within range of the effect of its explosion.

There are two difficulties in carrying out this otherwise certain and simple plan. The enemy may not come within the range of the mine, and when he does you may not know he is there.

With the first difficulty we have nothing now to do.

The second must be considered, as on it depends the difference between the two electrical methods of firing mines.

The simplest, and in its usual form, perhaps the worst plan, is by the method of cross bearings.

To go back to our circuit.

There is a generator in this case, a battery that is on shore. The main wire goes from the battery to No. 1 observer, from whom the mine bears, say south, that is, the mine is directly south of him, then passes through his key ; then goes to No. 2 observer, who has the mine, say, due east of him, and who also has a key. The main then goes on to a fuse in the mine, and the return takes the current back to the battery.

A word about return wires: the resistance of a conductor depends, other things being equal, on its size; the earth being large does not offer much resistance, and is often used as a return wire.

Now the circuit is not complete unless No. 1 and No. 2 both press their keys. A ship comes in. If ever she is south of No. 1 he presses his key. If ever she is east of No. 2 he presses his key ; but the keys are never pressed together unless the ship is south of No. 1 and east of No. 2, that is, over the mine.

This system has lately been well described by an eye-witness, and I dare say you will understand his description better than mine.

"And now we are going to fire ' by observation.' There is a mine of eighteen pounds of gun-cotton down yonder, two feet under water, and that barrel there is an enemy's ironclad steaming up the harbor. But she may also run close by without actually touching it. This contingency has been provided for by putting the mine in electrical connection with two observing stations. Yonder is one perched up there some feet above the water. It is a wooden shed, constructed so as to be readily taken to pieces and put up again wherever it may be desired. In actual service, it would probably be half buried in the ground, and the front of it protected or rather concealed by a bank of turf. There are two of these observing stations at different points of the compass, but both on the same electric circuit. The observers within them are keeping the object-glasses of a couple of small telescopes following the ship there as it approaches the mine.

"These telescopes are so mounted, that until they both point exactly to the destructive area around the mine, the electric circuit by which it is to be automatically fired is incomplete. The enemy might pass too far from the explosive underneath the water to be much affected by it. In that case there would be no use in firing. The two telescopes looking from different points of view, would not at any instant converge their lines of sight at the mine, and there would always be a break in the circuit. The ship would go on her way. She is working straight for the mine, however. The gear of one telescope clicks into a sort of notch, and one break in the circuit is repaired. Click goes the other telescope. The circuit is complete; a tiny piece of platinum wire is instantly raised to a white heat inside the mine, and up goes the ship, a volume of water leaping into the air, some of it to the height of a church steeple, bearing with it fragments of the unlucky tub that has done duty for the foreign ironclad, which, under similar conditions, would not have gone up in the air probably, but would have had a hole knocked in her bottom which would speedily have sunk her."

Other methods are the camera obscura; the plane table by a telegraph from the second station; firing all the mines in the neighborhood of the ship, so that one of them must hit her, and so on.

The plane table is electrical. The telescope at one station works a ruler at the other, and when the observer finds this line and his cut over a mine, he fires.

"Observation" firing cannot be used at night or in a fog.

The other system, that of contact mines, is different. To start from the battery, the circuit goes to a contact-key in the torpedo, and on to the fuse; when the torpedo is struck, then back by the return.

A ship must actually hit this mine to set it off. The ship in fact blows herself up. She may pass close to any number of mines, but only a small charge is required.

The electrical disadvantage of this system is, that you cannot send a small current through for testing, unless a boat or a friendly ship bumps the mine for you. This has led to complicated additions. The simplest of these is a very high resistance which bridges over the break in the circuit, so you can always send a small testing current round the circuit; but when the mine is struck, enough current will go through the fuse to fire it.

The next addition was by means of a further appliance, so that the action of a ship striking the mine could be imitated.

This has been arranged by causing the magnetic effect of the current passing through the high resistance to attract the other side of the break in the circuit, so as to cut the high resistance out.

This is useful in two ways,—it gives a far more trustworthy test than a simple resistance, as it stands to reason that a delicate instrument which works all right in the mine shows no serious damage is done to it; and again, it is possible by this means to fire a mine as well as by the contact of an enemy's ship.

There is another means of testing an electric contact mine, viz., to have a telephone in the mine with a ball on the diaphragm, so that the motion of the mine in the water makes a noise in the telephone.

Electro-mechanical mines are those which carry their own battery inside. This saves wire, but if the mines are picked up, is extravagant in boats and men's lives.

In these mines means must be used to keep the mine safe while being laid down. This is effected in the simplest form by keeping the wires apart, and joining them at a safe distance when the mine is laid.

The dynamiters imitated a very common form which works by means of some chemical action. They put acid on blotting-paper, and got away while the acid was eating through it. This mine was without a circuit-closer.

These electro-mechanical mines were used for the defense of Suakim, and were very successful, or seemed so, for after the explosion of one mine, the night attacks, to guard against which they were laid, ceased for two months.

### *The Torpedo Detector.*

This consists of a sinker, which is a heavy case, and a box, designed to be carried in a boat, from which the cable hangs. It can be so adjusted that no sound is heard in the receiver. If, now, the boat is pulled slowly through the water and the sinker is thus dragged along the bottom, no noise will be heard in the receiver unless the sinker comes into proximity with some mass of magnetic metal, such as a torpedo case. In this event, however, a humming noise will be heard in the receiver.

A slight and imperfect sketch has now been given of the appliances which come under the heading of this paper, and I think you will agree with me that no trouble, no care, no money is wasted, which is spent in teaching our men to make a proper use of electricity, which as a servant has been aptly compared, for ability and docility, to the slave of the lamp, but which as a master is always mysterious and sometimes terrible.

# THE FUNCTIONS OF CAVALRY IN MODERN WAR.[1]

BY MAJOR GRAVES, TWENTIETH HUSSARS.

PART II.

(Concluded from page 344.)

THE points remaining for our consideration and discussion to-day are (1) *Cavalry dismounted service;* (2) Cavalry with an army in *retreat;* (3) Cavalry with an army in *pursuit;* and (4) some concluding remarks on formation, armament, and education.

First, then, with regard to *cavalry dismounted service.* A considerable amount of controversy has been raised on this subject, owing in part to the prominence lately given to the question as to whether or not a force of mounted marksmen should be raised and maintained in this country. It has been suggested that owing to the shortcomings of the cavalry dismounted service, a certain portion of the cavalry should be organized as corps of mounted marksmen, who would combine the best qualities of good infantry and of good cavalry. The predominant feature in this force would naturally be that of infantry, owing to their being marksmen.

Were this carried into effect it would reduce our cavalry proper by some two thousand men, all trained, and efficient with sword or lance and carbine. Further, it would take away from some twenty regiments something like twenty-five per cent. of their best men, and thus for a time render them inefficient in many respects; and to gain what? To gain what Jomini describes dragoons to be, "amphibious animals."

I consider our cavalry force to be too few by some thousands now, and this would only add to a confessedly existing evil were we to still further reduce it.

I consider that, owing to this numerical weakness from which we suffer, this is no time to attempt any such new experiment, which must be bought and paid for out of a very small and valuable capital, namely, our small force of cavalry. The interest on that capital is efficiency, and I think that this is no time to reduce that interest by

---

[1] Read before the Royal United Service Institution.

adopting any such speculative scheme. We most likely, judging from the experience of the dragoons of by-gone days, should find our capital squandered, with the initial certainty of reducing the interest, as above, on some twenty regiments.

Some cavalry officers have said to me, "Oh! if you are going in for making our men fight on foot, they will lose their characteristics as cavalry," etc. But let us consider this. We have our cavalry trooper. He is a trained soldier; he is efficient as a horseman, at drill, with the sword or lance, and has a fair idea as to what is required of him on outpost duty or reconnoissance. So far, good. We put into his hands a carbine, very effective up to five hundred and six hundred yards, and possibly up to one thousand. Will it mar his riding to encourage him to become a good shot? Will his becoming a good shot induce him to go to the left when he should go to the right? Will his liking for shooting, increased by efficiency, cause him to dismount with carbine when the "charge" is sounded? Certainly not. Well then, having trained him as above, and having developed his shooting powers, we find him in a position where his horse and lance or sword are useless to him, but where a carbine is the one thing needful. Having his carbine, and being able to shoot, is there anything contrary to cavalry economy in placing him in the best available position to use it with effect, namely, on foot? I know nothing, provided always that his instruction is based on the principle that the functional expression of cavalry is in the main founded on the united action of man and horse, and that the function of dismounted service is demanded of him for the fulfillment of a special purpose which could not be carried out on horseback. I decline therefore to admit that shooting on foot converts a cavalry man into an infantry man, as strongly as I deny that an infantry man mounted is a cavalry man. The trooper dismounted is a cavalry man still, and finds himself in that position under exceptional circumstances,—to shoot. The infantry man mounted is still an infantry man, and finds himself in that position for a special purpose,—to get to a certain place in much less time and with much less fatigue than if he went on foot. If we can train our mounted infantry up to a certain point of efficiency in outpost and reconnoissance work, I am sure that this efficiency would only add to their already proved usefulness. At the same time, I do not think it would be advisable to raise regiments or corps of mounted infantry; I think the necessities of the case would be met by having a certain number of men in each regiment taught to ride, and to do this I do not see why the depôt at Canterbury could not be utilized by the addition of a few horses and rough-riders; or why a riding depôt could not be formed at Aldershot with a certain number of horses and an instructing staff. The system of borrowing horses from cavalry regiments is certainly most annoying to commanding officers; but this point will be urged later on.

Part II., Section 23, of the cavalry regulations, is very clear and concise as to the object and rules to be kept in mind with reference to dismounted service, and alongside this section I would quote Von Schmidt; he says, " . . . The experience of the late campaign has proved irrefutably that it is indispensably necessary that cavalry should to a certain extent be able to fight on foot. . . ." Again, " . . . Through its ability in this respect it will under all circumstances gain enormously in independence and self-confidence as well as usefulness." Again, " When owing to circumstances, ground, or to enemy's occupation of localities and defiles, it is not possible for cavalry to attain its object on horseback; when it is very difficult to turn such places; *when nothing can be hoped for from mounted action, and there is no infantry on the spot, nothing remains to cavalry but to dismount.*" " *In acting thus we shall not become mere mounted infantry, which is the last thing we could wish to be; we have no desire to fulfill the rôle of infantry.* . . . In this way there will be an enormous development of that desire to take the initiative, that love of enterprise and longing for personal distinction which should animate us as cavalry soldiers, which alone we wish to be.

" It is not our place to stand fast under fire in positions under cover; our object must be to approach the enemy and dislodge him. To this end every cavalry soldier must be trained in the use of his carbine, and in fighting on foot in dispersed order; taking the fullest advantage of the ground and the cover it affords. . . . The following then are the things most required of us: More thorough training in the use of the carbine than hitherto; for this duty has been very much put in the background, instead of being developed like every other one for the highest instruction of the men. . . ." " An increased expenditure of time over this duty is not necessary, provided that the musketry is thoroughly carried out with real interest and intelligence. . . ." " More extended instruction . . . in taking full advantage of the accidents of ground." " We must make better use of peace time, and prepare ourselves more thoroughly and systematically."

Speaking of the regulations of Frederick the Great, and his constant use of dismounted cavalry, he says, " In this glorious period, however, cavalry lost nothing of its true spirit. They did not forget to charge with *les armes blanches*, although they had much more fighting on foot than nowadays."

May we not apply the greater part of this to ourselves? If all this is so necessary, and of such emphatic importance to the German cavalry, which outnumbers our own to an enormous extent, how much more important for us, the importance increasing in proportion to the smallness of our numbers?

It would be needless to quote the use made of dismounted service in the Franco-German war in detail, and I would simply refer to the valuable services of the mounted infantry in Africa and in Egypt from the very first. The American war furnishes us with many instances of the value of dismounted service, whatever the value of those performing it in other directions. The battle of Five Forks is a notable example of what may be effected by efficient dismounted service, when Sheridan's dismounted men dealt with the Confederate right, while the Fifth Infantry Corps turned their left, and acting thus together caused a total loss to the enemy of some thirteen thousand men, and won a battle which decided the war.

The action of Tamai affords an example in which cavalry is shown as coming up in the nick of time, dismounting, firing, and thus checking the enemy's advance, gave our infantry time to re-form. An eye-witness writes in speaking of the temporary retreat of the left brigade: "We came back about eight hundred yards. . . . By this time the fire of the First Brigade, on our right as well as front, and the cavalry on our left, held the Arabs. . . . It was some moments before the retreat could be checked, and then the check was in a great measure due to the action of the cavalry. When first the infantry were engaged, the cavalry withdrew to the rear, where they were hidden from the enemy by a fall in the ground. In the panic, the cavalry advanced at a trot, meaning to afford aid to the infantry by a charge. This happily was unnecessary. The enemy seeing a large body of cavalry bearing down upon them, hesitated; this gave time to the soldiers to listen to their officers, and to re-form. . . . the rebels soon began to come on again. . . . Here again the cavalry did good service, some of the squadrons dismounting and firing volleys at the rebels who were collecting in the rear and on the flanks." These examples, and a multitude of others that might be brought forward, prove conclusively the value of dismounted service. I am very glad that the question of the establishment of corps of mounted marksmen and the organization of mounted infantry has been raised, for I am confident that it will have the effect of indirectly increasing the efficiency of our cavalry dismounted service, which is the great desideratum, and also will give a stimulus to the training of at any rate a certain number of infantry in the use and care of the horse.

The second point for consideration is the functions of cavalry in relation to *an army in retreat*.

Jomini states, "Retreats are certainly the most difficult operations in war." He also says, "If the theory of war leaves any points unprovided for, that of retreats is certainly one of them." I will not therefore presume to enter into any theories as to the best methods of, times for, and order of retreats. It is sufficient to assume the fact of retreat of an army beaten in battle, but retreating in a fairly orderly manner, and that such retreat by an army of any magnitude should be conducted deliberately, "by short marches, with a well-arranged rear-guard of sufficient strength to hold the heads of the enemy's columns in check for several hours." The importance of keeping the touch between the various parts of the army retreating, and of the value of flankers, is shown by the mishaps that befell Napoleon during his retreat from Smolinsk, when the corps of his army retreated on the same road, but divided by a day's march, and having no means of information in the shape of flankers, the enemy cut in between the parts of his army, to his great loss, during three days at Krasnoi. Inasmuch as the chief function of cavalry in pursuit is to turn defeat into rout, so the chief function of the cavalry of the rear-guard of a beaten army is in combination with the other arms to prevent the defeat they have suffered being turned into a rout, and to cover the retreat of the army, so that order may be restored and confidence regained, with a view to a fresh struggle on arrival at a position suitable for the purpose.

A retreat under such circumstances is a very different matter from a movement to the rear of an army that has not been engaged, but is forced to move owing to the exigencies of supply, position, or political complications, etc. This is comparatively an easy matter; but, as Sir Edward Hamley says, "A beaten army is no longer in the hands of its general. It no longer responds to his appeal. The troops that have been driven from the field will be slow to form front for battle. Confusion, too, will be added to despondency, for regiments will be broken and mixed; artillery will be separated from its ammunition; supply-trains will be thrown into disorder, and the whole machine will be for the time disjointed." ... "It is partly to provide for this that generals usually keep part of their reserves out of action." And Lord Wolseley writes that the rear-guards "should be formed at least from the freshest troops; their strength should be one-fourth to one-fifth of the whole force," so, I would add, as to put a screen of unbroken and fresh troops between the retreating and confused and their confident and pursuing enemy. With regard to the duties of such a rear-guard the same writer states, " The great art of rear-guards is that of being able constantly, without risk and with very little trouble, to force the enemy to deploy for attack, and then to get safely away yourself without any serious fighting; in other words, the rear-guard should, by frequent occupation of strong positions, be continuously threatening to fight, as it is by so doing that it best fulfills its purpose." Jomini lays down that " it is generally sufficient if the rear-guard keep the enemy at a distance of half a day's march from the main body."

Now, owing to the important issues depending on the right performance of the duties of thus screening a retreating army; to the intimate interdependence of the three arms upon one another in this work; to the constant necessity for showing a front, and in so doing the constant necessity for screening, covering, and supporting each other by the three arms, how absolutely necessary it is for the leader of the cavalry to know something of the functions and capabilities of the other arms, and to have a well-formed idea of what should be done, and how to do it!

He and his troops maintaining a position nearest the enemy (except at the actual moment of passing through a defile, when the infantry would remain in most instances in rear to cover their retreat by fire, the artillery having passed over first), should be animated with such a sense of responsibility for the safety of the army as to be willing to sacrifice themselves for the safety of that army and the honor of their country; he should be ever watchful to seize and hold with dismounted men such points and positions as will force the pursuers to deploy, and advance to the attack, at the same time showing necessary vigilance towards the flanks and any parallel roads thereon, so as by a good system of flanking patrols he may prevent the enemy outmarching him and cutting him and the remainder of rear-guard off from the main body. A knowledge of demolitions would here be useful in the destruction of bridges, in the obstruction of deep cuttings by cutting or blowing down trees, etc.

I will here mention as very useful for examinations in tactics, the lectures by Major Dyke, the garrison instructor, Eastern District. In that on rear-guards he states, " Military history abounds with instances of victories more or less thrown away owing to feeble pursuit, . . . in fact, vigorous immediate pursuit is rather the exception than otherwise." He instances that after the battle of Weissenburg, "on the evening of 4th August all contact with the foe was lost." Again, after Wörth, "the pursuit instituted by the cavalry was discontinued at the entrance to the difficult mountain passes, and thus all contact with the enemy had ceased to exist." In like manner, after Spicheren, night set in and the ground was unfavorable, and so pursuit ceased. Therefore the cavalry leader with the rear-guard of a retreating beaten army should be self-reliant and resourceful; should be bold yet cautious; and should do his utmost to wear out the patience of his pursuers, while carefully nursing his own force.

We now come to the functions of cavalry with an *army in pursuit*. We must remember that a most important element in the value of a victory is that the results should be brought to hand and made the most of. To this end a vigorous but not reckless pursuit is essential.

Where the victory has been decisive, the cavalry should be, if possible, pushed forward at once to prevent a rear-guard being formed, and to harass and rout the mixed crowds now in full retreat, to overtake them and hang on to them until they have thrown down their arms, and have practically dispersed. Should a rear-guard have been formed, the pursuing cavalry should keep the touch of it continually; when it presents a front, it should be thus held as long as possible, while a turning movement is attempted with a view to cutting it off. Its flanks should be continually threatened with this object in view. One of the best examples of such a pursuit is that afforded by Sheridan's pursuit of General Lee after the battle of Five Forks. Denison gives an excellent account of it. The pursuit lasted from the morning of April 3 until the whole of Lee's army surrendered at Appomattox Court-House on the 9th. The chief point of interest is to be found in the turning movement made between Dratonsville and Sailor's Creek. Lee's rear-guard turned there and stood firm, some ten thousand strong. Sheridan held them in front while he sent forward the leading division of his cavalry, who dismounting on their flank harassed and checked their supply-train and escort. Whilst this was going on, three other divisions passed along the rear of the dismounted men, crossed Sailor's Creek before Lee's rear-guard, took up a position on the high ground on the far side, and dismounting placed themselves across the path of the rear-guard, whom they received with such a murderous fire from their long-range repeating rifles that the result was that they captured six thousand prisoners, sixteen guns, and four hundred wagons. The same system of tactics brought about the surrender of the whole army as above.

History affords us but few such examples on this point. The Prussian pursuit after Waterloo was first-rate; and earlier the French pursuit of the Prussians after Jena was another noteworthy instance of the results of victory made good by a really vigorous pursuit.

I would close this part of the subject by referring to two other cases of such pursuits which stand out in bold relief. First: After the great battle of Arbela, Alexander with his cavalry pursued Darius. After leaving the battle-field he crossed the river Lycus, halted there to refresh men and horses until midnight, again started in pursuit, and reached Arbela the next day, distance seventy miles. Darius had gone on. Alexander followed him, until after three days and nights his infantry could no longer keep up; but knowing that Darius was bound to fight, he dismounted five hundred cavalry, and put on their horses five hundred of his best infantry, pushed on all night, and came up with the Persians in the morning, and routed them at once, whilst Bessus, having murdered Darius, escaped with only six hundred horse. The fruits of victory were not only gathered in by this splendid exploit, but the fate of one empire was sealed, and the position of the other made sure.

The second and last instance I would refer to is, of course, the pursuit after Tel-el-Kebir, and the marches on Zagazig and Cairo. The whole of the cavalry and mounted infantry was on the right, under Sir Drury Lowe; and while the infantry were assaulting the position, they made a turning movement against the enemy's left, and, working round, cut into the stream of Egyptian fugitives, causing them great loss. I understand that the Fourth Dragoon Guards and the Bengal Lancers reached the railway and canal in rear of the Egyptian position at 7.30 A.M.; they proceeded along the canal to the lock, and one Indian regiment struck off at once to Zagazig, where it arrived at about 4 P.M. the same day; and another Bengal regiment went on at once to Belbeis, followed shortly afterwards by mounted infantry, and later still by the Fourth Dragoon Guards. They bivouacked there that night, and starting again next morning about 4.30, reached Cairo about sunset, to find that the tidings of the victory had preceded them, and that their arrival so soon after had produced such an effect that the governor with a garrison of some ten thousand men surrendered to a handful of jaded and weary heroes, who would have found it almost impossible to have urged their horses into a gallop. Such is the force of moral effect when applied at the fitting opportunity.

The result of this victory, the further result of this close-following pursuit and march, so well conceived, so ably carried out, was that the enemy collapsed and the war was finished.

We have now concluded the consideration of what I must admit is a very imperfect consideration, as far as I am concerned in its setting forth, of the " Functions of Cavalry in Modern War."

Before, however, entering on the discussion, we might do well, I think, to look around and see what we can learn from our neighbors.

And first, as to the question of *armament*. As we are armed at present, our dragoons and hussars carry sword and carbine, and our lancers carry the lance in addition. Some of our Indian regiments have lance and sword in the front rank, and sword and carbine in the rear rank; officers, some non-commissioned officers, and trumpeters, carry sword and revolver.

In 1878 I was permitted to give a lecture in this theatre, which was published in pamphlet form, on " Military Equipment," and in it I advocated the plan of arming front ranks with lance and revolver, and the rear ranks with sword and carbine. I still believe that principle to be correct, but I fear that it would not be workable in our service, and I know that the general feeling is against it.

Nolan says, " All seem to forget that a lance is useless in a *mêlée*," as was demonstrated at Aliwal. Marshal Marmont says, " It would be better for cavalry to have both the lance and sabre, . . . the lance should be the principal weapon, the sabre an auxiliary arm." Jomini says, " In charges in line the lance is very useful; in *mêlées* the sabre is much better." De Brack also affirms this. I think therefore that the principle would find effectual practical expression if it were recognized as the general rule to support lancers with dragoons or hussars. We should then avoid such disasters as Aliwal, and should be in a fair way to realize the benefits obtained by this method at Meangunge. Touching the *revolver*. In November, 1864, a fight took place in Virginia between a squadron of Federal cavalry armed with the sabre, and a squadron of Mosby's armed with the revolver. The loss to the latter was one man killed and several wounded, and the loss to the Federals was twenty-four men killed, twelve wounded, and sixty-two prisoners; thirty-six killed and wounded out of one hundred. On another occasion, under similar circumstances, the sabres lost twenty-six killed and wounded, fifty-four prisoners, and eighty horses; the Confederates, who were armed with the revolver, *lost not a single man*. As before said, *we* only put revolvers into the hands of our officers, some non-commissioned officers, and the trumpeters; what is the state of things in Continental armies on this point?

I am indebted to the courtesy of an Italian staff officer, and to the military attachés of Austria, France, Germany, and Russia, at our court, for full information on this head.

The Italian officer informs me that up to two years ago their lancers had lance, sword, and revolver all through; now they have copied us, and have armed them with lance, sword, and carbine,—the revolver being distributed throughout their cavalry as with us exactly.

In the Austrian army, the lancers have front rank lances and revolvers, the rear rank carbines, all other cavalry twenty-eight revolvers per squadron.

In the French army, the whole of the cuirassiers have the revolver. The letter I received dated the 4th of June last states, "d'une manière générale" every man in the army who has not a gun has a revolver. Infantry, ordnance, and also in horse artillery, gunners and drivers, who have no carbine, have revolvers.

Lord Wolseley, who was in the chair on the occasion of my lecture, said on this point, "The next point is about revolvers; a good deal has been said upon that subject, and I fully concur in the remarks which have been made. I certainly agree with reference to the advisability of giving the revolver to artillerymen. At the present moment an artilleryman is really in a most defenseless condition: for if his battery is charged, unless he uses his handspike, he has actually nothing to defend himself with. *Every gunner should be furnished with a good revolver.*" I say the same; but I am not sure that I should give one to the driver, who would in most cases have enough to do in looking after his horses.

In the German army, the whole of the Prussian cuirassiers are armed with the revolver, and the corresponding heavy regiments of the other German states. In the other regiments, all officers and non-commissioned officers are thus armed.

The Russian military attaché in London writes me: "Cuirassiers and lancers have, in their front ranks lances, swords, and revolvers (six chambers); the rear rank of the cuirassiers carries sword and revolver; the rear rank of the lancers sabre and rifle." Now are America, Austria, France, Germany, and Russia all wrong in this matter? I do not invite discussion on my theory in this question; I respectfully invite discussion on the actual practice of these nations. Will wisdom die with us in this matter? No; but it looks as if our men without revolvers will die for want of wisdom. Let us look this matter fairly in the face. The weakest moment of cavalry, however armed, is immediately or shortly after the shock. But suppose one of our lancer regiments has charged a lancer regiment carrying six-barrelled revolvers; in face of and compared with the revolver not only *in posse* but *in esse*, does not our weakness become weaker, and compared with our weakness, does not their weakness become strength? I would simply refer again to the two instances quoted from the American war, adding that they might be indefinitely multiplied.

I have been asked to touch upon the question of the use of machine-guns in relation to cavalry. I see Lord Charles Beresford has quoted the opinions of several officers of the different branches of the service.

The opinion of a colonel commanding an infantry regiment is, "To me it appears as if cavalry is the arm which will profit most by the introduction of machine-guns." He states, "It has practically always with it one hundred and fifty infantry, ... and not a *single man has to dismount.*" If this be so, then we should return our carbines into store and abolish musketry instruction. A colonel of artillery states, "A machine-gun to be of any use for this purpose must be able to manœuvre at the same pace as the battery which it supports." If this be so, it is a necessary sequence that it should also manœuvre at the same pace as the cavalry regiment to which it is proposed to attach two machine-guns permanently. Is this generally possible? Who is to command the battery of two guns? an artillery officer or a cavalry officer? In what relation is the officer commanding the cavalry regiment to stand towards the guns? I humbly think he will find plenty to do in giving practical expression to the functions of his cavalry proper. The same officer says further, "For horse and field-batteries the problem is more difficult. No carriage with small wheels can be relied on for transport purposes. ... How can you transport them (machine-guns) so as to be suitable for rapid movements under service conditions?" If this problem is difficult of solution in relation to field artillery, it is more so in relation to cavalry.

A colonel of engineers says, "I cannot conceive their being permanently attached to cavalry or artillery without constantly hampering them, as it would only be on rare occasions they would be required." I quite coincide with this view so far as my present limited knowledge of the subject permits me to form a judgment.

As our pace is regulated by the capabilities of the slowest, I fear the machine-guns would be found a very slow horse. In any case, I think, as at present advised, their best place is with the horse artillery attached to the cavalry brigade, in which position they would, as occasions arise, render most valuable moral and actual help.

I trust a few remarks upon our tactical and administrative units and formation will not be considered out of place here. I am not a worshiper of everything foreign that differs from our own usage; but I confess I think we can learn something from the Germans here. We have four squadrons per regiment, and only three majors, the infantry having four. (I cannot see the justice of this, taking into account the interests of the senior captain of cavalry.) Owing to our squadrons being divided into two troops only, as compared with the four Zugs of the German, we lose the services of some officers from leading, they being relegated to the serre-file rank. I should like to see the tactical and administrative units reduced to the same denomination, the squadron, commanded by a major, with one captain and two subalterns under him. I should like to see the guide done away with, and the squadron divided into three divisions, the centre one under command of the captain, and the others led and commanded by the subalterns. The difference in handiness and mobility between three such divisions and two troops up to war strength should be obvious.

I have had to do with the instruction of a regiment composed of five squadrons of close on one hundred of all ranks in each, and can quite enter into the advantage it would be to have squadrons of three Zugs in each of some, sixteen front rank. We should gain in mobility and in the development of the powers of the younger officers.

It is in no spirit of carping criticism that I venture to suggest that the method adopted in the instruction of junior officers on joining is in very many cases very unsatisfactory, and does not attain the object which should be kept in mind by those who carry out their instruction. An officer is posted to a regiment, and finds himself on the barrack square among the recruits; he goes through the course of drill from the goose step up, together with the sword or lance and carbine drill, etc.; and as soon as he can perform these fairly well he is "dismissed." The same obtains with reference to his riding and musketry. *Seldom indeed is any account taken of his ability to impart to others that which he has learned.* As for meat, bread, hay, straw, and oats, he is supposed to know all about their quality, etc., by inspiration.

Surely this is not as it should be. No wonder then that many of these duties are irksome, and therefore improperly performed in many cases. No man can take a real pleasure or intelligent interest in doing, or attempting to do, that which, from ignorance and want of instruction, he can do only in a consciously imperfect manner.

We have at Aldershot a school for auxiliary cavalry, which, if developed, would prove of much more general use than at present. This school has to borrow from the cavalry regiments some twenty to twenty-five horses during certain periods of the instruction carried on there.

This is obviously a great tax upon the patience of the officers commanding the regiments thus depleted *pro tem*. They have also to lend a certain number of men who are required for foot-drill instruction, and who draw working pay for this duty. Now if this school were enlarged and had a riding-master (who would act as adjutant as well) attached, a couple of rough riders, forty horses (sound, but cast from regiments on account of age), and a deputy commandant, I think we could solve the difficulty of instructing the officers and staff sergeants of auxiliary cavalry, and teaching a certain number of infantry how to ride and groom their horses, besides affording young cavalry officers facilities for going through a course which, from personal experience, I can vouch would be very helpful to them in the matter of *imparting instruction*,—a point becoming of greatly increased importance under the new regulations for squadron instruction by officers. It might be replied that such an institution could not cover so much ground at one time. It would not be at all necessary, because there are certain months in the year during which it would be most unwise to press the attendance of auxiliary cavalry officers. This also holds good with reference to the sergeants of the permanent staff. Some of these very months fall at a time when it would be most convenient for infantry men to be attached for a course of riding, etc., namely, the furlough season, months when there is little done in the way of field days.

If the infantry are attached by twos and threes to cavalry regiments, they must necessarily fall to a greater or less extent into cavalry ways and ideas; but drilled together and working and living together as usual at such an establishment, the infantry spirit would be kept up.

Again, the troopers permanently posted from the cavalry with the horses would no doubt be men who have re-engaged for twenty-one years, and they would be available both for mounted and dismounted instruction drills. This method adopted, we should gain the advantage of one system of instruction for mounted infantry and the junior officers, as well as the auxiliary cavalry, and at a very small cost.

I cannot help thinking that our methods of instructing young officers are too cramped and too much confined to the subjective. It is very necessary under existing methods of war to obtain clear views as to the best way of acting and manœuvring in combination with the other arms. I need not say how little opportunity is afforded junior officers for this, except what they can pick up out of books or from the war game. This does not sufficiently *train the eye* to grasp the general idea of movements being executed by other arms of the service than our own. Would it not be a good way of spending a forenoon upon which there is no parade or other duty such as courts-martial, boards, etc., for a major to ride out with his squadron officers and watch the drill of an infantry regiment, or when possible a brigade, not to see how they worked so much as to discuss together the best means of supporting their advances or retirements, their various manœuvres and attack? As the movements are being executed, to guess their purport, and to suggest the best means of screening their movements from a supposed enemy, taking the character and features of the ground into consideration. To watch the movements of artillery in the same way, and to prospect the best methods and places for escorting and supporting them; then to get a distance from them and discuss the most favorable opportunities, means and direction for attacking them, taking into account the features of ground and the position of supposed support.

Colonel Chapman, military secretary to the commander-in-chief in India, delivered a lecture at the United Service Institution of India last May, his subject being "The Last Autumn Manœuvres of the German Army." He drew attention to the complete separation of the several arms of the service, and how they manœuvred in utter independence of each other. He says, "The cavalry acting under its own leader sought more to extend itself in isolated attacks on the enemy's cavalry, and instances of its dismounting and holding positions until the infantry came up were never noticed." Touching artillery he says, "Apparently there were no artillery tactics at all, and officers brought their batteries into action and opened fire without any study of the ground, and any particular object save that of firing upon the enemy." Cavalry did not care for the artillery, and the artillery and infantry did not work for each other.

I cannot understand the principle underlying the spirit of parsimony in a certain direction which limits the opportunities for the instruction of all ranks, from generals down, by means of autumn manœuvres. It is a principle of penny wise in times of peace, but must be pound and many pounds foolish in war. But then those who exercise this principle do not go to war; they stay at home and fight with the screw instead of the sword, drive their non-combatant teams with the quill, and harness them with red tape; and then when anything breaks down, throw themselves heartily into the, to them, congenial recreation of hunting the scapegoat.

A few words as to the rank and file of our cavalry service. I think it is a matter of sincere and unmixed congratulation that the reports from the various recruiting districts as to the class of men joining the cavalry were such, that the inspector-general of recruiting was able to state in his last annual return that they were without exception satisfactory. On reading this I immediately began to look up the question of education in this connection, and I am deeply indebted to the kindness and courtesy of General Sir Beauchamp Walker, to whom this Institution and the army at large owes so much in this matter, for information on this head, as also to Colonel Orr of the same department for the following tables, which show that the rate of progress in general education among the rank and file of our cavalry is an encouraging feature in our condition.

*Percentage of Men (Non-Commissioned Officers and Men) in possession of Certificates of Education.*

| 1873. | | 1881. | |
| --- | --- | --- | --- |
| 1st class | 0.75 | 1st class | 1.0 |
| 2d " | 8.3 | 2d " | 15.31 |
| 3d " | 11.35 | 3d " | 12.94 |
| 4th " | 9.3 | 4th " | 30.89 |
| Not certificated. | 70.30 | Not certificated | 40.37 |

The summary of appendix to General Order 121, 1st September, 1883, shows that in branches of the service of a strength of over one thousand the percentage of passes is as follows:

| | | | |
| --- | --- | --- | --- |
| 1. Foot Guards | 97.72 | 4. Royal Engineers | 90.60 |
| 2. Cavalry | 91.48 | 5. Infantry (line) | 89.33 |
| 3. Commissariat and Transport | 90.99 | 6. Royal Artillery | 87.65 |

The latter table places cavalry very high on the list in the matter of passes gained; the former proves that there is an eminently satisfactory rate of progress in mental capacity and intellectual culture; and in face of this growth of capacity and culture obtaining among the rank and file of our cavalry service, one hears with apprehension of the great difficulty met with in obtaining recruit officers for the cavalry; of special facilities being offered to candidates willing to accept commissions in the cavalry; of the necessity of modifying the terms of admission from being absolutely competitive to competitive combined with qualification. I welcome the modification, while I am bound to regret the necessity for it; but the necessity having arisen, I think the authorities are bound to grant us larger opportunities for instruction in those duties which lead us into combination with the other arms. As the hearing of the ear may bring the foot into readiness to move; as the seeing of the eye reveals the direction for the blow of the hand; as the foot may not say to the ear, "I have no need of thee;" and the hand without the guiding eye would strike wide of the mark, so cavalry, artillery, and infantry should have ample opportunities granted them of cultivating those inter-relations, for exercising those characteristic and individual functions which, carried out in union, weld eye, ear, hand, foot, and body into one corporate entity, form one harmonious whole, complete and perfect in all its parts.

To conclude, what does this marked intellectual and educational advance exhibited among the rank and file of our cavalry service demand of us regimental officers? It demands that which I humbly believe we, as a body, are seeking and striving after as never before, namely, a proportionate increase of capacity and knowledge for ourselves. We, who most of all exercise a direct personal influence on our men, should see to it that that influence is exercised for good; that we set them an example of diligent application, of scrupulous conscientiousness in the performance of our duty; that no detail of that duty is too petty or insignificant to be done carefully and well. Duty thus done becomes a pleasure; but duty done in a half-hearted and grudging spirit, as if it were a bore, makes that duty in time a bondage, and begets a spirit that soon infects those under our immediate influence to their grievous harm. On the other hand, as I trust will be admitted, the "Functions of Cavalry in Modern War" demand of officer and man increasing intelligence, self-reliance, and resource, increasing knowledge and efficiency for their effectual expression in action; thus that increasing knowledge, that resulting efficiency will necessarily add an unconscious dignity to the character and bearing of the individual, and will make him a valuable entity in that branch of our queen's service to which I deem it a high honor to belong.

LIST OF WORKS LIKELY TO BE USEFUL IN THE STUDY OF TACTICS.

*General.*

Hamley, Art of War.
Tactique des Trois Armes, Mazel.

Jomini.
Denison's History.
Clery, Minor Tactics.
Tactique de Combat, Brialmont.
Home.
Traité d'Art Militaire, Perizonius.
Modern Tactics (Wilkinson and Shaw).
Lectures, Dyke.

*Cavalry.*

Cavalry Regulations.
Von Schmidt, Instructions (for detailed instructions).
Conduct of a Contact Squadron, Bell.
Verdy du Vernois, Troop Leading.
Catechisms (Cavalry Regulations), Colonel B. Bell.

*Artillery.*

Field Artillery, Pratt, 1883.
Tactique de l'Artillerie, Von Schell.
Defense and Attack of Positions, Schaw.

*Infantry.*

Field Exercise Book.

# THE LITERATURE OF THE THIRTY YEARS' WAR.

BY J. WATTS DE PEYSTER, BREVET MAJOR-GENERAL S.N.Y.

"The History of Gustavus Adolphus," by Walter Harte, Stockdale's (the Third) Edition, London, 1807; "The History of Gustavus Adolphus," by B. Chapman, Vicar of Letherhead, London, 1856; "Gustaf Adolph, König von Schweden, und Seine Zeit," by A. F. Gfrörer, Dr. Onn Klopp's (the Fourth Edition), Stuttgart, 1863; "The History of Gustavus Adolphus," by John L. Stevens, recently United States Minister at Stockholm, New York and London, 1884; Geijer's "History of the Swedes" (comprising the first three volumes of the original down to the end of Christina's administration), translated by J. H. Turner, London, 1832 to 1836; "The Civil and Military History of Germany from the Landing of Gustavus to the Conclusion of the Treaty of Westphalia" (in reality of the whole Thirty Years' War), in three volumes or parts, by Frances Hare Naylor, London, 1816; "Geschichte des deutschen Reiches unter der Regierung Ferdinand III.," by M. Kock, Wien; "Eulogy of Leonard Torstenson, by H. R. M. Gustavus III.," Stockholm, 1787; "The Lives of the Warriors," by General the Hon. Sir Edward Cust, B.A., London, 1865-67; and at least two hundred other works or volumes in Latin, French, German, and English in the possession of the author.

THE following article is intended as a Review, but to partake at the same time of the nature of an Essay. The number of works of more or less value in regard to Gustavus Adolphus and the Thirty Years' War is very great; but in spite of the prominent names which appear as authors or inspirers, both the biography of Gustavus and the history of the Thirty Years' War has even yet to be written. From all the lives of the great king we do not learn the whole truth in regard to him. In some respects he is more a myth than the Washington of Weems. He was not a *saint* in the ideal sense of the word, but he was a MAN, and his motives, while they were subordinated to religious principle, were tinctured with selfishness and founded on policy. A successful leading politician in this country is said to have remarked that in a very large city he had found that virtue had a number of representatives, and vice had none; that he would unite the suffrages of vice on himself. He did so, was elected again and again, until all the virtues marshaled their champions under one leader, and then, and not until then, was he defeated. Again, it was said in an army that a number of especial classes rejoiced in more or less distinctive representatives, but that religion had none, and that whoever trained under that flag would succeed. A standard-bearer offered himself and did so. Thus it is: policy and interest walk hand in hand, and, as Lear said, the godlike and the devilish divide the empire of the *microcosm*, man.

Although Harte devoted heart and soul to his work on Gustavus, and accumulated an immense amount of information in regard to the king and the war under consideration, it is by no means satisfying any more than the most recent biography of Stevens, who from his position enjoyed advantages such as very few men in writing up a subject have possessed. The fact is that until the manuscript treasures at Skokloster are carefully arranged and indexed and published somewhat like our "Official Records,"—" War of the Rebellion,"—and are translated into a language familiar to the majority of historians, there is no use of expecting a true picture of the exterior actions and interior motives of this momentous period, or a clear revelation of the characters of the chief actors. As yet most writers have followed each other in the same rut. It is said that the two sides of the face of Gustavus III. were so dissimilar that a profile portrait from the left would never have been recognized as a likeness of the same person when painted from the right. Just so in regard to the prominent characters in the greatest religious war that was ever fought out between modern titular Christians. Nor are students anxious to arrive at the truth, more capable of doing so from pen-portraits than they are of judging of the real characters of the Joabs, Ahithophels, and Davids of the period from their actual portraits. Lying before me is Salmzon's exquisite series of likenesses of the leading men of the Thirty Years' War, published at Stockholm, within about thirty or forty years. Some of the finest faces belong to the weakest men, and to any but adepts in physiognomy the strongest men are by no means characterized by general features indicative of their strength. One man who looked what he was, " with a mind steeped in beer," was John George, Elector of Saxony. To a woman's fancy Gallas would certainly prove attractive. Banér has traits which recall those of Richelieu and Mazarin. Piccolomini shows himself completely: a bad, bold, Italian of the worst type. Horn, who had the character of being so humane that he disarmed war of its worst horrors, has a very harsh face; and Königsmark, whom the French represent as positively ugly, because he saw through their tricks, and would not submit to their imperiousness, has a portrait handsome enough to justify what they said of him, that he was a " woman's man," as well, as he really was a most enterprising soldier and sagacious leader. The finest head, however, grander even than that of Gustavus and Banér, who is said to have resembled his master closely, is that of Leonard Torstenson,—whose name, translated, signifies the Lion, strong, son of the (memorial) stone (or pillar) of the Thunder God (Thor),—in its blended grandeur of unmistakable goodness and greatness.

If called upon to recommend the best work in every respect for the period from the beginning of the war to the death of Gustavus, I should select, for whomsoever can read German, Gfrörer; as a general history, Naylor; as a military essay, Cust's "Lives of the Warriors;" and for the political or civil aspects, Gindely. For military details the last is almost worthless, and, as before remarked, there has not, as yet, been a real military history published. In his "*Geschichte des Kriegswesens,*" von Brandt has furnished some exquisite episodes replete with the most valuable information; and Feil, in his "Die Schweden in Oesterreich," has presented facts, in detail, in regard to military operations within the Imperial Hereditary States in 1645 and 1646 which are astonishing in their revelations. Although I say it myself, and it may sound like egotism, I have never seen a book which contains such a mass of information (however undigested and shapelessly thrown together) as my life of Torstenson, which cost many years of the hardest labor and a large amount of money, willingly expended to obtain every authority accessible in any language open to me.

" Few modern nations can vie with the Swedes as historians; . . . in Sweden history don't stand on her dignity, pared down to barren facts, but is alike simple and amusing" [witness the series of historical novels of Topelius. Lagerbring in this respect resembles Topelius.] " Geyer [or Geijer], a greater genius far, . . . is the driest of the series. When selected by [his] government to write the History of Sweden," he recommended Afzelius as the best calculated to weave in interesting anecdotes and legends necessary to the full understanding of the matter. Fryxell is "quaint and legendary till the death of Erik XIV., when his style changes." Lastly we have Stjernholm,—" most painstaking writer of the century," of " unwearied industry." He can scarcely live, with his details, to bring his work down further than the rise of the Vasa dynasty,—all that is of interest to any but his own countrymen.

By the way as a parenthesis, there is a curious fact connected with Ten Broek's translation of Gindely's history, published by Putnam's Sons, which I once reviewed in *The United Service.* In his note to page 288, vol. ii., he alludes to the following passage in Gindely: " Für die unterhaltung der Reichs-armée wurden 120 Römer-monate bewilligt." Ten Broek observes, "This is the only passage of the work thus far the application of which I have not *supposed* that I understood." He translates it, "For the maintenance of the imperial army, 120 Roman months were granted." The real signification is that the Diet voted a contribution from the States of the Roman Empire (for which they were bound in carrying on a common war), equivalent to the aggregate of 120 monthly allowances, or six-tenths of the extreme amount for which they could be held liable, or the utmost ever granted,—*i.e.*, 200. "*Römer-monate*," is a technical term.

With these preliminary remarks what follows is a crystallized or perhaps, more properly speaking, a digested presentation or review of what occurred after Gustavus Adolphus, for astutely political and strictly military as well as actual religious motives, determined to take part in the great German war. "The pear had been maturing for years; it was now ripe and ready to fall;" the slightest breeze awakened by the pen or the sword was alone necessary to break it off. The Siege of Stralsund by Wallenstein precipitated events. The "pear" fell! Gustavus landed in Pomerania. It was the real beginning of the great end.

H. R. M. Oscar II. delivered an Address on the one hundred and fiftieth anniversary of the death of Charles XII., which proves that, in these times, kings are better educated and as intellectually able as any other class. He shows that however brilliant was the career of Charles, it was fatal to his country, but not fatal because Charles was "a madman," as he is generally styled, but because such a hero, king, soldier, and general, needed a kingdom more commensurate with his own greatness than Sweden.

Gustavus III., another king of Sweden, in a note to his Eulogy of Leonard Torstenson, written in 1787, makes a remark which shows that the Swedes were not always unanimous as to the permanent advantage of the military triumphs of Gustavus Adolphus, although the injurious effects were *remote* not *immediate*, as in the case of Charles XII.: "There was a time when, owing to particular reasons and purposes, it was attempted to dispute the great services Gustavus Adolphus rendered to the realm. *It was insisted upon that his glorious reign was more brilliant than advantageous to the kingdom; that it contributed more to the nation's honor than to its happiness.*"

Horace Marryatt, in his "One Year in Sweden," reads to the point in this connection: "That contest lasted thirty years, though it destroyed the power of Romanism in the German Empire,—*half ruined* Sweden;" after Charles XII., "the curse and glory of Sweden," "A RUINED COUNTRY."

In both cases it was like an individual of great vitality and strength of constitution but of feeble physique, enabled by strong and quickly-repeated stimulants to perform great feats of strength,—terrible exhaustion necessarily followed. In the case of Sweden the stimulants were foreign triumphs, administered in heroic doses by boldest practitioners. The reign of Louis XIV. is nearly a parallel, and that of Napoleon. Both achieved marvelous military successes; both reigns ended in a prostration, which, as old Blücher feared for the cause of the Allies, would be the case,—*i.e.*, that

> "Pens would lose by writing
> What swords had won by fighting,"

or otherwise the *righteous* dismemberment of France in 1871 would have been more thoroughly executed, in one case one hundred and fifty, and in the other case fifty-six years before it did occur.

The deeper a student examines into the undeniable facts of history, the more it will become evident that there is absolutely nothing new in the world, and that what is accepted as new is nothing more than another form, or presentation, or application of the old—the *Vieux-Neuf* of Edouard Fournier—in some shape or another, justifying the declaration of Solomon, or of whoever was the author of Ecclesiastes, that wonderful production of the human intellect, that "there is nothing new under the sun." It almost would appear as if the adage is true, "The more folks learn, the less they know," or as Byron sung it, perhaps, better,—

> "——Knowledge is not happiness, and science
> But an exchange of ignorance for that
> Which is another kind of ignorance;"

all culminating in the remark of the famous Prime Minister, Oxenstiern, to his son when starting out as representative at Osnabruck, "Go, see with what little sense the world is governed." One thing is unquestionable, the practical development of modern war dates further back than the seventeenth century, and is due not to one man nor two, but to many, and it would not be saying too much if it were asserted and maintained that war as well as religion owes its first real modern impulse to *printing*. Polybius hit the centre when he wrote that "Truth is to history what eyes are to animals. Tear out their eyes and they are useless. Even so take Truth from History and it is no longer of any use [or value]."[1] Before printing, except as copyists, writers

---

[1] Any one who honestly desires to appreciate "what history can teach us," let him read the article by W. S. Lilly in the *Contemporary Review*, republished

drew upon their imaginations or their prejudices for their facts. Printing came to the rescue and just in time. All that the moderns knew, in 1500–1625, of real war was due to the Romans; that is to say, to their adaptativeness and adoption and conversion of the systems they encountered, so far improved and amalgamated, as they appear in the perfect praxis of the Legion. The Phalanx of the intellectual Greeks was a simple application to armed organizations of men of the laws of mass and momentum; the Legion of the less refined but more practical Romans was the perfect recognition of the power of momentum without the necessity of mass. It was the substitution of the manœuvring cannon for the ponderous and fixed artillery,—the ballista or battering-ram of the ancients,—the flexibility of intelligence and the education of individuals for the stiffness and unaccommodativeness of overarmed aggregated numbers. Printing diffused knowledge and reproduced the wisdom and works of antiquity, and Gustavus studied the classics, and in them found and from them derived his inspiration. His tactics were the reappearance of those of the Legion, destined to shatter the massed formations of his opponents as did the legions under T. Quinctius Flaminius, the phalanx of Philip V. of Macedon at Cynoscephalœ. Hallam, however he may be in less or greater degree correct in his "Europe during the Middle Ages," claims for the English Condottiere, Sir John Hawkwood, died A.D. 1394, the honor of being—

"The first distinguished commander who had appeared in Europe since the destruction of the Roman Empire. It would be absurd to suppose that any of the constituent elements of military genius, which nature furnishes to energetic characters, were wanting to the leaders of a barbarian or feudal army; untroubled perspicacity in confusion, firm decision, rapid execution, providence against attack, fertility of resource, and stratagem. These are in quality as much required from the chief of an Indian tribe, as from the accomplished commander. But we do not find them in any instance so consummated by habitual skill as to challenge the name of generalship. No one at least occurs to me previously to the middle of the fourteenth century to whom history has unequivocally assigned that character. It is very rarely that we find even the order of battles specially noticed. The monks, indeed, our only chroniclers, were poor judges of martial excellence; yet, as war is the main topic of all annals, we could hardly remain ignorant of any distinguished skill in its operations. This neglect of military science certainly did not proceed from any predilection for the arts of peace. It arose out of the general manners of society, and out of the nature and composition of armies in the Middle Ages. The insubordinate spirit of feudal tenants, and the emulous equality of chivalry, were alike hostile to that gradation of rank, that punctual observance of irk-

in *Littell's Living Age*, No. 2152, 19th September, 1885, and reflect upon the influence of a great man upon the world's progress,—an influence which is due to the direct action of the Infinite upon the Finite, through the inspiration of genius, the individual, the Man of and for the Time upon Men.

some duties, that prompt obedience to a supreme command, through which a single soul is infused into the active mass, and the rays of individual merit converge to the head of the general. In the fourteenth century, we begin to perceive something of a more scientific character in military proceedings, and historians for the first time discover that success does not entirely depend upon intrepidity and physical prowess. The victory of Muhldorf over the Austrian princes in 1322, that decided a civil war in the empire, is ascribed to the ability of the Bavarian commander Schwepperman, [who] is called by a contemporary writer Struvius, 'CLARUS MILITARA SCIENTIA VIR.' "

Many distinguished officers were joined in the school of Edward III. Yet their excellencies were perhaps rather those of active partisans than of experienced generals. Their successes are still due rather to daring enthusiasm than to wary and calculating combination. Like inexpert chess-players, they surprise us by happy sallies against rule, or display their talents in rescuing themselves from the consequences of their own mistakes. Thus the admirable arrangements of the Black Prince at Poitiers hardly redeem the temerity which placed him in a situation where the egregious folly of his adversary alone could have permitted him to triumph [Lee and " Stonewall" Jackson are most apposite examples of these remarks in the Pope campaign]. *Hawkwood, therefore, appears to me the first real general of modern times,*—the earliest master, however imperfect, in the science of [Maurice of Nassau, Gustavus Adolphus, Banér, Torstenson, Mercy] Turenne and Wellington. Every contemporary Italian historian speaks with admiration of his skillful tactics in battles, his stratagems, his well-conducted retreats. Praise of this description, as I have observed, is hardly bestowed—certainly not so continually—on any former captain. Hawkwood was not only the greatest but the last of the foreign condottiere, or captains of mercenary bands."

It is useless to enter into an argument as to who did truly give the first impulse to systematized modern war; but it is worth showing, and susceptible of proof, that on the field of battle in the application of the " Three arms combined," Gustavus Adolphus was the MAN and HIS Leipsic, in 1631, the model. Torstenson's Leipsic, in 1642, was finer as an exemplar of simple direction and fighting; but the Leipsic of Gustavus was equivalent to the quiet daring of Franklin when he elicited the electric spark from the kite-string and demonstrated the feasibility of the application to buildings, of conductors. Gustavus in one sense as Franklin in another *eripuit fulmen.*

This flexibility, this individualization of force, is more and more manifested ever since in the less and less rigid tactics of each succeeding war, due as much to the dissemination of intelligence by *printing* as to the invention of more and more destructive firearms and their accumulation on the battle-field; of which the enormous susceptibilities were discerned by Gustavus Adolphus or by Torstenson, his famous chief of artillery; which of the two was the man who now can see or determine.

The Thirty Years' War constituted one of the decisive periods in the great process of human development and the liberation of Thought from the trammels of priestcraft and superstition. Without it, Thought would not now be *Free*. What is more, this contest was only a critical crisis in a conflict which may be said to have had a prelude in the struggle of the Seven United States of Holland for their emancipation from the yoke of Spain, and it was the latent continuing virus of the disease which required so much firing and bloodletting,—a virus manifested even as late as in the Franco-German struggle of 1870–71, which developed a new Empire and Emperor in Germany,—both firm in the belief and relief which the principal factors adverse to freedom of soul and body strove to crush throughout the Thirty Years' War. The most dangerous enemies to Human Progress in Europe were the Papacy and the House of Hapsburg, and their power was not thoroughly broken until Sadowa, in 1866. Claiming to be German the Austrians were the direst foes to Germany and to human freedom. They were the sworn tormentors and executioners of a church, which, if triumphant, would have plunged humanity back into a condition analogous to that of the " Dark Ages," and victorious, they would have crippled Mind for centuries. Ferdinand II., who made the Thirty Years' War, expressed as to will and wish exactly the idea of Tacitus: " They make a desert and they call it peace." Such may not have been his intention, as regarded a desert, for a waste cannot pay taxes or tithes, but such would have been the inevitable result had success crowned his resolve. Little did he think that when his organized or "disciplined savages," wasted the Mark of Brandenburg, that he was only preparing the way for the Rise of a new authority in Germany, which should place its heel, within about two centuries, upon the very head of his successors. Max Nordau, in his awful work, " The Conventional Lies of Civilization," prohibited in Europe, which has passed through seven editions in seven months in this country—in the fearful aggressive of his chapter entitled " The Lie of a Monarchy and an Aristocracy," is nevertheless compelled to admit that the Prussian Dynasty, " The Hohenzollerns of Germany, have at least a clean record of which they need not be ashamed." Frederick the Great, one of the greatest kings who ever simultaneously grasped the sceptre of a despotic monarch and the sword of a great soldier and general—one of these Hohenzollerns—within one century after the close of the Thirty Years' War, inflicted a deadly wound upon the Hapsburg power which has never closed and is still bleeding. Thence its life-blood has been ebbing slowly away, until now the third successor of Frederick is Emperor of Germany, and the Austrian

Imperialty, once the German Empire, is so little German that it is compelled to move in accordance with the influence and direction of other races upon which it formerly looked down as the master upon the serf.

Whatever skeptics, or worse, may say, philosophical and critical history proves indisputably that as the Moslem says, "There is no God but God," and God[2] "the Most High, ruleth in the kingdoms of men, and giveth it to whomsoever He will, and setteth over it the basest of men,—doeth according to His will in the army of Heaven, and among the inhabitants of the earth; and none can stay His hand, or say unto Him, 'What doest Thou?'"

Whether this Rule is applied through direct interventions or by inevitable laws; by immediate miraculous operations or fixed decree, has ever been a disputed point, and cannot be settled even through comparative citations from the Holy Scriptures. The weight of the argument lies in the scale of predetermined regulation, which leaves no fissure or hiatus for the voluntary action of mortals. To this is conjoined an intimate relation not only between the *microcosm* (man) and the *macrocosm* (universe), in cause and effect subordinate to law, and close affinity, step by step, grade by grade, from the lowest order of creation,—through the animal culminating in the highest order of men,—to the lights which burn by myriads in the measureless expanse of ether, as Pope rhymed,

"So, from the first, eternal order ran,
And creature linked to creature, man to man."

According to Fraunce:

"Man is all symmetry,
Full of proportions, one limb to another,
And all the world besides.
Each part may call the farthest brother.
For head with foot hath private amity,
And both with both moon and tides.

---

[2] The Buddhists seem to demonstrate this in *their* universal prayer, "*Om mane padmi Oum*, Oh God, the jewel [only Supreme] in the Lotus, Amen!" and the Zoroastrians in theirs, "the purest and noblest religion of antiquity," recognized a One Almighty Supreme over Ormuzd, the principle of good, and Ahriman, the representative of evil—ONE WHOLE.

——"Joy above the name of pleasure,
Deep self-possession, an intense repose. . . .
No other than as Eastern sages paint,
The God [Om] who floats upon a Lotos leaf;
Dreams for a thousand ages, then awaking,
Creates a world, and, smiling at the bubble,
Relapses into bliss."—COLERIDGE.

> "Nothing hath got so far,
> But man hath caught and kept it as his prey.
> His eyes dismount the highest star,
> *He is, in little, all the sphere.*
> Herbs cure our flesh because that they
> *Find their acquaintance there.*"

This was exactly the idea of the great Paracelsus, so abused by empirics, pedants, and people unable to reach the height of his genius understand him.

Wallenstein, whose horoscope (talisman [or astrological amulet]) is still preserved in the "Treasury" "Imperial Burg," at Vienna, stands by no means alone in his firm faith in the influence upon, and revelation of, the stars as regards the fortunes of men. The horoscopes of Gustavus, and of Pappenheim, and of Christian IV., made in accordance with the stellar conjunctions at their birth, were strangely fulfilled; that of the first exactly. The appearance of comets, "importing change," has always been regarded as ominous, and no one who beheld it can forget the huge meteor which passed over our country before the Slaveholders' Rebellion, in 1860, first separated into two with a mighty explosion, sailed on portentously, and, thus divided, across the arch of heaven and, then, became reunited into one orb before it disappeared; nor that which in the Northwestern heavens shone like a vast sword dripping blood, in 1863. Examples might be multiplied, but to whoever disbelieves in these appearances there is no need to say more or enter into further proofs or even more extraordinary examples of cause and effect or influence.

It is very doubtful if any of the leading men of the time were not more or less superstitious. Among the Positivists it has been asserted by his friends and admirers and by historians that "Banér was elevated far above fear and *credulity.*" Above fear unquestionably, yes; but whether he was superior to the superstitions of his time is not so certain, especially if Parival, who published in 1656, is correct in his "History of this Iron Age," which comprises one of the most reliable accounts of the Thirty Years' War. This author appears to have been acquainted with all the secrets of the time, and, for some reason or other, was able to obtain information in regard to the peculiarities of every one of note. In Part II., Chapter vii., page 179, he says, speaking of Banér and Torstenson's campaign of 1639:

> "*Bannier* went into *Bohemia, Torstenzon* into *Lusatia,* and *Stalhans* into *Silesia;* and God knows into what condition they put that country, where they found more friends than the Imperialists did in *Pomerania.* He defeated General *Marizini* neer *Chemniz,* and incamped before *Prague,* where he also defeated General

*Hofkirck. All the world was amazed at this progress, which against all apparence and all expectation, and which cost so much blood, so much desolation, and so many inflagrations throughout all Saxonie, and even to the very gates of Prague. Fortune had again turned her back upon the Imperialists, who changed their commander. For, the Arch-Duke Leopold was declared Generalissimo or Chief-General, and Piccolomini his Lieutenant. Many encounters hapened, in which the Swedes had almost still the better and Fortune accompanied them even to the last, according to the assurance which was given Bannier, by a certain* PEASANT, WHO WAS BECOME HIS PROPHET."

During the Thirty Years' War there were manifest examples of the stultification of those whom the Almighty had predestined to fall, to stumble, or to go astray, as the prophet coarsely but forcibly expressed it,—in language which seems unpolished to the nicety of the hypercritical ears of this generation,—when he speaks of the oppressor becoming brutish in his arrogance and erring in every work as a drunken man staggereth in his vomit, slipping and finally falling in it. For example, Gustavus could not have acquired all he did and have established his base securely, in 1631, if Austria had not, in consistence with her fatal greed, attempted to grasp all and in the futile attempt periled everything. Had the "disciplined savages," sent into Italy to sack Mantua, been present in Saxony, Gustavus could not have won at Leipsic; and if Ferdinand had not had Wallenstein assassinated in the nick of time for the Swedes, Nordlingen would have arrived two years before it did and the sagacious diplomacy of the murdered Great Captain, Friedland, would have rendered the League of Heilbronn and the recuperation of Oxenstiern and Banér an utter impossibility.

Colonel Malleson, B.A., in his paper or address, read before the Royal British Historical Society, 7th February, 1884, entitled "The Lost Opportunities of Austria," shows that the Peace of Westphalia, 24th October, 1648, left Germany divided into two camps. "Internally—that is, within the limits of Germany—the Peace of Westphalia settled the religious question. Whilst it confirmed the dogma, held by every prince, great and small, as an unquestioned prerogative, that the religion of the prince was to be the religion of the people (*Cujus regio ejus religio*), it left, with rare exceptions, the people practically free to worship God as they chose. (The expulsion of the Protestants of Styria, by the Emperor Charles VI., is an exception to this general rule.) But as, generally, the people of Southern Germany adhered to the old, and those of Northern Germany embraced, in some form or other, the [Evangelical, so styled] reformed religion, the practical result was to divide Germany into two camps,—the Southerners, allied by sympathy with Austria; the Northerners, more or less divided, but prepared, as the sequel has proved, to follow *the lead of a strong Man* whenever *that* STRONG MAN should appear." ...

"That strong Man" did appear in Frederick the Great, and it was against him, when he had weakened with age and trials, that Austria, in 1778, again manifested her incapability to profit by opportunity.

"Again, after a term of years, did the question arise [the question of Austria's possession of Bavaria]. Again was the opportunity offered. In the interval had occurred the two Silesian Wars, and the Seven Years' War. The daughter of Charles VI., the illustrious Maria Theresa, ruled over all her father's dominions, lost Silesia excepted. By her side, invested nominally with equal powers, but obliged to conform in matters of high policy to the strong will of the Empress, stood her gifted son, Joseph II. Once again offered the opportunity of incorporating Bavaria, although, this time, not without a battle. The opportunity arose in this wise Charles Albert, of Bavaria, had lived to enjoy a fleeting gleam of prosperity by his election to the imperial dignity ; and had then died, all his ambitious hopes shattered, in 1745. His son, Maximilian Joseph III., had, by the Peace of Fussen, April 22 of the same year (1745), become reconciled to Austria. He died childless December 30, 1777. He was the last of the Bavarian line of the House of Wittelsbach. His nearest of kin was the Elector Palatine, Charles Theodore. But, in virtue of the title of investiture drawn up more than a century before by the Emperor Sigismund, the House of Habsburg had claims, on the failure of heirs to the Bavarian Wittelsbachs, to the whole of Lower Bavaria. Joseph II. then represented, in co-regency with his renowned mother, the House of Habsburg. He did not allow the opportunity to slip. Charles Theodor was childless, and had no hope of children. A lover of pleasure, given to profuse expenditure on his own gratifications, he readily acceded to the claims of Austria to transfer to her the territory indicated in Sigismund's old parchment.

"But his nearest relative and heir, Charles II., Duke of Zweibrücken, stepped in to prevent the transaction, appealed to the old jealousy of the aggrandisement of the House of Austria, of Frederic II , of Prussia, and incited that Prince to invade Bohemia, in order to maintain the right of the ruler of Bavaria and his successors to the possessions of the territories intact, just as they had been at the death of the last of the Bavarian Wittelsbachs. This action on the part of Frederic brought on the War of the Bavarian Succession. Joseph, meanwhile, had taken up on the Bohemian frontier, behind the Elbe, a position so strong by nature and so fortified by art, that Frederic found it unassailable. He did all he knew, tried all the tricks and stratagems which had served him so well during the Seven Years' War, to entice Joseph from his strong position, to divide the army, or to leave an opening for an attack. Joseph was not to be tempted, and his quiet persistence completely baffled the great warrior-king. But Frederic did not renounce hope. He had ordered his brother, Prince Henry, to march through Saxony and endeavor to break into Bohemia through Lausitz. With the aid of the army under his orders he would have at his disposal a sufficient superiority of numbers to force the Austrian position. But Joseph had placed in the field, to observe and baffle Prince Henry, an army fifty thousand strong, under the command of his best general, Field Marshal Loudon, a man who had shown his capacity to look even Frederic himself in the face. Able, then, as were the dispositions made by Prince Henry, Loudon baffled them. He did more; he forced the Prince to retreat. He followed him and was on the point of forcing him to deliver, under very disadvantageous circumstances, a battle which [according to Austrian critics and others friendly to them], if success had crowned his efforts, would have been fatal to Frederic, which would not only have secured the whole of Lower Bavaria, but have recovered Silesia [!?], when his [Loudon's] hand was stayed in the most marvelous manner. The story is thus graphically told by the Freiherr von Janko, in his 'Life of Loudon :' 'On September 3, 1778, information reached Loudon that Prince Henry had crossed the Elbe near Leitmeritz, and had taken a firm position. Exclaiming, "Now, at last, I have the Prince in the position in which, since the beginning of the war, I have wished to see him," Loudon sent an express to the Emperor to promise him, if he would send him only twelve battalions, he would finish the war. The Emperor dispatched the battalions. Loudon, meanwhile, had concentrated his troops; and, hearing that the battalions were proceeding by forced marches to join him, hastened from Munchengratz [where the emperors of Austria and Russia and the king of Prussia met in 1833], to Benatek, crossed the Elbe at Brandeis, the Moldau at Weltrus, and on September 20 took up a position opposite Prince Henry at Budin. His position was in every respect most advantageous for an attack, one of his corps occupying a commanding post on the enemy's left, whilst his front and right were so placed that Prince Henry could not retreat without fighting, whilst in case of defeat his army had no means of escape.'

"I now relate, in the words of the author, the incident which prevented the destruction of the Prussian army: 'With an overstrained anxiety every one in both camps,' writes von Janko, 'beheld the arrival of the moment which was to decide the question of superiority between the two generals, who, according to the judgment of the best-approved strategists, had, during the Seven Years' War, made no mistakes—[for had not Frederic himself declared, to his generals, one day, speaking of the events of the Seven Years' War, " *We all committed faults, except my brother Henry and Loudon.*"'  And yet this Loudon, the capturer, in 1761, by a brilliant stroke, of Schweidnitz, was rewarded for the astounding success by a partial eclipse, until events made his employment in the highest command a matter of absolute necessity.]

"But just as Loudon was preparing, on the 23d, for an attack which should be decisive, Loudon was surprised by the arrival in his camp of the Emperor. Joseph had come himself, in order to soften, by his presence, the unpleasantness of the orders of which he was the bearer. The Empress, absolutely determined to bring to an end by peaceful means the dispute between Frederic and herself, had commanded her son to forbid at all costs the risking of a battle, even were a brilliant victory the certain consequence. Maria Theresa, in fact, saw opposed to her only the warrior who, having robbed her of Silesia, had kept that province against all continental Europe. She did not realize the fact that Frederic was no longer the Frederic of Leuthen and Torgau [?], but an overcautious warrior, fearing to risk much lest he should lose all; she dreaded lest, as in former days, a defeat should only make him the more terrible in his revenge. On the eve, then, of a battle which [according to the story of the Austrians and their partial friends] could not have been lost, and which would, in its results, have amply avenged her earlier wrongs, she ordered Loudon to abstain. Loudon did abstain. Peace was concluded. Austria renounced her pretensions to the whole of Lower Bavaria and was forced to be content with the acquisition of the Inn Circle and Braunau, a territory of about a hundred and ninety square miles. The fears of Maria Theresa had lost the opportunity of incorporating the whole of Lower Bavaria and of recovering Silesia!"—(Pages 246-249.) *Transactions of the Royal Historical Society* [*of Great Britain*], *New Series, Vol. II., Part III.*, London, 1884.

Space precludes the opportunity of following out to completeness this line of proof, but it is simply necessary to close the presentation here with the remark of one of the ablest statesmen who has ever lived, William Pitt, that "Austria has always been one year behind the rest of the world with an idea and with an army," or as a military critic worded it, "one idea, one year, and one battle behind time." The Austrians never dared to fight a doubtful or prolonged battle *out*, as Grant said unjustly of the Army of the Potomac, and then, to prove that he was right, proceeded recklessly to fight it to pieces.

Before leaving this subject for good it might be sensible to dwell upon the stupid bigoted arrogance of the Emperor Ferdinand II. and his ghostly advisers, who had several glorious opportunities to pacify the discord, by the application of simple justice: 1, after the battle of the White Mountain in 1620; 2, after the temporarily decisive battles of Wimpfen in 1622, of Lutter in 1626, of Nordlingen in 1634. After those dates neither he nor they had any other such an opportunity, and they had shown their hands too clearly and had aroused passions which nothing but defeat or victory could exhaust or annul, or gratify or avenge. "Extraordinary times," says Becker, "developed equally extraordinary forces, and even more extraordinary men." This was peculiarly the case with the Thirty Years' War. The "Wars which grew out of the French Revolution," which comprise the Napoleonic conflicts of seventeen years, developed no such succession of marvelous leaders. Of all who influenced the end of those more recent twenty-three years, not more than three will live in the far future as "directors of the storm." Wellington! Blücher! and Napoleon! The Archduke Charles[3] might have been added, to convert the trio into a quartette, if he had had more than six hours a day working power in him.

During the Thirty Years' War there was a succession of HEROES. They are named here, not in order of time, but in order of greatness and authority. Gustavus Adolphus, "the foremost man—according to accepted general history—of all this modern world," and his great

---

[3] Croker (1, 314) asked Wellington "whether the Archduke Charles was really a great officer?" *Wellington*—"A great officer? Why, he knows more about it than all of us put together." *Croker*—"What, than Bonaparte, Moreau, or yourself?" *Wellington*—"Aye! than Bonaparte or any of us. We are none of us worthy to fasten the latchets of his shoes, if I am to judge from his book and his plans of campaign. But his mind or his health has, they tell me, a very peculiar defect. He is admirable for five or six hours, and whatever can be done in that time will be done perfectly; but after that he falls into a kind of epileptic stupor, does not know what he is about, has no opinions of his own, and does whatever the man at his elbow tells him."

antagonist, Wallenstein. Schmidt, v. 1, quoting, remarks, "In fact, it is probable that the Protestant party and perhaps the Lutheran (form of) religion in Germany would have been blotted out if Fortune, tired of serving the vast designs of Ferdinand; or, rather, if *Providence by a secret judgment, the depth of which every one must adore*, had not then (at the crisis) raised up the most formidable enemy which the empire ever had, in the person of Gustavus Adolphus, King of Sweden." Bougeant, i. 150; Naylor, ii. 382, justly adds, "A curious confession for a Jesuit!" It is questionable if Wallenstein ranks very far below the former in intellect, *fore*sight. In *far*sight he was fully equal to Gustavus. In *in*sight he seemed to have failed terribly, especially in his selections of confidants, executives, and what the world generally styles friends.[4]

---

[4] The rise of Wallenstein—like that of Wellington—was much more honorable than that of Napoleon Bonaparte, and his fall infinitely more dignified and manly. He was the son of his own great actions, and not one of his promotions but was earned. It is stated by Gfrörer that he commanded, under Dampierre, a squadron of the cuirassiers who delivered Ferdinand II. at the crisis of his fate in 1620, at a moment on which the future of the emperor and his family and the empire turned. He at once became a necessity, and he simply, but grandly, improved his opportunities. Again and again he preserved the Emperor, and he was assassinated by that cruel bigot because he had become too powerful as a subject, when, in addition to his influence, he exhibited a perfect insight into the fanaticism and administration which was ruining his country, and when he gave indications that, with time and opportunity he would traverse the plans of the Jesuits and their pupils, and establish a toleration and justice far ahead of the time and their power of conception. He was an extraordinary compound of crime and virtue. His crimes were those of his period and position; his virtues were all his own. He was mean, but seldom; he was magnanimous, but often. He performed noble and glorious actions, which few men are able, under similar circumstances, to bring themselves to do. He was never little in punishments nor rewards.

The former were annihilating as the other munificent. His great mistake was his conduct at the siege of Stralsund, and even there he would or might not have failed if the Danes and the Swedes had not interfered. The first he disarmed; the second he could neither terrify nor cajole, because their king felt that if he permitted Stralsund to fall, Sweden must inevitably suffer and succumb.

Wallenstein would now appear a very great general if he only had a Jomini, who, after all, was a courtier—often making good appear bad, and evil show as meritorious—and in spite of the injustice manifested by Napoleon towards Jomini, his very selfishness made him a very mild critic of that heartless tyrant and greatly overestimated man.

"The invasion of Gustavus Adolphus, the defeat of the Imperial armies at Leipzig, the conquest of Bavaria by the Swedes, and the death of Tilly" were accomplished facts. The empire was on the brink of ruin, and there was only one man who could save it. This man was Waldstein. When the emperor requested and, at last, implored him to resume the command, he showed that he felt all his

Tilly enjoys an exaggerated estimate. He was a lucky evolution of circumstances which he certainly did not improve anything near to the uttermost, and he was very weak in so far that he allowed himself to be swayed by rash counsels,—for instance, as at Leipzig, 1631, against his own better judgment. In this weakening he sinks exactly to the level of the old Mohawk Valley militia general, Herkimer, who plunged into the slaughter-pit of Oriskany simply because his militia colonels charged him with cowardice and treason if he did not push on blindly, a course which his common sense told him would be suicidal, as it proved to be. Pappenheim's rashness dragged Tilly into the battle he sought to shun and then down to disgrace and death. Ward styles Tilly "an honest old savage, whom a recent refreshingly audacious attempt [of Klopp, Kevin and Company] has failed to whitewash into

importance. After having declined the position several times, he at last agreed to it on the following conditions:

"That Waldstein should have the sole control of the army, which he promised to raise; and there should be no imperial authority within his camp; no peace should be concluded without his consent, he, as Duke of Mecklenburg, being one of the belligerent parties; *he should have full power to manœuvre and to take up his quarters however and wherever he should find it convenient;* that he should have the sovereignty of the provinces that he might conquer; and that the emperor should give him as reward one of his Hereditary States (Bohemia?), of which he was to be the sovereign, though as a vassal of the emperor."

"The campaign of Waldstein against Gustavus Adolphus has been told in the article on the Thirty Years' War. [*It would require the knowledge of a consummate general to decide whether Waldstein or Gustavus was the greater captain.* ☞ But from the moment that Waldstein resumed the command, he directed all operations, and Gustavus Adolphus acted under the impressions which he received from the plans of Waldstein. In his life of Turenne (i. 23) the Chevalier de Ramsay asserts 'Waldstein's fortune balanced that of the Swedish hero.'] Waldstein's defense of the lines near Nurnberg can only be compared with the defense of the lines of Torres Vedras by the Duke of Wellington. The march of the King of Sweden towards Bavaria, after his fruitless attempt on the lines near Nurnberg, was a great fault; and although the king soon perceived his error and changed his plan by rapidly following Waldstein, this circumstance is another proof of what we have just said. It is true that Waldstein lost the battle of Lutzen (6th of November, 1632), but able judges have given it as their opinion that on this occasion Waldstein showed his superiority to the king in the choice of the battle-field, while the king is said to have shown greater ability in the direction of his attacks. But the successful part of these attacks was the merit of Duke Bernhard of Saxe-Weimar, the king having fallen in the beginning of the battle, while engaged in rallying his troops, which were disorganized in consequence of those fruitless attacks which he directed."

"As to the military conduct of Waldstein after the battle of Lutzen, we shall only add that he punished with death many generals, colonels, and inferior officers who had not behaved well in that battle. He soon repaired his losses, and his arms were victorious in Saxony and Silesia."

a Christian hero!" How different the decision of Schuyler, the real conqueror of Burgoyne, in regard to the relief of Fort Stanwix!

Mansfeld, "the German Attila," was a far more remarkable man than Tilly, more bright, resolute and endowed with greater individual resources, although far less moral than the old lay-Jesuit. Although not handsome or well-formed he loved the other sex, and he always had a bevy of beauties about him, but with his amorousness and acquisitiveness he was destitute of fear, and could rule the ruthless hordes around him with a hand of iron which made the fiercest quail. Witness his putting down a mutiny : Gfrörer tells us that in a small most unattractive body dwelt an ever-restless soul. Nature had formed him to be a military leader, and with a power almost unexampled he knew, when he chose (which, however, seldom happened), how to curb his lawless troops. Once, during the Bohemian War (1520), a crowd of soldiers thronged his doors and demanded their pay, long since due. All alone he came out, cut two down, and wounded a lot more. Then some six hundred pikemen rushed upon him whom he drove off. Fearlessly, Mansfeld, followed by three captains, mounted, rode right into the mass of mutineers, shot eleven, wounded twenty-six, and made the whole submit. As a rule, Mansfeld let his soldiers have free course in a country. He was Wallenstein's instructor in demonstrating how to make the people maintain his army through sheer robbery. In this he was mightier than a king. The British general, Sir Edward Cust, author of the "Annals of the Wars," and a number of military biographies of the highest order, states that Mansfeld "is regarded as one of the greatest generals of the seventeenth century; but he was too reckless of gain to have been a good disciplinarian, and his strategy was rather the effect of experience than of study." If trustworthy reports of his improvements have been handed down, he developed "a well-organized system of vedettes and patrols, which constitute the eyes and ears of an army." The claim for him that he was "the first to employ dragoons in warfare," or horse-musketeers, must simply mean that he assigned them to duties most proper for their peculiar arms, etc., and discipline, for they were an arm apart long before, as shown in J. W. de P.'s Articles on "Cavalry," in *The United Service:* I., September; II., November; III., December, 1880.

Mansfeld was a diminutive, sickly-looking, deformed man, but he possessed the soul of a true hero. Constantly persecuted by fortune, he was to the last [bore himself] superior to his fate, and he merits immortality, for he had always proved himself [personally] superior to adversity. He was a very eloquent, persuasive, and successful negotiator, raised armies with incredible rapidity, was bold in council, fearless in danger, fertile in resources, resolute, and never shrinking even under the most adverse circumstances. The French, who felt the weight of his blows, gave him a nickname equivalent to "Bloody Bones;" the Imperialists styled him the "Attila of Christianity ;" and disinterested military critics, "the Ulysses of Germany." Romanists and politicians may abuse Mansfeld as they will, but they cannot destroy the proof of his frequent exhibitions of magnanimity and consistent heroism. Nor did Christian of Brunswick fall behind him in the latter exalted quality.

Christian of Brunswick, the Achilles to this Ulysses, was his pupil. Schiller speaks of them as "two men worthy of immortality, had they been but as superior to their times as they were to their adversities." They, private individuals, by their force of character, kept alive the war against an empire and a league for six years, and had these troops enjoyed the advantages of those of Tilly and Wallenstein, they would have checkmated both Emperor and Princes. The world rolling on, subject to inevitable law, as Seneca wrote eighteen hundred years ago, expressing the ideas of philosophers long antecedent, and indorsed by the deepest reflection ever since, must attribute the failures of the good, the honest, the truly brave, and the rarely unselfish to the fiat (Fate) which the good and wise Arnold adduces as the only valid excuse for Hannibal's not marching on Rome after Cannæ, "God did not will it to be so."

"All accounts of the times are full of numberless stories of Christian's contempt of death, of his fury in combat." Like Mansfeld, his preceptor, he was fond of beauty and liked to see it around him. He is the only leader of the period who appears without beard or moustache. He died before he was twenty-six, of poison, it is supposed, administered by the emissary of his enemies.

As a levier or creator of armies out of apparent nothing, the almost Boy-Bishop Christian of Brunswick, or the Halberstadter, dubbed Knight of the exalted British Order of the Garter by James I., in 1624, rises up almost like a giant. Greater than Murat as the leader of a charge of cavalry, he was already a captain of dragoons in the Dutch service before he had any sign of down upon his lip. This is the best proof of his fitness to lead men, because the Dutch were too economical to trust a squadron of those horsemen which cost them so much money, to any one who did not know how to command and handle them to commercial as well as to military advantage (Dalgetty). His cavalry charge at Fleurus is admitted to have been one of the most gallant of the kind during the whole Thirty Years' War,—superior to any made by Pappenheim. Gfrörer corroborates this, in that he reads, "The day of Fleurus was the most brilliant of the whole of Christian's warlike career."

It is claimed that Gustavus Adolphus styled Pappenheim "the Soldier." Mark the title; *not* General, but Soldier; and, drawing the attention to the true distinction between the definitions, the intrinsic difference between these two titles " Let him (Pappenheim) fleet on,"— " Be air !" and disappear among the shades.

Of the Germans, Bernard of Saxe-Weimar was *the* hero, and wherever undaunted courage without pure generalship could win, he won. The triumph at Lutzen was solely his,—always remembering the extreme ability of the Swedish lieutenant-generals, and the gallantry of their troops, pretty much all expended on that field. The same rashness or desperation lost Nordlingen, which almost neutralized Lutzen. At Rheinfelden, his career of success would have ended had it not been for the generalship of the " Perfect Captain," the mortally-wounded Huguenot, Duke de Rohan. It is questionable if the partisan, the sly Königsmark, was not equal to Bernard in military capacity and enterprise, yea, even to Turenne; during this war, as a lieutenant or subordinate he was far his superior. But oh, what a succession of heroes did Sweden bring forth. As one fell, another took his place, great, greater, the greatest, Torstenson, "under Sweden's crown Sweden's greatest commander;" greater as a general than even his sovereign, Gustavus, greater as a fighter than Banér, greater as a disciplinarian and humanitarian than Horn, greater than all the rest in his combination of genius and talent, as a commander of infantry, as a leader of cavalry, and as a handler of artillery; a *Feld-herr*, a diplomatist, a man of culture, learned in classic lore, a lettered man with a developed taste for the fine arts. "*My* LENNART," as Gustavus affectionately was wont to style him, who thought that next to Torstenson came Nils Brahe, killed at Lutzen. Then came Banér, hyperbolically styled "the second Gustavus," who owed his greatest triumph and much of his other successes to Torstenson; then Lilijehoek, killed at Leipzig second, who was esteemed much higher than Wrangel, Jr., who had the luck to finish the war, a good fortune due in a great measure to his having been dry-nursed by Torstenson when the latter could no longer keep the field in person and command. Last in this list, which cannot be extended for want of time, comes the nephew of the great Gustavus, afterwards known as Charles X., Gustavus, king of Sweden, who would have superseded Wrangel had the war lasted a few months longer, and have enjoyed the credit of finishing it. He rather belongs to the Germans than to the Swedes, and it is as hard to rank him as a general as it is to place him as to race. He did great deeds. He was the conqueror of Poland and of Denmark, and if the Dutch and English had not interfered with their fleets and diplomacy, he might have accomplished the union of the "Three Northern Crowns," and constituted a kingdom strong enough to act as counterpoise to Russia. Neither Bernard of Saxe-Weimar nor Banér surpassed him in audacity and enterprise, but he lacked all the discreet characteristics of Torstenson, whom he recognized as his preceptor in the Art of War.

Without forgetting or depreciating the solid, *the cube-like* greatness of Gustavus Adolphus, or the brilliant soldiership of Charles X. Gustavus, more than one historian who has considered their careers with philosophic clearness and calmness, has come to the conclusion that it is questionable if the enterprises of both were not as exhaustive to Sweden as what has been styled "the madness" of Charles XII. (Horace Marryatt's "One Year in Sweden," II. 229, de P. alcove N. Y. S. L.) Gustavus Adolphus and his immediate pupils in war were to Sweden what Epaminondas was to Thebes, but just as Thebes was too weak to keep up the exertion requisite to maintain her supremacy in Greece, which Epaminondas, "the greatest of the Greeks," bestowed upon her through, and solely through his supreme individual force, just so Sweden was too poor a country to stand the drain made upon her resources by Gustavus Adolphus and Charles X. Gustavus. She was bled so profusely by them that, had not the cool-bloodedly astute or cruelly sagacious Charles XI., intervened and stopped the hemorrhages and allowed her veins to fill again, and administered cordials to reinvigorate her, through his "Edict of Restitution," or seizure or reappropriation of the prodigal gifts of the crown-lands and appanages, etc., to favorites deserving as well as undeserving, Charles XII. would have found no strength left to expend on his wild career of conquest and military crusades, for they were little less, however boldly and ably carried out, until arrested at Pultowa by superior multitudes of barbarism piled upon him, suffocatingly, by a semi-barbarian despot, Peter the Great. (See the Vicompte de Vogue's "True Story of Mazeppa.") As it was, the Rise, Increment, Apogee, Decline, Fall, and Syncope of Swedish influence began with the coronation of Gustavus Adolphus in 1618 and ended with the death of Charles XII. in 1718. This unnatural strength almost reminds the observer of the effort of the empiric called in during the last illness of Louis XIV., who by his "heroic treatment" and stimulants, seemed to restore the moribund. When the effects, however astonishing for the moment, passed off, the gangrene resumed its progress or sway and hope was at an end.

A thorough study of all accessible authorities, and they have been very numerous,—Swedish, German, French, and English,—leads to the conviction that in some respects the character of Gustavus Adolphus has never been correctly presented. He was not the faultless man that his eulogists would have people to believe. His violent temper, which often carried him to extremes, his love episode with Ebba Brahe, —"the memory of this early love cast a gloom over his whole existence,"—and his amour with the Dutch maiden of Gottenborg, who gave birth to his only son—afterwards a Swedish general, Count Wasaborg,[5] who was wounded at Wittstock by the side of Banér and Torstenson—and a hundred other incidents of his life, show that he was simply a mortal after all; an exceptional one, however, and therefore greater in that he was not a miracle or a demigod, but one, as St. Paul exclaimed, when the citizens of Lystra would have worshiped him as a god, " We also are men of like passions with you." In fact, Gustavus was not so faultless or perfect a man as generally held up to be by moralists and optimists, because he often displayed human weaknesses and human policy; but when his nobler qualities of heart and mind are weighed against all the blemishes which can even be alleged, he was indeed GREAT, because represented as he is, or can be, he was after all a MAN, and what the world—humanity—needs in its crisis is a MAN, and " MEN AND DEEDS," as Duncan Macgregor sings so grandly in his " *Clouds and Sunshine:*"

"Wanted: MEN!
Not systems fit and wise,
Not faith with rigid eyes,
Not wealth in mountain piles,
Not power with gracious smiles,
Not even the potent pen;
   Wanted: MEN!

"Wanted: DEEDS!
Not words of winning note,
Not thoughts from life remote,
Not fond religious airs,
Not sweetly languid prayers,
Not love of cant and creeds;
   Wanted: DEEDS!

"MEN AND DEEDS!
MEN that can dare and do;
Not longings for the new,
Not pratings of the old;
Good life and action bold—
These the occasion needs,
   MEN AND DEEDS!"

---

[5] After the death of his daughter Christina, unmarried and without issue, the direct line of Gustavus was extinct, but has still representatives in Sweden through this Count Wasaborg, whose eclipse and disappearance is another proof that great

There are always two sides to every story, although one may be strongly authenticated and the other comparatively weak and even only problematical, nevertheless in a number of cases the latter may eventually prove to be the most trustworthy in its realization of the spirit,—that spirit which maketh alive when the letter killeth or seemeth to kill. Gustavus Adolphus was not the disinterested man he is held to have been by simple panegyrists. He was not the saviour, pure and simple, that he appears in his biographies. He did not enter upon the German War directly from the impulse of religious duty or sympathy. He was impelled by state policy, by military strategy, by ambition,—yes, as he regarded the matter, by necessity; by all these motives, as well as by religious duty and feeling, and by devotion to the truth.

Gustavus was learned in classic lore and took Cæsar and Scipio for his models (Becker ix. 56). The former taught him to seek out the enemy abroad, as Cæsar did in the country east of the Adriatic to keep war out of Italy, and away from Rome, the aim of that war as Washington was the grand objective of the "Slaveholders' Rebellion;" and Scipio was an example that it was wiser to carry war into the Africa of Gustavus (Germany) than to let an imperial Hannibal (Wallenstein) bring its miseries into Sweden. Memnon gave the same military advice to Darius, and had it been followed, the career of Alexander the Great in Asia would be read very differently, if indeed it would be read at all.

The chief element of Sweden's intrinsic strength lay in its peninsular position, which justified Gustavus Adolphus in electing an aggressive which was eminently a defensive-aggressive, instead of submitting to a purely defensive, the latter a course which, in the long run, is inevitably suicidal. Sweden—under the circumstances of the period, with naval strength untrustworthy as to time and combination—occupied the same position as to Wallenstein and as to the Empire as England did to Napoleon; or, more properly, that England under Elizabeth did to Spain and its imperialty of wealth and force—Scotland paralyzed by intestine greeds, rivalries, and religious antagonisms, just as Denmark had been too much crippled by Tilly and Wallenstein to interfere again in a quarrel in which, had it been true to its own hates and perhaps interests, it might have been wise to interfere or else keep quiet ever after, which the Danes had not the sense to do. Denmark

---

men must have great mothers as well as great fathers. This justifies the rule of the Semitic and other races, who only trace descent through the mothers.

at this time acted just as Prussia operated in 1805, when in cordial, active union with Austria and Russia, Napoleon, the Wallenstein of another period, must have been beaten. Again, in 1806, Austria was equally derelict, when Prussia and Russia were combined, justifying the fear of Jomini, who expected that the Hapsburg—if the leopard could under any circumstances change its spots—would take advantage of Napoleon's defeat at Preuss-Eylau—for defeat it was if Benningsen had only had one or two more roast potatoes to give him physical strength to hold on—should issue forth from the sally-ports or passes of its bastion of Bohemia, take the French in the rear, sever their communications, and annihilate the common enemy. Alas! human beings, even those esteemed the wisest, in accordance with "the Conventional Lies of Civilization," seldom, if ever, act in obedience to horse common sense, but are almost always submissive to what is oftenest most foolish policy and sheer diplomacy.

It was through this endeavoring to combine the spirit of worldly policy and gain and the spirit of religious conviction and dedication that he fell at Lutzen, or failed. Remember that the bitterest denunciation was launched against Laodicea, not because it was the most derelict of the Seven Churches, but because it was "neither cold nor hot." "You cannot serve God and Mammon." So far as ability and learning are concerned, Zwingli was a far greater man than Luther, but he strove to overcome through a coalition, through the sword of spirit and the sword of flesh; to unite religion, military force, policy, and politics; and he fell, comparatively young, at all events in his prime of intellect and strength, on the field of Cappel, just as Gustavus was slain in his prime at Lutzen. Luther held fast solely to the sword of the spirit and abided firmly thereby, and, as he triumphed through that at the Diet of Worms, he stands triumphant to-day and realizes the inspired language of the prophet and chronicler in regard to David:

"And I [the Lord] was with thee whithersoever thou wentest, and have cut off all thine enemies out of thy sight, and have made thee a great name, like unto the name of the great *men* that *are* in the earth."

Gustavus Adolphus, to repeat for emphasis, strove to combine religion and ambition, piety and policy, and diplomacy and the sword, and when he stood highest, he fell. He seemed to realize this at the last and to comprehend the terrible truth, as if the light of eternity shone upon his spirit through the veil of mortality. When the population of Naumburg prostrated themselves adoringly before and about him, this idea flashed upon his mind and he became prophetic in the presentiment which was realized within a few days.

To demonstrate that Gustavus is not altogether regarded as a model of disinterestedness, consider the words of one of his greatest admirers, an English clergyman, B. Chapman, London, 1856, in his "History," vii. 191 :

"It is common fashion with German writers to attribute the interference of Gustavus Adolphus in the Thirty Years' War to a grasping ambition; and one of the latest 'historians of that nation [Gfrörer] has not scrupled to say that he came to Germany as a robber.'[6] This

---

[6] The word "*robber*" has eluded careful search in the revised edition of Gfrörer of Dr. Klopp, but Gfrörer certainly emphasizes his idea that Gustavus came into Germany on his own account and for his own purposes, *against*, especially not with, the will of Duke Bogislaus, of Pomerania, and almost all the other princes who had reason to be most interested in his advent.

Even Menzel, so lavish in his praise of Gustavus, says a great many hard things of the Swedes. He says (384) : "Peace, nevertheless, could not be concluded (1641); France and Sweden still sought to tear the *prey* from each other's grasp ;" and (385) "Sweden solely aimed at the conversion of the German coasts of the Baltic into a Swedish province." He calls (392) Turenne's army a "robber band ;" styles (381) Königsmark one of the boldest robbers of the day (388), who "pillaged the country on his own account," and Gindely (124) charges Banér with having amassed through plunder and left one million dollars ; an enormous fortune for the period ; Schiller (321) states that, in 1638, "booty was his [Banér's] sole object." Burgus (71) (Naylor II. 406) an enemy, in opposition *to all*, thus eulogizes the Swedes as soldiers : "Constant and patient in adversity, bold and determined in battle, and modest and affable to the peasantry and those upon whom they were quartered." The strength of the Swedes was in their hardy recruits and disciplined veterans, led by generals trained and instructed by theory, practice, and example. The imperialists, Bavarians, and Germans, generally, had nothing to compare with the latter. Their leaders were kinglings, princelings, and court favorites, like our own political humbugs and members of rings—military and administrative. Therefore to Germany could be applied the terrible invective of Ezekiel, "Thou land devourest up men," and the graphic first chapter of Joel, describing the successive desolations of Tilly's, Mansfelds, and Christian of Brunswick's bands, of the Friedlander's hordes, of the merciless army of the Empire, and finally of the contending forces, Swedish, French, Bavarians, Empire, and Circles.

The clear, accomplished, celebrated military critic, VON CLAUSEWITZ, in his "*Militarische Briefe eines Verstorbenen an seine noch lebenden Freunde . . . für Eingeweihte und Laien im Kriegswesen, Dritte Sammlung*, Adorf, 1844, goes into a close comparison between the careers and their results, of Gustavus Adolphus, Frederick the Great and Napoleon. This comparison covers many pages but can be summed up, briefly, as follows : von Clausewitz begins with the just remark that kings endowed with military capacity cannot be compared with other generals, because they are in possession of greater power in every way and are likely to be more implicitly obeyed and better sustained by their subordinates. Wallenstein understood this, and with reason attributed his coming short of success on many occasions

grave charge has no real solidity. Not without repeated solicitations from the depressed and deprived among the Germans themselves, not until the war (through the element of Catholic aggression involved in it) had become, as Geijer truly observes, 'the common concern of Europe and mankind,' did Gustavus invade the empire. And though, no doubt, he expected great rewards for himself and nation, if his efforts in the common cause should prove successful, the nobler motives which prompted him to engage in it were tainted by no base cupidity. His expectations were founded in reason and justice. He had a right to look for requital—in the event of victory—for the risk he ran, for the great service he rendered, either from the honesty or gratitude of the restored, or from the spoils of those who had provoked the contest. Nay, more; without exposing himself justly to the charge of a greedy ambition, well might he have meditated the dissolution of that confederacy which was no longer the result of a harmony of feelings and interests, and sought by a new combination of a part of the Germanic body under his own protectorate substantial guarantees for Protestant independence and peace. Various indications of such a policy, not absolutely determined, but roughly shaped out, to be developed and modified according to the course of events, and the counsel and inclination of the Protestant states in alliance with him, will be seen in the following pages [of the history quoted], and especially in the account

---

to his not being adequately supported. And here let it be remarked that, strange to say, there are only two generals in history who never had a mutiny in their armies, although composed of the most heterogeneous elements, and were never disobeyed either by present or distant subordinates,—Hannibal and Torstenson, " the modern Hannibal." Few are aware that Gustavus had open mutiny in his camp at Nuremberg on the 22d July, 1632. His troops rebelled against the strict discipline which he attempted to enforce (Gfrörer, 767), and when he desired to lead them out against the enemy they refused to fight before their arrears of pay were given to them; and the citizens of Nuremberg had to lend two tons of gold (two hundred thousand rix-dollars, equal, at least, to $1,000,000, if not $2,000,000 of to-day). Wellington was of opinion that Napoleon " was in more awe of his marshals than was generally supposed. He acted as if he was not sure of their obedience; for instance, he would order one of them to take another under his command, but he never ventured to tell the other to obey him" (Croker Papers, i. 312); and he was several times positively disobeyed. Wellington was often disobeyed in the most startling manner. Sir William Stuart imperiled the army by direct disobedience after, or during, the retreat from Burgos. Crawford, at times would do just as he pleased in the teeth of his orders, and Picton was " consistently disobedient." It was astonishing how Wellington could put up with it, unless he had to do so. Torstenson would not stand the slightest nonsense. He was emphatically what the Romans styled "*Vir Auctoritatis*" and the Greeks " *Anax Andron.*"

of the king's conferences with the Council of Patricians at Nuremberg in the summer of 1632."

Chapman, in citing one of the latest German historians, means Gfrörer (p. 1016), whose words are: "*Niemand hat Gustav nach Deutschland gerufen. Wie ein Räuber ist er in unser Reich eingebrochen*,"— *i.e.*, "No one invited Gustavus into Germany. Like a robber did he break into our Empire." Gfrörer has written the best Life of Gustavus Adolphus and History of the Thirty Years' War, down to the death of that king, which the writer has ever read or examined with care; not, it is true, in the original edition, but in the fourth, revised and improved by Dr. Klopp, after the death of the original author. In this, the direct assimilation of Gustavus to a robber is not to be found in the exact words quoted by Chapman, but it is implied again and again. Gfrörer said (522) that Gustavus had determined on the invasion of Germany long before he carried his plans into execution. That "war he would have, and war at any price" (536), and compares his impulse to the ambition which spurred Alexander to attack Persia, concealing his real motives with the blinding words of religion and the Gospel. Gfrörer undertakes to prove it, and again and again returns to the subject, quoting still existing testimony. For instance, among many other arguments, the Swedish party claim that Gustavus crossed the Baltic to deliver Duke Bogislav, of Pomerania, from the oppression of the Emperor, whereas Gfrörer declares, even when the king was about to embark, Bogislav, so far from welcoming the fact, conjured him in the name of Heaven to stay at home. Gustavus could not heed this beseeching appeal of the Pomeranian Duke—afraid of being ground to pieces between the upper millstone of the Imperialists and the nether millstone of the Swedes—to stay at home, because it was impossible and contrary to the only plan of operations which could promise eventual success. Pomerania was the inevitable Swedish military base. They already held Stralsund, and they needed the other fortresses and strong positions in the Duchy to insure their "lines of communication and supply," and cover their retreat in case of ultimate remediless reverse. Pomerania was indeed subsequently more than once their refuge, without which they might have been driven into the sea. So Bogislav had to receive with open arms, as friends and defenders, the self-constituted allies who, he fondly hoped, would not force themselves, sword in hand, upon him as such. Many of the most touching episodes of history resolve themselves into grim jokes when the naked truth is revealed, when denuded of its clothing of arguments, its mask of hypocrisy, and its veils of deliberate lies.

Yet when Gfrörer, an absolute German and no more, presumes to say Gustavus broke in as a robber, and the eulogists of the Swede that he entered as a deliverer pure and simple, they both falsify facts. He came as neither. He came as a great king, captain, and statesman, because it was his true policy to do so and the end justified his calculations. (Naylor, II., 382.) He was to the Germans what Isaiah prophesied Cyrus would be for the Jews,—" called and chosen,"—but nevertheless he was exactly what the Prophet styles such deliverers in another chapter, " a punishing-rod and an instrument of vengeance," to be broken—as was Gustavus—when his work was complete, although incomplete to his own mind.

There is not the slightest doubt that after admitting, which is incontrovertible, that the origin of this most horrible of all awful wars was the result of Jesuit planning and teaching and inciting, it would not have assumed its terrific extent and form, if greed, state policy, individual selfishness and ambition had not grasped the opportunity to add fuel to the flames. Priestcraft and its pupils converted Germany into a Gehenna. Without them it would have been a war like our civil war, the "Slaveholders' Rebellion," vast and costly enough, but still free from the unparalleled atrocities which characterized it; whereas the "Slaveholders' Rebellion" only presents hideous blotches, all on one side, such as Belle Isle, Libby, Andersonville, and other prison-pens. What is more, cruel as were the Romanists towards the Protestants, they were equally oppressive to their own people, and set an example which, a Protestant regrets to say, was imitated on all sides and in every direction, until even the most humane found it necessary to "fight with fire." Admit that the Gothic Cæsar was selfish and ambitious, and even yet enough virtues must be conceded to him to justify his elevation to the highest rank among the great and good men in all ages. His great fault was that he did not at the opportune moment shut his eyes to the lure of ambition and solely remember that the Protestants of Germany, as Gfrörer himself admits, yearned for his appearance among them as a saviour, as the Jews looked forward to the coming of their Messiah. Had he been that Deliverer, pure and simple, he would have gone to Vienna after Leipzig and have indeed delivered his co-religionists of the Austrian Hereditary States from the horrible oppression to which they had been subjected through the Jesuits and their plans and pupils.

Butler, in "Hudibras," has four witty, and, at the same time, truthful lines in this connection:

" For none but Jesuits have commission
To preach the Faith with ammunition,
And propagate the church with powder;
Their founder was a blown-up soldier,"—

their founder Ignatius Loyola,—who, originally a courtier and soldier, aspiring to the love of the highest lady in the land (his queen it is said), having been crippled by a wound in the leg at the Siege of Pampeluna, in 1521, became transformed from a man of the world into the astutest priest and religious organizer in the world.

In an imaginary conversation between Mars and Minerva—whom Homer, by the way, makes superior in military gifts and powers to the god—the goddess asks if the war-god had not severely blamed Gustavus for not having marched directly upon Vienna after his victory at Leipzig (I. p. 10), and Mars does not give a positive answer. Afterwards he goes on to excuse the king, even against such high authority, that it is impossible not to cite, again and again, the opinion of Oxenstiern, who held to it firmly throughout his life, and yet it is well known that the chancellor was by no means an enthusiastic man.

In the action of Dirschau, Gustavus, reconnoitering, was wounded in the arm. Oxenstiern remonstrating respecting his reckless exposure on this and other occasions, the king replied, "You are of too cold a temper;" or, "You are so cold, upsetting my plans when most prepared for a bold expedition." "Possibly," replied the great chancellor, "but if my ice did not sometimes cool your fire, your Majesty might have been consumed before this;" or, "I am so, if I did not throw cold water on your Majesty's fire, you would long since have been reduced to ashes." As to the feasibility of the march upon Vienna after Leipsic I., the admission of the king himself is all-sufficient. The battle was fought 7th September, 1631. On the 14th Gustavus wrote to his sister, " *The enemy has been so much destroyed that* WE COULD GO UNHINDERED WHERE WE WISHED." This language is too clear and decided to admit of question.

Of the three great modern captains, Von Clausewitz considers Frederic the Great entitled to the palm, because he attained the object at which he aimed from the beginning. Crowned with the laurels of victory Gustavus certainly received a very serious check when he came in contact with Wallenstein, and who would have eventually remained master of the field is one of the unsolved questions of history,—insoluble because Gustavus' fell a victim to his own rashness or to assas-

---

[7] If the careful singling out of a redoubtable adversary with the intention of putting him out of the way surreptitiously is assassination then was Gustavus

sination at Lutzen, and Wallenstein was soon after assassinated in turn by an ungrateful master whom he had served too well. As for Napoleon, he actually overstepped the limits of the possible, and he was an utter failure. Frederic never once transgressed or passed beyond the limits of his abilities. He fully comprehended and steadily kept in view the objective of his original plans, and as "old Fritz" is the only one who brought his work to a perfect conclusion, to him must be conceded the honor of being the greatest commander of modern times, and he deserves the credit the more because he contended triumphantly and longer against greater odds and difficulties than the others.

As an evidence of the effect of the glamour of a great name upon all but a very few, the majority accepting its subscriptum as an incontrovertible authority upon the minds of the vast majority of even thinking people, take the utterances of Napoleon Bonaparte, as recorded by Count Montholon, in regard to Turenne. Napoleon cites Turenne as one of the seven great military exemplars of all times. There was nothing like genius ever evinced by Turenne. He was the soul of cold-blooded calculation. Napoleon admits this (M. iii. 57). Comparing the conduct of Marshal Ney in 1815 with that of Turenne in 1650, he says, "Turenne acted from calculation and moved by the ambition of ruling the councils of the regency, when, forgetting his oath to Anne of Austria, and declaring himself in favor of the opposite party, he marched upon Paris. Ney did nothing similar to this."

Again (M. iii. 241-42), he enunciates another *dictum* in which it can be proved he makes as many mistakes as there are sentences.

Turenne made *five* campaigns before the treaty of Westphalia. . . . "In 1646 he set out for Mayence, descended the left bank of the Rhine as far as Wesel, where he crossed that river and ascended the right bank till he reached the Lahn; formed a junction with the Swedish army [as if it belonged to him !] passed the Danube and the Lech, and thus performed a march of two hundred leagues across an enemy's country. When arrived on the Lech, he had all his troops united under his own command, having, like Cæsar and Hannibal, abandoned his communications to his allies, or rather, having consented to separate himself for a time from his reserves and his communications, reserving only one place of depot. There was nothing extraordinary in this. Armies were very small and had to live from hand to mouth, and Menzel considers the Turenne's army a ' band of robbers.' "

In 1648 he passed the Rhine at Oppenheim, formed a junction with the Swe-

---

Adolphus most assuredly the victim of such a crime. Maurice de la Châtre, in his "Histoire des Papes," Paris, 1843, writing evidently without bias, for he condemns Wallenstein while painting the character of Ferdinand II. in repulsive colors, says, Vol. IX, page 13, "Gustave Adolphe et Wallenstein se recontrerent dans les plaines de *Lutzen*, et livrerent une *bataille terrible* dans laquelle le *roi de Suede* succomber *victime de la trahison."*

dish army at Hanau, advanced along the Rednitz and retrograded on the Danube, which he crossed at Dillingen; defeated Montecuculi at Cusmarshausen, passed the Lech at Rain, and the Isar at Freising; the court of Bavaria became alarmed for its safety, and quitted Munich. He next fixed his headquarters at Muhldorf, which he laid under contribution, and ravaged the whole of the electorate to punish the elector for his insincerity."

Now to criticise the great Corsican!

After the annihilating overthrow of the French and Weimarians at Tuttlingen, 24th November, 4th December, 1643, Turenne was sent to take command of the French army of Germany. This was in December, 1643. If he accomplished anything worthy of note his successes seem to have made little impression on the French ministry since, in July, 1644, he was superseded by the Duke d'Enghien (the great Condé) and served under him until the troops went into winter quarters, October-December, 1644. In March, 1645, Turenne, left to himself, again advanced into the Palatinate, and on the 2d-3d May he was surprised by the Bavarian Field-Marshal Mercy, and, according to existing circumstances, was whipped as disgracefully as Rantzau at Tuttlingen, in 1643. Mercy took almost the whole of the French infantry, ten guns, and all the baggage. Shortly after he was joined by four thousand Hessians under Königsmark—a man of royal mark, a king among generals of ordinary calibre. With this assistance Turenne forced Mercy to raise the siege of Kirchum (Kirchheim). His defeat at Mariendahl or Mergentheim, and whatever he did or did not do, subsequently resulted, much to his mortification, in his second supersedure, 1st July, 1645, by the Duke d'Enghien. On the 3d August, 1645, occurred the battle of Allerheim, or Nordlingen second. At the crisis of this battle, Mercy, who considered the victory secure, was killed and the French enjoyed the glory of a drawn battle like Antietam. (Koch thinks Mercy was killed by the accidental shot of one of his own men, as is claimed, incorrectly however, to have been the case with Stonewall Jackson, and undoubtedly was true of the desperate wounding of Longstreet. The Third Corps A. of the P. pretty clearly prove Jackson was killed by a volley of one of its Regiments, the First Massachusetts Volunteers.) To prove that this could not have been any decided success for the French, the opposing forces continued facing each other not more than five or six leagues apart, for over two and a half months, until 17th October, 1645. All this time, Turenne was responsible for the paralysis, since he was in full command, the Duke d'Enghien having left the army after winning the field of Allerheim.

This brings the story down to 1646, when Napoleon commences his *dictum*. Turenne did nothing of note in this campaign by himself, for he was united with the Swedish Field-Marshal Wrangel, who was always acting under the inspiration of Torstenson, if Wrangel was not all the time conched or dry-nursed by that great captain. In regard to Torstenson, Turenne exhausts eulogy in exalting his superior abilities; not that Torstenson needs his approval. For Turenne to endorse Torstenson recalls the words of St. Paul to the Corinthians (II. Cor., iii. 1), "Need we, as some *others*, epistles of commendation to you, or *letters* of commendation from you?" Turenne and Wrangel were likewise assisted by Königsmark, who ranks with the ablest commanders developed by the Thirty Years' War, and with less means accomplished a great deal more than Turenne ever did.

What is more, Wrangel waived the chief command in favor of Turenne as a mere matter of policy, to propitiate the vanity of the French court, for Turenne had brought up only nine thousand men; Königsmark five thousand; and the Hessians four thousand six hundred; and Wrangel had twenty-three thousand. The fact is the allies had pretty much everything their own way, since the Imperial commander-in-chief, the Archduke Leopold, did not dare to venture a battle and "buried himself under accumulated earthworks,"—as Birney said of the heavy artillery regiments in the Wilderness—which the allies did not deem it advisable to attack. This conduct of the emperor's brother so disgusted the Elector of Bavaria that he entered into an armistice with the allies. This campaign of 1646 is the first mentioned by Napoleon as indicative of Turenne's greatness. If Turenne did win any laurels he must assuredly share them with Torstenson who planned, and Wrangel and Königsmark, who had so much to do with the execution.

In 1647 Turenne was recalled to the command in Flanders, and in the course of the summer lost, through his own or his (the French) government's injustice to them, the greater part of the Weimarian troops, who went back to the Swedes, to whom they originally and rightfully belonged.

In December, 1647, as the Elector of Bavaria had broken his pledges in taking up arms again in favor of the emperor, Turenne was ordered back into Germany, where he once more united with the Swedes and their confederates under Wrangel and Königsmark, and advanced again in May into Bavaria.

Napoleon says that Turenne defeated Montecuculi at Ousmarshausen. This is an error. The Allies defeated Melander at Z(S)usharsbausen. Montecuculi was a mere subordinate, a general of cavalry, and Gronsfeld, who commanded the Bavarian contingent, and Montecuculi stopped the victorious career of the Allies and saved the remnants of an army which Melander had nearly sacrificed by his mismanagement. There was now no Imperial army fit to resist the Allies until Piccolomini got back from the Low Countries and gathered together a new army and forced the Allies in turn to retreat. In the midst of a "Campaign of Manœuvres" (ironical), peace ended hostilities,—a peace due in a great measure to an independent, bold, and happy stroke of Königsmark.

Now it would bother even Napoleon to demonstrate conclusively to a competent critic what great genius Turenne showed between 1644, when he first held command in Germany, and during the four years which intervened before the war closed. He was subordinate in two indecisive victories, and he was surprised and utterly cut up in the only conflict in which he was exercising an independent chief command. It has been observed again and again that "even a great general may be defeated; but there is no general of any capacity whatever who can find an excuse for allowing himself to be surprised." Koch shows up Turenne and justly disposes of the French claims to doubtful victories, at best drawn battles. Without the great Swedish Leaders, in Camp and Court, the French would have been nowhere in this war.

What is more, Turenne and the Swedes had no great general opposed to them in the campaigns, or three years cited, by Napoleon.

It suited Napoleon's policy to compare himself to Charlemagne (Charles I., *Karl der Grosse*, Charles the Great) and to Louis XIV., the *magnificent*, claiming the one as a French emperor, and both as French sovereigns. He chose to forget that Charlemagne was one of the great Germans and not a Frenchman at all, and that the career of Louis XIV. terminated anything but gloriously in spite of Turenne,—almost as bad as his own did for him. Turenne was one of the ablest of the generals of Louis XIV., but to justify his appearing in the same class with Alexander, Hannibal, Cæsar, Gustavus, and Frederic, requires more proof than truth can furnish, or even the *dictum* of Napoleon can establish.

And now let us examine the claims to greatness on the part of the other six of the Great Seven. Alexander the First, like Sesostris, inherited an incomparable army and very able generals from great fathers, Philip of Macedon and Amenophis III. In a large measure the same was the case with Frederic. Napoleon

Bonaparte received into his control "the magic sword of the Revolution, which would cut in the hands of any one, would cut of itself," veteran troops and officers inspired with the loftiest enthusiasm, highest ambition, perfect confidence in themselves and their cause. Cæsar, who almost touches Hannibal in the exceeding altitude of his powerful individuality, was certainly the architect of his own fortunes; but then he had Rome's constant, courageous commonwealth behind him, its resources, administration, armament, as a basis, as a reinforcement and as a reserve. Hannibal had to make and remake his armies; to supply them from the word "Go"; to exchange their imperfect arms for better; to find, extract, and supply food, in fact, everything needed to the moment and occasion. No greater commander or citizen, soldier, or Soffete (civil-executive) ever lived. Gustavus, like Frederic, was a wise, despotic king, and a great general. Neither Hannibal nor the "modern Hannibal," Torstenson, were kings, but simply servants of states, the one niggardly from policy or politics, the other from poverty; both had to crush mutinies once and for all, to organize their forces, and reorganize forces as fast as they were expended. How Hannibal ruled with such perfectness is an enigma, unsolved and unsolvable. His secret died with him. How Torstenson administered and carried on war is a problem which has puzzled experts, and none as yet have found the demonstration of it, or to the investigation of his system and campaigns have been able to append the triumphant Q. E. D.

Restricted, as it seems I am always to be, as to the space accorded, and at times for preparation,—for it takes more time to condense than to conceive, it is necessary to confine the attention to certain considerations which are undoubtedly the least known. First, the slaughter upon the battle-field, enormous as it was, sinks into insignificance before the depopulation occasioned by absolute murder, through famine, and through consequent endemic and epidemic diseases. The second matter of astonishment is the enormous sums of money, almost inconceivable when added up, squeezed out of the country, day by day, month by month, year by year, and, sometimes, more than once a day, by successive visitations of armed extortion and civil requisition. Writers stand appalled at the vast contributions levied by Wallenstein, and argue against fact, that the figures are incorrect. Conceding, however, that mistakes may have been made, he was only one of many who robbed systematically. He *acquired* millions for himself when a silver dollar had a purchasing value equal to a double-eagle to-day and *required* millions to maintain his tens of thousands of wolves, who were always hungering and never satisfied. Banér, who is not generally charged with cupidity, left a fortune of Rx. 1,000,000, equivalent to at least $10,000,000 of to-day, and after twenty-eight years of this plundering, Wrangel looted a single town to the extent of Rx. 4,000,000, which is said to have represented an equivalent within the present century of $40,000,000. All this goes to prove what immense hoards derived from industry, economy, and even parsimony must have been piling up in the countries thus raided for thirty years, which had not only to pay for raising, paying, maintaining, supplying, and rewarding vast native armies but the successive invasions of Danes, Spaniards, Swedes, French, Transylvanians, Cossacks, and other barbarians who either temporarily or continuously occupied one or another portion of Germany, and shot through it to and fro like a shuttle through the warp.

Third, the armies of this war, however small in comparison with the armies of the present century, were like the small body of the Octopus in comparison to the mass and extent of its tentacles and their powers of injury to a peaceable population. They resembled Eastern armaments in which the fighting force is to the servants and camp-followers as the meat of the peach-pit to the fruit itself. Even under the administration of Gustavus, while Swedish discipline was at its best, and loose women were prohibited, soldiers were permitted to have their wives and children in the camp, so that the number of mouths to be fed almost exceeds belief. Afterwards when morality ceased to be a consideration, loose women were tolerated to an almost inconceivable extent. Brigaded under a regular hierarchy of control, and according to regulated grades of respectability, there was no such thing as shame about it. It was recognized and regulated, and those who are curious on the subject will find ample information in Freytag's "Vergangenheit," and in technical treatises on army life and administration of the period. The Germans were bad enough, and the French worse, but the Spaniards almost inconceivably bad, with this difference that sometimes in a playful mood they ripped up the unfortunates supplied to them. In the latter years of the war, the armies resembled migratory Tartar hordes.[8]

---

[8] Between the armies of the Thirty Years' War—in fact, all the armies of that and previous wars subsequent to the decay of Roman discipline, with the exception of the Swedish and English, proper, and those of the present era—one great difference presents itself. The former were accompanied into the field by not only wives and mistresses, but children, and worse characters of both sexes. Sometimes the number of effectives in a regiment scarcely exceeded that of the women attached to or dependent upon them. In 1620, when a regiment, newly raised, started out from the place where it was "mustered in," it numbered three thousand men and two thousand females.

In the last decade of the war, the camp-followers rose to threefold and fourfold the numbers of those who bore arms regularly. Freytag in his "Vergangenheit" presents a startling picture of this condition of affairs.

As an instance of this constitution of an army, worthy of the days of Xerxes, at Susmarshausen, the strength of the Imperial army, proper, was thirty-three thousand eight hundred soldiers, whereas that of the women, children, and camp-

To sum up the whole matter, the literature of the Thirty Years' War is as worthy of study as the incidents of which it treats are full

---

followers reached the startling number of one hundred and twenty-seven thousand. General Gronsfeld writes, 31st March, 1648, that in the two armies (Imperialist and Bavarian) there were certainly more than one hundred and eighty thousand men, women, and children ; . . . provisions were issued for forty thousand every twenty-four hours; how the remaining one hundred and forty thousand persons were to live [except by robbery] passed his comprehension." Even as early as 1632, when Wallenstein advanced against Nuremberg, his march was closed by upwards of four thousand wagons,—fifteen thousand women,—according to the estimate of Burgos ; and that chronicler supposes the number of sutlers and servants to have been nearly equal (King, 180). Such an aggregation made the march of an army nothing better than a visitation of locusts, with the difference in favor of the insects, since the latter confined their consumption to the vegetation, which was bad enough, whereas these human hordes consumed or carried off everything else. In a few days a comparatively comfortable district with its private or farm dwellings, steadings, outbuildings, etc., etc., would be converted into a perfect waste, just as it is stated that an invading column in 1780 entered the Schoharie and Mohawk valleys—then for the period well settled and cultivated—and, after it marched off, left nothing but the soil and ashes and stone walls to mark where buildings had stood.

Such a state of things has always been common in Eastern countries, even down to the present day.

"It is related by the monks that so sure were they [the Spanish-Saracens] of success and of subduing the whole country [France] that it appeared as if the Moslem army of occupation [which was defeated at Tours by Charles Martel, 3d–4th October, A.D. 732] had come to stay permanently, for they brought with them their wives and childen, flocks and herds, and all their belongings. It was an invasion with a purpose."

For instance, in April, 1799, the English General Harris, in addition to his thirty-five thousand fighting force, was accompanied by one hundred and twenty thousand non-combatants. The proportion of the latter in Asiatic armies, as a rule, has always been at least four ineffectives to each real effective fighting unit. ("Famous and Decisive Battles," by Capt. Charles King, U.S.A., page 180.)

"At the present" (Brockelhurst "Mexico To-Day" 1883, p. 256) "the Mexican army, twenty-five thousand strong, has no commissariat; *crowds of women* follow the troops wherever they move, and provide the soldiers with food."

It was such an Imperial and Bavarian horde of mingled iron and clay of over one hundred and sixty thousand human beings of both sexes and of all conditions that the Allies, Swedes, French, and Associate Germans—doubtless themselves very much encumbered with useless adjuncts—caught *in flagrante delicto* astraddle of the small but not fordable river Zusam. In this affair Z(S)USMARSHAUSEN, the Imperial general, Melander, or Holzapfel, very much resembled a man who goes out to shear and comes back shorn, or starts out to hunt a bear and is hunted instead and hugged to death. The river Zusam, in this district, continually winds like an *s* or *S* or S.

To cover Augsburg, Melander had sufficient strategy to perceive the best position to be assumed to protect the passage of the Danube, was at Zusmarshausen. Suddenly he heard the Allies were about to cross the river at Lauingen further up, and instead of remaining quiet at a central point to observe and strike, he marched off to Glottwang. Finding at that place that he had been misinformed, and that

of interest and instruction. "There were giants in those days." As statesmen, Oxenstiern and Richelieu have never been surpassed. The

---

instead of catching the Allies napping—as Grant expected to surprise the Rebels on the morning of the 26th April, 1862, at Shiloh (as Browne says, page 187, in his "Four Years in Secessia")—he was himself surprised.*

Discovering his mistake too late, Melander hurried back to Z(S)usmarshausen and got half his army across the Zusam when Wrangel and Turenne were upon him, catching him "astraddle of the fence," just as Lee might have occasioned fearful losses to Burnside, while falling back across the Rappahannock, after Fredricksburg 1st, in December, 1862, and Meade should, at least, have caught Lee at Williamsport and Falling Waters, in July, 1863, and again at the Rappahannock, in the autumn of the same year. Gronsfeld with his Bavarians were just about across when Melander galloped back to the rear-guard to make some dispositions to arrest disorder and strive to avert defeat. As he reached the scene of confusion, Montecuculi's cavalry were just routed, and the other troops became "clubbed" and driven *en masse* without his being able to effect anything to restore order among

---

* Quite a number of battles in the course of the world's history, resemble this last collision of importance at Z(S)usmarshausen during the Thirty Years' War, in more than one of its phases.

The first and most remarkable is Timoleon's victory at the Crimessus, in Sicily, B.C. 343; when the good and great Greek, with about 10,000 men, defeated some 70,000 Carthaginian mercenaries. This overthrow, due to a variety of circumstances, all traceable to natural causes, seems scarcely less miraculous than the discomfiture of the host of Midian by Gideon, or that of the army of Mesha, King of Moab, by King Jehoshaphat of Judah, and Jehoram of Israel; if the facts of these cases could be laid open to critical investigation. They were due to panics to which all ancient and Eastern armies are subject.

Are they more remarkable than Marathon, B.C. 490, achieved in the face of day; or Hemmingsted, A.D. 1500, in the Ditmarsh district of Denmark, by a mere handful of brave peasants, over a Royal army of 30,000; or Narva, 30th November, 1700, when 8000 Swedes under Charles XII., advancing in the face of a snowstorm and a numerous artillery, defeated 80,000 Russians in an entrenched camp, garnished with 150 guns? What is to be said of the "Castlebar Races," 1796, or as to Plattsburgh, 11th October, 1814? On the latter occasion between 12 and 14,000 British veterans, fresh from their glories under Wellington in Spain, after defeating superior numbers of veteran French under Napoleon's ablest lieutenants, abandoned field and fame and wounded, in the face of a few American regulars and not over three thousand militia, almost without cover. In the Class of Battles to which Z(s)usmarshausen belongs, may be included in some respects more or less resemblant, the Persians at the Zaab, after Arbela, B.C. 331; Hannibal's victory at the Trebbia, B.C. 218; (Evesham, 1265, "Art of War in the Middle Ages," 52?) Wallace at Sterling on the Tweed, 1298; Blorebeath, Stafford Co., England, 1459, (See "Art of War in the Middle Ages," p. 120), exactly as to principle; ("Drowning of the Hungarians after the Battle of the White Mountain," 1620) Prince Eugene's utter defeat of the Turks at Zenta, on the Theiss, Hungary, 1696, after Pultown, 8th July, 1708.

Sobieski's victories on the Plain of Nimiron, in Gallicia, whence he drove the Turks across the Dniester, Stryi, and Schewitz, 1672; Suworrow's Rymnik; Blenheim on the French right, 1704 (Oudmarde might have been made a partial or complete *disaster*, to the Allies while crossing the Schelde, 11th July, 1708, if the French had had a general of any real ability at their head), Campo Santo, 8th February, 1743; Ratisbon, 1809; Aspern, 1809; Beresina, 1812; Katsbach, 1813; Leipsic, after the conclusion of the last of the Three days' "Battle of the Nations," 1813; Ostrolenka, Poland, 26th May, 1832. A number of other instances might be added did time permit their consideration.

former, Pope Urban VIII.—an able man himself—regarded as a being superior in degree to humanity. Under some aspects, he was one of the most extraordinary men that ever lived. After the death of Gustavus, he had to pilot the ship of state amid reefs and shoals and swift tides and eddies almost equal to whirlpools. He conned the craft safely through. After Nordlingen, he was in command of the same vessel, dismasted amid a cyclone, and he brought it triumphantly into port. No prime minister ever had a harder task. Œdipus himself was not called upon to solve, to ordinary experience, a more unsolvable riddle. Salvius, another Swedish representative, was pitted against the greatest diplomatists of Europe and carried his points. As to the generals they have been sufficiently dwelt upon. They were worthy children of Thor, the ideal leader of the Northern races; perhaps one of the few mortals justly deified by superstition, if apotheosis could be justified in any case. The "Theatrum Europæum," equivalent to one of our finest illustrated periodicals, is a marvel of painstaking collaboration. It is the copious source of every sort of information in regard to the period.

Our "Rebellion Record" was conceived with the same idea, but is as inferior in comparison in value as copper to gold. The battle and siege plans in the "Theatrum" are unique. Without them nothing would be known trustworthily of any of the important collisions and sieges. The maps for the period are excellent. Chemnitz and a few other writers constitute the authorities to which every historian must resort. Without them, any one attempting to write on this war would be a

---

the Imperial regiments, proper, or hold them up to their work. The Elector of Bavaria subsequently charged certain of their Colonels with cowardice. At this juncture, a bullet struck Melander in the body, and with a last exhortation to his broken troops, he fell mortally wounded from his saddle.

It was here almost as it was to be at Aughrim, 1689, after St. Ruth was killed. All was inevitably lost there, before Sarsfield (Lord Lucan) could gather up the reins of command. Gronsfeld, who had gotten across with almost all the Bavarians, posted them to defend the river, but soon discovered that unless he destroyed the bridge his own force would be annihilated as well as the other half of the army, the Imperialists, who were still on the west shore. It was a type in 1648 of what occurred at Leipsic in 1813. The premature destruction of the bridge and the subsequent heroic resistance of Ulric Würtemberg, saved a portion of the Imperial army, but delivered up the rest to the swords of the Allies. The result of this German (1648) Little Sailor's Creek of (6th April, 1865), delivered over Bavaria to the invader, and they made the most of their victory. Just as the sovereign and Elector Maximilian abandoned his dominions and subjects to the Swedes under Gustavus Adolphus, in 1632, just so, again, he repeated his flight to Salzburg, the capital of the Archbishopric of that name, leaving everything a prey to the irruption which his own duplicity, bigotry, and cruelty had brought thus again and again upon his unhappy people.

mariner at sea without compass and charts. As a study for everything but strategy—which was, perhaps, precluded by circumstances—for grand tactics, for tactics, for logistics, in the most comprehensive sense, for demand and supply, for marches, for everything pertaining to the carrying on of war, the raising of armies, the feeding, the furnishing, and the fighting them, there are no such lessons to be learned from any similar term of years as from 1620 to 1648. After the peace of Westphalia (1648), war continued, here or there, almost without cessation, but there was very little scientific improvement until the time of Frederic the Great; and although enormous armies were brought into the field, until the great Hohenzollern arose, science was under an eclipse. In his strategical acuteness of vision Napoleon ranked very high, but in no other way. To him cannot be traced a single step in advance, such as characterize the daybreak of Gustavus and of Frederic. It may seem almost a paradox to conclude with an assertion so startling as this which follows: the four years of the great American contest for the suppression of "the Slaveholders' Rebellion," developed more novelties in the combination and applications of the sciences and arts of peace as coadjutors to the arts and sciences of war, demonstrating that the useful may be made the handmaid of destruction and invention, the best servants of force, than any like period of hostilities in the history of the world. With the impetus then and there given, war entered as to tactics, arms, and everything inseparably connected with it, into, as it were, a new plane of existence.

That the views expressed in this article have been strongly corroborated, can be proved from recent works which have appeared of late years since different national archives were thrown open to investigation; Professor Ward in his Lectures on the "House of Austria in the Thirty Years' War," and Koch's "History of the German Empire during the Reign of Ferdinand III.," etc. It is only very lately that historians have appeared, who were not absolute champions of the religious doctrines they professed. With the abating of intolerance, due rather to skepticism or indifference than to charity, truth has come to the front.

Professor Ward is very clear and very just, although he does deal slashing blows to those who deserve it. Towards Wallenstein he is in so far just, in that he shows that in getting rid of him, his only great general, the emperor committed the *great* error which gave to the enemies of his realm and religion, victory in the end; that Wallenstein understood Gustavus Adolphus, and that the Swedish hero was by him, "the Friedlander," drawn away from his own plans to act as Wallenstein intended. As to Gustavus, Ward makes it clear that, from the first, he intended to have a hand in the German war; whatever may have been the original impulse or extent of his aims, "Gustavus Adolphus—of this there remains no doubt—aspired to no less a prize than the Imperial crown." "The sack of Magdeburg—which, even were its captors freed from every stain of criminality, would remain a monstrous political blunder—threw Saxony into his arms; the victory of Breitenfeld placed the fate of the empire in his power. *Then, had he marched upon Vienna, it must have fallen.* And so must the same city have fallen into the hands of the victors of Sadowa, and so must Rome into those of Hannibal after Cannae. But, whatever we may think of the Prussians of our own day, neither Hannibal nor Gustavus were politicians of the event." The first complaint of Gustavus against Ferdinand III., the exclusion of his ambassador from the conferences at Lubec, was a manufactured grievance. "The object of Gustavus Adolphus was obviously to be insulted." The cases of his representative and that of Benjamin Franklin were identical. Both were treated most disrespectfully, Salvius by the Imperial Commissioners, Franklin by the English Ministers, and both lived to play a principal part in the humiliation of the powers to whom they were previously objects of discourtesy almost amounting to contempt.

Koch is the first historian who gives a fair account of this conflict at *Susmarshausen,* which is generally styled no better than a bloody skirmish, and is more worthy the title of a battle than most engagements which are classed as such. In a measure he excuses Melander, and shows that the fighting lasted over nine hours and was lively and bloody, adding that Melander's career had an unfortunate but glorious termination. Considering the fact that this general was a rigid Calvinist, and that a bigoted Romanist emperor made him commander-in-chief of his army, is excellent proof that he must have possessed and displayed unusual military ability, which by one historian at least has been claimed for him.

# THE ACTUAL AND OSTENSIBLE CONDITION OF THE RUSSIAN CAVALRY.

By H. von Dewall, Rittmeister à la suite of the Old Mark Ulan Regiment No. 16, Instructor at the Military School, Potsdam.

(Translated from the *Jahrbücher für die Deutsche Armee und Marine* by Stanislaus Remak, late First Lieutenant Fifth U. S. Artillery.)

It will be remembered how animated a discussion was maintained not long ago in daily and technical periodicals with regard to the question whether, in the event of a war with Russia, the menacing of our Eastern frontiers or even an interference with our arrangements for mobilization might be efficiently warded off, inasmuch as the Russian cavalry could pour itself forth upon East and West Prussia, as well as over Silesia, before we could make suitable dispositions to prevent it.

The Russian cavalry possesses an organization similar to our own in so far, in that in a condition of peace it closely approximates its war strength; so that independently of the period requisite for the instruction of recruits, it is enabled to leave its garrisons in a few days,—in part, perhaps even in a few hours. In a certain sense, it has, indeed, an advantage, as compared with ours, as the dispositions with regard to its assignment and incorporation, necessary in war and especially for the purposes of the great operations, are already met in a state of peace. When we moreover bear in mind that the great majority of its divisions are distributed in the Western provinces, in part in the very frontier territories, while the remainder are suitably located along the railway lines, the significance of the question above propounded will appear in no degree lessened and a ready explanation will be found of the fact that a keen eye is kept on the part of the Germans upon the Russian cavalry, which, quite regardless of its tactically cavaleristic[1] value or the want of it, is calculated, in view of its great masses alone, to play an important part in future wars. That this part was not a conspicuously prominent one in the last Turkish war, is due to circum-

---

[1] The word is adopted from the original. Repeatedly employed in the further progress of the article, it carries within itself its meaning, which could not otherwise be rendered without a somewhat labored circumlocution; nor then always, without detriment to the adequate forcibility of expression of the precise thought intended to be conveyed.—Translator.

stances, the more detailed explanation of which would lead us beyond the purport of this paper; but the plains of the Vistula and the Niemen are conducive, in other fashion than the mountainous regions of the Balkan peninsula, to the active participation of the mounted troops in the great battles, in which it may be demonstrated that the cavalry can yet coöperate in the achievement of decisive results there, as well as in the service of the strategical operations before and after. If anywhere, the Russian cavalry can there demonstrate what it can achieve; if the aims, which it has heretofore affected and still affects, be the correct ones, and if the expectations at the present time formed of it by the people and by the leaders of the Russian armies, be justified. *There* will the greatest masses of horsemen in the world contend with one another; *there* will be found the opportunity to bring our ancient knightly arm anew in good stead, to show that without it the great armies of the present era are inadequate colossi and not only that, but also to prove to the dismayed infantry, that the breech-loader can yet be conquered, if only the cavalry shall have remained as of yore and shall ground its attacks upon those principles, which aforetime have been taught us under the ægis of the great Frederick, by a Seydlitz and a Zieten. The time of peace and inactivity, which ensued after that period of highest fame, cannot be to us a sign of incipient relaxation, but only a time of collected deliberate readiness and expectation. The ban is now broken, that rested upon us. This is the avowed tactical creed of the *German* cavalryman!

And the Russian? He boasts of his numbers and relies—he, the trooper,—upon his musket! The numbers, yes, these are considerable; doubly as great as ours! But are these masses, over whom he holds sway, filled with the same spirit, which is solicitously nourished and cherished in our horsemen? Were this the case, the solution of a knotty problem would undoubtedly stand in our way. But it is not so and cannot be so, if horse and sabre and lance are to be made subservient to, nay, are to give way to, the fire-arm.

Already as long ago as at the time of the Franco-German war, a revolution became manifest in Russia in the views upon the employment of the cavalry; the experience, which it was thought had been gained in the conflict with the Turks, gave this new impulse; the possibility of the practical success of cavalry attacks against the fire-arms of the day appeared to be beset with perplexing doubts; and continually greater and greater force was acquired by the tendency to gravitate towards the belief, that the fire-arm alone could restore to the cavalry what it had lost—*i.e.*, that it could only yet hope to operate with unqualified success if the rapidity of the horse were united with the readiness of fire of the infantry and that, therefore, these two desirable elements must be incorporated with one another. Thus all these years are filled up with a succession of important changes in organization, which constantly tended to deprive the cavalry regiments of their character as regiments of horsemen and sought to remodel them into a body of troops, which should be in the position of rivaling the infantry, but which, in the natural order of things, in proportion to the growth of confidence in their rifles, were bound to suffer in cavaleristic peculiarities. With the transformation of the regiments of ulans and hussars, attached to the fourteen European cavalry divisions, into dragoons,[2] which ensued after the close of the autumn manœuvres of 1882, this labor of re-organization came to a close for the time being, and it was hoped that now, at last, a body of cavalry adapted to present demands had been secured.

From this alone we would be already enabled to determine the spirit with which it is proposed in the future to cause the cavalry to be indoctrinated. For the Russian dragoons had for years aimed to achieve preëminent efficiency in fighting on foot; they even seek with a sort of pride, to all appearance, to render the cavaleristic element itself, of ulterior account. But the best evidence of the ideas entertained by the Russian authorities as to the future sphere of action of the cavalry, appears from the fact that a similar armament and employment is also contemplated for the Cossack regiments; so that, when this transformation shall have been completed, the existence in Russia of a body of actual cavalry, fighting with sabre and lance, will scarcely be any longer in question.

The Russian cavalry, it will be remembered, is divided into:

I. The regiments of the regular cavalry (cavalry of the guard and army);

---

[2] We are indebted for a portion of our observations to a work which has recently appeared and which seems to us worthy of the widest dissemination: "The strategical cavalry manœuvres under General Gurko in Southern Russia, in the fall of 1882, and the reform tendencies in the Russian cavalry, By A. von Drygalski" (R. Eisenschmidt, Berlin). Owing to the difficulties, consequent upon the lack of knowledge of the Russian language, the few literary productions upon the army institutions of Russia which come into the world, must be doubly welcomed, especially when written, as in the case of the work above mentioned, from the critical point of view of the professional soldier. While the first part of the book gives a clear description of those strategical manœuvres, which is interesting in itself, he who seeks instruction upon the spirit now animating our comrades-at-arms over there, will be amply rewarded by studying the second part of it, designated "reform tendencies."

II. The Cossack regiments,      ⎫ which in time of peace are
III. The so-called irregular troops, ⎭ only in part organized.

I. Of **regular cavalry**, since the before-mentioned re-organization, there are:

    4 regiments of cuirassiers of the guard,
    2   "    " dragoons  "  "  "
    2   "    " ulans     "  "  "
    2   "    " hussars   "  "  "
   46   "    " dragoons  "  " army.

Total,   56 regiments of cavalry, consisting
  of 2 divisions, of 2 squadrons, each,    = 224 squadrons.[3]
To which is to be added: the Crim Tartary division, consisting of 2 (in time of
war 4) squadrons,                          = 4  "
which in certain respects belongs to this
enumeration.

    Total, in time of war, 57 regiments    = 228 squadrons.

Independently of insignificant differences, the strength of each of these organizations on a war footing, is: 31 officers, 48 non-commissioned officers, 17 trumpeters, 512 men[4] = 608 combatants. These 57 regiments have, therefore, a war strength of 34,656 combatants.

II. Of **Cossacks** there are, *i.e.* are newly organized in war:

    (*a*) THE DON COSSACK WOISKO.

In peace are present:
The combined Don Cossack regiment (body
guard), consisting of 4 squadrons    = 4 squadrons.
15 Don Cossack regiments (army), first category = 15 regiments, consisting each of
                       6 sotnias  = 90 sotnias.

Carried forward                        94 squadrons and sotnias.

---

[3] The fifth squadrons serve as reserve squadrons and are so named even in time of peace; they are disregarded in the above calculation.

[4] Presumably intended to include corporals, who in the Russian army do not attain to the rank of non-commissioned officers.—TRANSLATOR.

Brought forward                94 squadrons and sotnias.

Newly organized in war:

The Don Cossack regiment (body guard), consisting of
The Ataman Cossack regiment (body guard) consisting of
} formed out of the combined Don Cossack regiment (body guard), of the peace footing.

6 squadrons = 6 squadrons.

6 " = 6 "

15 Don Cossack regiments, (army), second category, consisting each of 6 sotnias = 90 sotnias.

30 independent sotnias, second category, = 30 "

15 Don Cossack regiments, (army), third category, consisting each of 6 sotnias = 90 "

Total, 52 regiments, consisting of     316 squadrons and sotnias.

The war footing of these organizations is:

The Don Cossack regiment, (body guard), 53 officers, 96 non-commissioned officers, 25 trumpeters, 960 men = 1134 combatants    1134 combatants.

The Ataman Cossack regiment, (body guard), has apparently the same war footing = 1134 combatants    1134 "

The Don Cossack regiments, (army), 21 officers, 86 non-commissioned officers, 19 trumpeters, 686 men, each = 812 combatants; in all:    40,600 "

War strength of the Don Cossack Woisko:    42,868 combatants.

### (b) THE KUBAN COSSACK WOISKO.

In peace are present:

2 squadrons, His Majesty's convoy     = 2 squadrons.

10 regiments of horse, of 6 sotnias each     = 60 sotnias.

1 division of horse, of 2 squadrons     = 2 squadrons.

Carried forward                64 squadrons and sotnias.

| | |
|---|---|
| Brought forward | 64 squadrons and sotnias. |

Newly organized in war:
 20 regiments of horse, second and third categories, of 6 sotnias each = 120 sotnias.

 Total 30¾ regiments = 184 squadrons and sotnias.

Their war footing is:
 The squadrons of the convoy, 6 officers, 18 non-commissioned officers, 2 trumpeters, 160 men, each = 186 combatants; in all  372 combatants.
 The Kuban Cossack regiments of horse, 23 officers, 86 non-commissioned officers, 13 trumpeters, 768 men, each = 890 combatants; in all  26,700 "
 The Kuban Cossack division of horse, 11 officers, 18 non-commissioned officers, 7 trumpeters, 266 men = 302 combatants, = 302 "

War strength of the Kuban Cossack Woisko: 27,374 combatants.

(The squadrons of the convoy are detached from the Woisko in time of war, but are counted in the above enumeration to arrive at the total strength.)

### (c) THE TEREK COSSACK WOISKO.

In peace are present:
 2 squadrons, His Majesty's convoy = 2 squadrons.
 4 regiments of horse, of 4 sotnias each = 16 sotnias.
Newly organized in war:
 8 regiments of horse, second and third categories, of 4 sotnias each = 32 "

 Total 12½ regiments = 50 squadrons and sotnias.

Their war footing is:
 The squadrons of the convoy, 6 officers, 18 non-commissioned officers, 2 trumpeters, 160 men, each = 186 combatants; in all  372 combatants.

Carried forward  372 combatants.

Brought forward  372 combatants.
The regiments of horse, 17 officers, 58 non-
commissioned officers, 9 trumpeters, 512
men, each = 596 combatants; in all  7152  "

War strength of the Terck Cossack Woisko:  7524 combatants.
(The squadrons of the convoy are detached
from the Woisko in time of war.)

### (d) The Astrachan Cossack Woisko.[5]

Total, 3 regiments  = 12 sotnias.
War strength of the Astrachan Cossack Woisko: 1782 combatants.

### (e) The Orenburg Cossack Woisko.[5]

Total, 18 regiments of horse  = 108 sotnias.
War strength of the Orenburg Cossack Woisko:  16,488 combatants.

### (f) The Ural Cossack Woisko.[5]

Total, 7⅔ regiments  = 46 squadrons and sotnias.
War strength of the Ural Cossack Woisko:  7059 combatants.

### (g) The Siberian Cossack Woisko.[5]

Total, 9 regiments  = 54 sotnias.
War strength of the Siberian Cossack Woisko: 8190 combatants.

### (h) The Semirjetschensk Cossack Woisko.[5]

Total, 3 regiments  = 12 sotnias.
War strength of the Semirjetschensk Cossack
Woisko:  1842 combatants.

### (i) The Trans-Baikal Cossack Woisko.[5]

Total, 3 regiments,  = 18 sotnias.
War strength of the Trans-Baikal Cossack
Woisko:  2676 combatants.

### (k) The Amur Cossack Woisko.[5]

Total  = 1 regiment of 6 sotnias.
War strength of the Amur Cossack Woisko:  910 combatants.

---

[5] The detailed enumeration of the original in the case of these Woiskos has been omitted for want of space.—Translator.

III. Of irregular troops, which though so called, have also a fixed status, and are to be newly organized in war, there are:

| | Officers. | N.-C. Officers. | Trumpeters. | Men. | | Combatants. |
|---|---|---|---|---|---|---|
| 1. 1 Sotnia in Irkutsk. | | | | | | |
| War strength | 6 | 12 | 1 | 120 | = | 139 |
| 2. 1 Sotnia in Kravsnojarsk. | | | | | | |
| War strength | 6 | 12 | 1 | 120 | = | 139 |
| 3. 2 Ussuri sotnias. | | | | | | |
| War strength | 5 | 9 | 3 | 133 | = | 300 |
| 4. The Kutais irregular regiment of horse of 4 sotnias. | | | | | | |
| War strength | 23 | 30 | ... | 600 | = | 653 |
| 5. Standing militia. | | | | | | |
| 1 Kuban sotnia. | | | | | | |
| War strength | 1 | 7(?) | ...(?) | 80 | = | 88 |
| 11 Terek sotnias muster | 22 | 66(?) | ...(?) | 1177 | — | 1265 |
| 11 Daghestan sotnias muster | 22 | 66(?) | ...(?) | 975 | = | 1063 |
| Ssuchum guard (1 sotnia). | | | | | | |
| War strength | ...(?) | 10(?) | ...(?) | 160 | = | 170 |

War strength of the irregular troops: 32 sotnias with 3817 combatants.

To these are to be further added those unenumerated thousands, available for organization in case of need out of the multitude of men and horses, of whose sum however, it is impossible to make a calculation, or even an estimate.

If, therefore, all these organizations come into existence in time of war, Russia would be able to bring into the field of cavalry:

| | | | | | |
|---|---|---|---|---|---|
| 1. The cavalry of the guard and army, including the Crim Tartary division | 57 Regts. | = 228 Squads. | with | 34,565 | Combts. |
| 2. The Don Cossack Woisko | 52 " | = 312 Sotnias, | " | 42,868 | " |
| 3. " Kuban " " | 30¾ " | = 184 " | " | 27,374 | " |
| 4. " Terek " " | 12½ " | = 50 " | " | 7,524 | " |
| 5. " Astrachan Cossack Woisko | 3 " | = 12 " | " | 1,782 | " |
| 6. " Orenburg " " | 18 " | = 108 " | " | 16,488 | " |
| 7. " Ural " " | 7¾ " | = 46 " | " | 7,059 | " |
| 8. " Siberian " " | 9 " | = 54 " | " | 8,190 | " |
| 9. " Semirjetschensk Cossack Woisko | 3 " | = 12 " | " | 1,842 | " |
| 10. " Trans-Baikal Cossack Woisko | 3 " | = 18 " | " | 2,676 | " |
| 11. " Amur Cossack Woisko | 1 " | = 6 " | " | 910 | " |
| 12. " Irregular troops | ? " | = 32 " | " | 3,817 | " |
| Aggregate strength | 196⅔ regts. | = 1062 squadrons & sotnias. | | 155,186 | combts. |

These are, it must be confessed, significant numbers, as compared with which our 93 regiments with their 57,939 combatants (counting 23 officers and 600 men to the regiment), would have a hard struggle, if numbers were anything else than—numbers. By themselves they as yet prove nothing. Of what use to the Russians are these 155,000 horses, if they cannot be made available in good time? Even if the Russian regiments could be recruited up to the full standard as rapidly as the German, it would be impossible, in view of the colossal dimensions of the Russian realm, and in spite of the railways, to forward them to their destinations before the lapse of months. No proof is needed of this. Without going back further than to recent times, we know that in the Crimean war, as also in that against Turkey, Russia has had to suffer from the impossibility of accomplishing a timely union of her combatant forces. The former came to an unsuccessful issue, principally in consequence of these causes. Russia, though immeasurably superior to the allies in combatant strength, was powerless to effect the transportation of her forces before the decisive moment. It was the same in 1877 and 1878, and so it will be for a long time to come, in future wars. To accomplish with adequate dispatch the junction on the frontier of military organizations like the Russian, will remain a difficult, and perhaps, indeed, an insoluble problem, even if Russia shall be, some day, traversed by a widely disseminated railway system, answering the demands of military necessity.

There can, however, be no question as to a recruitment of the Russian cavalry to its war strength, as rapid as that of our own, when we recollect that large parts of the regiments of Cossacks and of horse, and notably all those which are not regularly organized except for war, belong to the second and third categories. It is true that the troops of the second category are not only armed and equipped in time of peace, but have also their horses; but the troops of the third category are prepared with their armament and equipment alone and have no horses. Thus, the regiments of the latter category may be primarily left entirely out of consideration, and even those of the second category will in all cases require a certain time,—perhaps several weeks,—before the completion of their formation and before they shall be ready to march. In so far as can be predicated, therefore, there would, under any circumstances, be no question as to a transportation of these latter organizations, until the march to the field of the regular army of operations should have been accomplished. We, for the time being, would consequently not have to concern ourselves even as to the regiments of the second category. Those who know what it means to push forward an army of so and so many hundred thousand men into the field, on four railway lines, and to make all the dispositions for their current and eventual wants and subsistence, will perceive, without the necessity for the exhibition of detailed calculations, that there can be neither time nor room for following them up at a very early day, by the dispatching of further masses of troops. Russia does not, at the time, possess more through railway lines than these, in which is already included that leading out of her Southern provinces, from Charkow, by way of Balta, to Lemberg, on the Austrian frontier. From its terminus, Dubno, the troops would have before them to the Prussian frontier, a distance of 460 versts = 305 English miles in an air-line, that is to say, a march of about four weeks.

For immediate employment Russia has only those regiments which are already formed in time of peace. The remainder will furnish, it must be admitted, a highly respectable reserve, increasing in importance the longer the war may continue, and the more impaired in strength our own cavalry, which cannot command equally powerful second and third lines, may become. At the outstart, however, these regiments may be disregarded as having any bearing on the strategical development of the campaign, upon the issue of which they could exert no appreciable influence, perhaps for months.

Bearing in mind the foregoing remarks, we will perceive that Russia has organized in time of peace 504 squadrons and sotnias, with a war strength of 77,001 combatants. And even from this number deductions must be made. As the combined Don Cossack regiment of the body-guard is to serve as a nucleus for the two Cossack regiments of the body-guard of the Don Cossack Woisko to be formed in case of war, it can scarcely be assumed, if a systematic mobilization be had, that it will move into the field with the regiments of the first category; but on the contrary that, in all probability, it will not do so until the completion of the organization of these two regiments, that is to say, with the second line. In the same way the irregular troops, taking into consideration their constitution and organization, appear little adapted to be brought into immediate service. Altogether, then, there would be 4,575 combatants, which may well be deducted from those 77,001; so that the actual strength of Russian cavalry moving into the field at the outbreak of a war would amount to 72,426 as against our 57,939 men. It is true, it cannot be presumed that these figures are infallibly correct, as they are not directly taken from official sources, but depend essentially upon the statements made in the latest yearly issues of the "Yearly reports upon the changes and progress in military matters." But in reality, a few hundred or thousand men more or less need not be regarded as of consequence in affecting the questions with which we have to do.

All the regiments of the cavalry of the guard and army, as also those of the Don Cossack Woisko and a few of those of the other Woiskos, are attached to permanent cavalry divisions, which are moreover provided with artillery for their support. In *time of peace*, there are of these divisions:

    2 cavalry divisions of the guard,
  14    "      "      "      "    army,
    1 Caucasian cavalry division,
    2      "      Cossack divisions,
    1 Don      "      division.

Total, 20 cavalry divisions.

Out of the extraordinarily strong second cavalry division of the guard (seven regiments and one independent squadron), two divisions are formed under an order of mobilization,[6] there being consequently in time of war a total of twenty-one cavalry divisions, consisting each of two brigades (the second cavalry division of the guard, of three brigades), of two regiments, with two horse batteries, each; excepting, however, the cuirassier division of the guard, which then includes the Ural Cossack squadron of the body-guard, and the first Caucasian Cossack division, which numbers five regiments. It should, at the same time, be mentioned that the two Caucasian Cossack divisions have only one battery each.

As, from the point of view of their strength, since Russia, excepting the few regiments of the guard, possesses only dragoons and Cossacks (or, what is, to all purpose, to the same effect, regiments of horse), so also in respect of other constituent elements, do we find a similarity between the various divisions. There are:

The cuirassier division of the guard, composed, as indicated by its designation, of the four cuirassier regiments of the guard and the before-mentioned Ural Cossack squadron of the body-guard.

The first and second cavalry divisions of the guard, composed of

---

[6] To this division belongs the combined Don Cossack regiment of the bodyguard, out of which the before-mentioned two regiments are organized in time of war. Thus, unless the division were divided, it would include eight regiments, which would undoubtedly be too many.

the ulan, dragoon, hussar, and Cossack regiments of the guard, equally divided between them.

The fourteen cavalry divisions of the army, composed, on the other hand, of three dragoon regiments and one of Cossacks, each.

The Caucasian cavalry division, composed of four dragoon regiments.

The three Cossack divisions, composed each of four (the first Caucasian division, of five), Cossack regiments, i.e. regiments of horse.

As to the *rôle*, which would be assigned to these divisions, it can be determined with tolerable certainty. It is true, that in time of peace they are attached and united to the army corps in such a manner, that the two divisions of the guard belong to the guard corps; the fourteen cavalry divisions of the army to the army corps Nos. 1–14; the two Caucasian Cossack divisions to the first Caucasian army corps; the Caucasian cavalry division to the second Caucasian army corps; while the Don Cossack division is apparently not assigned to any corps. But from this distribution among the army corps, it by no means follows that this relation is also intended to be kept up in time of war. Rather has the recognition of the necessity for an independent employment of the cavalry, rendered all other considerations of this sort of minor importance, and it exercises such a dominant sway over the entire instruction, organization, and being of the Russian cavalry, that it is to be expected with absolute certainty that, in time of war, the divisions will be assigned to the positions under the potent influence of that doctrine regarded as appropriate to them, which conclusion is also strengthened in view of the permanent assignment of artillery to them.

Now, though we have, to practical intent and primarily, to do only with the before designated available Russian cavalry of the first line, we must not be oblivious of the fact, that those regiments of the second and third categories, with their 82,760 men, are in the rear of the first line, preparing for the fray, and—though it may be a long time—will yet finally reach the front. It will scarcely be maintained, however, that the strategical importance of the cavalry would be of appreciable significance and influence during the first period of the war; let the *rôle* of the German combatant forces become developed in the course of it, how it may, whether as an offensive or defensive one, always will the side that shall be provided with a numerically superior cavalry (equal excellence being pre-supposed) be the better served, and in consequence possess a certain advantage. But that, in such later periods, the Russian cavalry will be numerically stronger is unquestionable and a matter of fact which those may bear in mind for whom our 93 regiments are already too many. It may be urged that the Cossack regiments have no reserve squadrons (such being only formed for the regiments of cavalry of the guard and army); and that, therefore, presumably, portions of the regiments of the third category would have to undertake these functions not only for those of the first, but also for those of the second, category. But with all that, whatever could be pushed forward *with us* in the way of reserves, would be of inappreciable account in comparison with the masses which would appear from the interior of Russia. In 1870 it was repeatedly demonstrated that our reserve squadrons could scarcely, nor in adequate time, cover the more serious losses,—and over there, there are 80,000 fighting men moving forward into the first line!

Herewith we have to a certain extent a definite notion as to the numbers with which we are concerned in regard to the Russian cavalry. But with no arm do numbers alone amount to so little, and in order to arrive at an approximately correct judgment as to the value of the Russian cavalry, it is first of all necessary to examine more closely the fundamental principles, which underlie its equipment and armament, its instruction and employment.

While formerly the cavalry of the guard and army was exclusively mounted upon the quite fairly useful but rather heavy-footed horses of Great Russia, these regiments in later times have also taken the majority of their remounts from the races of the steppes of the Southern provinces. In himself better adapted than any other to military service, by his endurance and tractability, the Cossack horse nevertheless furnishes in his build the type of the lightest imaginable cavalry horse (though in certain aspects the Hungarian may perhaps stand side by side with him); so that in point of fact the Russian cavalry of the present can scarcely be regarded as consisting of other than light regiments. One does not need to be a defender of the heavy cavalry, especially of the cuirassiers, to appreciate that as the mass must ever lend to a *choc* a certain preponderance of weight, the Russian cavalry must in this manner, in view of its system of remounts, fall short in its necessities and that it has little prospect in a closed attack, to withstand an adversary riding towards it upon more powerful horses, well held in hand in consequence of a rational training that ensures obedience and equanimity. And the more especially so, as there is to all appearance scarcely any more question as to artistic equitation in the Russian cavalry. The deer-necked, weak-backed, Cossack horse renders every systematic training well-nigh futile:— short gallop, side-steps, and such; indeed every species of well-executed evolution, upon which, with justice, a high value is placed among us, are with him demands totally impossible of fulfilment. A cavalry in which the spirit for equitation and the art of riding vanishes in the degree, to which it seems to have vanished in the case of the Russian, —such a cavalry must inevitably and simultaneously retrograde in its peculiarly cavaleristic elements. It has known better times, at least the cavalry of the guard and army; its riding-school horsemanship was even quite fair; but, in this respect, its *matériel* in horses is the ruin of it. Let us not deceive ourselves. Over there they have it, that the Russian cavalry with its system of to-day is giving proper importance to field-exercise and true horsemanship, as contradistinguished from the many years wherein that accorded to school-training, on its part dealing a death-blow to the cavaleristic spirit, had been inordinately exaggerated. As to the latter we might be conservative enough to offer to be convinced; but one goes from one extreme to the other. One forgets, that school-training forms the fundamental basis of field-exercise and that where it is proposed to progress by strides to the latter, without leaving to the former the place due it of right, this can only be at the cost of the horses, but above all of horsemanship. Of what use to the Russian cavalry are the races, for which prizes are offered on behalf of the state; of what use the prolonged rides for the testing of endurance, which latterly have come in vogue also in the garrisons; of what use, above all, to the Cossacks, are the various tricks practised, reminding one of the circus,—when, in spite of all, there is total powerlessness, by proper influence upon the horse, to control him in obedience during the attack? These are all things, which might quite gladly be accepted into the scale, after naught should have been found wanting; but they must never be dignified as of primary importance, or as the chief aim to be attained.

Even the equipment of the Russian cavalry horse cannot be conducive to horsemanship, *i.e.*, the art of riding. The peculiar form of the horse's neck appears to necessitate a rein rather lower than common. On the contrary, however, in consequence of the remarkable manner of saddling and packing, the bridle-hand inevitably assumes an abnormally high position. Upon a felt saddle-blanket surmounted with leather, rests the tree and upon this the quadrupli-folded horse-cover, or the schabraque, as the case may be. To the front of the tree there are arranged, as with us, the pouches; at the rear, an overcoat-sack. But as in the latter, there is, with the other respective articles of equipment, no room for the overcoat itself, it has been contrived to find a place for it at the front fork, where, after the fodder-sack has been wrapped around it, it has been fastened over the pouches. When, therefore, in view of the high seat of the rider on the felt saddle-blanket, tree and horse-cover, or tree and schabraque, a satisfactory seat upon the back and in consequence an easy bringing forward of the off hand is scarcely possible, which in certain respects, for that matter, on account of the soft back, may all be very well; so, on the other hand, through this seat and especially through the position of the overcoat, the bridle-hand is proportionately heightened. The result of this is that, as with such a rein the animal cannot be well held in hand, everything contributes in the more rapid gaits to a disorderly, uncontrollable dashing and tearing, while the unnaturally raised attitude and the inadequacy of the off hand impose the whole burden upon the weak back. A peculiar impression is also given by the further loading down of the horse. In a pocket fastened to the felt saddle-blanket, there are, in a similar position as with us, two horseshoes and sixteen nails; on one side of the overcoat-sack hang the cooking utensils. To the rear of the saddle, where with us lies the fodder-sack, hangs on one side a net with hay for two days and on the other side a sack[7] with two days' provender of oats; so that the whole load, inclusive of forage, weighs over one hundred and fifty pounds and the horse has altogether to carry, if we assume the rider, with arms and equipments, to weigh two hundred and ten pounds,[8] some three hundred and sixty pounds.[9] Now let one fancy the cavalryman in the act of mounting his horse, peradventure pursued by the adversary after an unsuccessful attack on foot. True it is, the animal is not large, but how far must the man lift the right leg out of the ball-and-socket joint, to get over the hay net, the overcoat-sack with the cooking utensils and the two days' provender of oats!—With the Cossack regiments, the method of saddling is the same, with slight differences, which are of no especial interest. That the Cossacks ride upon the snaffle and, instead of spurs, carry a whip, is well known.

The armament, also, since the regiments of hussars and ulans have been transformed into dragoons, is, taken all in all, the same in the entire Russian cavalry. While, formerly, the dragoons and Cossacks exclusively were armed with muskets available for fighting on foot, to-day the whole body of regiments, with insignificant exceptions (the cuirassiers of the guard, etc.) could dismount to the same weapon. Yet this revolution, as has been seen, has been no violent, sudden one. Es-

---

[7] Not to be confounded with the above-named "fodder-sack," the object of which, in addition to this haversack, we further do not quite clearly comprehend.
[8] V. A. v. Drygalski.
[9] About three hundred and seventy-one English pounds.—TRANSLATOR.

pecially with the dragoons had fighting on foot been regarded with peculiar predilection, as will be notably perceived, if we recollect the corps of dragoons of the tsar Nicholas. Indeed from the very beginning has the Russian cavalry had a certain tendency to attach predominant importance to fighting with the fire-arm in hand; and often it has been said that the cavalry of Peter the Great (dragoons) felt far more in its element on foot than on horse-back. The experience derived from the war of 1870-71, which clearly demonstrated the indubitable necessity of the fire-arm for the cavalry, could only give new impetus to this tendency; as a result the carbine was soon placed in the hands of the second rank of the hussars and ulans. But then even this did not seem to satisfy the increased demands of the case; it was believed that a successful contest by cavalry before the front of armies pre-supposed the possibility that in case of need it should individually possess characteristics enabling it to carry on a brisk combat with fire-arms, and then was brought about that transformation of the twenty-eight regiments of ulans and hussars of the army into dragoons, since which time the entire body of Russian cavalry (excepting the guard) virtually consists only of dragoons and Cossacks. In consequence, as a matter of course, the organization and armament are in keeping with this change; or, these latter have, rather, it should be said (in view of the fact that, as known, the Cossacks had already time out of mind carried the fire-arm in addition to the lance), been throughout adapted to an employment of the cavalry on foot.

Of blank hand-arms all the regiments (the regiments of the guard, army, and of Cossacks) carry the sabre;[10] in addition thereto, the Cossacks and the cuirassiers, ulans, and hussars of the guard, carry the lance. Of fire-arms, the cuirassiers of the guard have exclusively revolvers on the Smith and Wesson system; the ulans and hussars of the guard have, for the first rank and for the non-commissioned officers, the revolver; for the second rank, the carbine on the Berdan system (construction similar to the Berdan infantry musket but of lesser length,

---

[10] The sabre, similarly as at one time with us the side-musket of the infantry (e.g., the Prussian palace-guard company), is suspended from a bandolier worn over the breast. It thus acquires a quiescent position, which is recognized as a great advantage, while on the other hand, the bandolier interferes with the breathing of the man. It is peculiar, but in certain respects quite ingenious and useful, that the blade is sheathed in a wooden scabbard. By this arrangement the annoying rattling, through which a cavalry regiment betrays itself from afar, even on the softest soil, is intended to be avoided. Eye-witnesses, who are very enthusiastic over this device, picture to us as highly singular the impression conveyed by the regiments thus moving ahead in phantom silence.

the cartridge being the same as for the dragoon musket); the dragoons have for both ranks the dragoon musket provided with a bayonet (!) (Berdan system, but likewise of lesser length; the cartridge the same as that for the infantry musket, but with a weaker charge); and the Cossacks have the same musket but without a bayonet. Of ammunition pursuant to this armament,—taking no account here of the reserve quantum at hand in the trains, etc.,—there are carried: by the cuirassier of the guard, 20 revolver-cartridges; by the hussar and ulan of the guard, 20 revolver- or 20 carbine-cartridges, according to the rank; by the dragoon and Cossack, 40 dragoon musket-cartridges.

If one has, in Russia, a *penchant* for cavalry of a peculiar species and aims to attain, in so far as may be possible, the extreme theoretical standard, which has been apparently fixed upon, that is an affair with regard to which we would not in so far be lacking in conservatism as to deny that there may be justification, in a degree; though we are by no means enthusiastic for an exaggerated uniformity and are quite clearly of opinion that, without detriment to their appropriate spheres in action, the hussars and ulans may continue to exist along with dragoons, in fact, that the ulans, on account of the lance, *must* continue to exist. If, further, the entire cavalry receive the same firearm, in order that the independence of this arm of service shall not be impaired, that is also a matter, as to which no one can justly find fault. That every troop of cavalry must be in a condition to fight on foot, on occasion, requires no especial demonstration at the present day. But when the dragoons are also to carry a bayonet (!), with the avowed intention of attacking with it on foot, closed in mass, it is not too much to say that an arrangement of this kind must alienate, in no slight measure, even the judgment of the most conciliatory. As a matter of fact, forty-six regiments of horse, the dragoons, are thus armed; with the sabre they are provided with the means for making the bayonet available, and on each and every occasion, when they dismount to fight on foot, they are to fix the latter, to vivify by its moral influence, so we are told to believe, the spirit of the offensive.

That the offensive spirit should not desert the cavalry on foot, is clear, and that the bayonet strengthens the offensive, is also subject to no doubt. But must the dismounted cavalry, in fighting on foot, on the defensive, as also on the offensive, equal, nay even excel, the infantry? Such would certainly seem to be the drift of the reports, which come to us upon the matter, as they dignify such a capacity into especial praiseworthiness. And if, through the employment of the bayonet, such a preponderant value be given to fighting on foot, must not the cavalry necessarily become degraded into a sort of go-between, half cavalry, half infantry, neither one thing nor the other? We have every esteem for the infantry, as the principal arm of all modern bodies of troops, achieving the final decision of battles; but we have no esteem for an infantry, which is at the same time cavalry, or, what is to the same purpose, for a cavalry, which is at the same time infantry, and by which, therefore, it is proposed to represent a composite arm, possessing the peculiar attributes and adaptability of each. To be both with equally preëminent excellence, as much a cavalryman as foot soldier, is simply impossible, even with a vastly lengthier period of service than is everywhere in vogue at the present day in European armies, and though the Russian cavalryman were to remain his full six years with the colors;—the one is inevitably antagonistic to the other. The dismounted cavalryman is only the half of an entirety; what may be required of him on foot, can only be a service incident to occasion, but must not be made the chief end of his being. The future, perhaps, may have in store for us "mounted infantry." But then let it be what it is intended to be, "infantry" which, fully and absolutely organized, instructed, armed, and equipped as such, has learned the further lesson, to make proper use of its horses to the intent of reaching the spot where it shall act as infantry and which shall, at the same time, inspire that respect, which is commensurate with the inherent importance of this arm. To require simultaneously from it the service of cavalry, the closed attack, the making of *reconnaissances*, etc., would be preposterous. For our part, we are scarcely prepared to have much faith, even in such a mounted infantry. Heretofore it has nowhere sufficed for its intended purpose. The few companies of mounted infantry, which the French had created in Southern Algiers (the men rode on mules), were soon done away with; the formations contemplated by the English in the Egyptian expedition of 1882, were abandoned, because, apparently, the requisite *matériel* in horses was not forthcoming. In Southern Africa, where, alone, mounted infantry to an extent achieved results and played a *rôle* of some importance, considerations had weight which have no bearing whatever in the case of our European armies. From childhood, the Boer is as much at home with the rifle, as with the horse. The same remarks have force, to a certain extent, with regard to the cavalry in the American war of secession, especially that of the Southern states, at least with regard to a great portion of its reserves. It was incorrectly denominated as such; the name of "mounted infantry" would have been more appropriate, for of distinctively cavaleristic peculiarities, which would have admitted of its employment in battle, closed in mass, it possessed little. The great raids, which gave it fame, require from the troop itself, as shown by the manner in which these occurred or became developed, nothing more in the way of such cavaleristic peculiarities, than a certain endurance, as well as familiarity with and aptitude for riding, which qualities fall lamentably short of making a cavalryman of the individual in question. If Russia, as it would appear, have taken those swarms for her prototype, she cannot expect in the future other achievements for her bodies of horse than were there attained;[11] nor can there then be question of a stand to be taken by cavalry in dressed files, sabre in hand; and the practicability and utility of successes peculiar to the undertakings of cavalry, properly so called, must be acknowledged by her to be excluded from the limits of the possible.

And,—we report it with reluctance,—it is almost so. True, it is not quite proposed as yet to abandon a contest with cavalry in the open; but an attack upon infantry is regarded as purposeless, for the cavalry would be destroyed, so it is said, ere it could get at the infantry. And for this reason, the bodies of horse are to abandon this thankless field of activity, and are only to devote themselves exclusively to the solution of their other two problems, the strategical service of *reconnaissances* and fighting on foot, in the latter of which, utilizing the rapidity of their horses to approach unobserved, as well as on occasion to disappear with alacrity, they might still have chances. The Russians think of the cuirassiers of Woerth and of Sedan. But bravery alone can certainly not accomplish everything; to success are essential besides courage, prudence; besides gallantry and dash, also reflection and the military eye. In fine, so say the Russians, the few cases in which, in the last wars, cavalry had still found the opportunity to act with energy, had proved beyond the possibility of contradiction that the time of its successful achievements existed no longer. But they lose sight of the fact, so far as 1870 is concerned, that both sides, Germans as well as Frenchmen, only commenced to learn through this war.

Since that time all our efforts have been directed towards the ascertainment of the forms and conditions necessary to be arrived at, under a due appreciation of the altered relations appertaining to the efficiency and tactical requirements of the various arms of service; this one thought is almost exclusively the basis of all our exercises;

---

[11] V. the note to the translation of the "Russian criticism" upon this paper, in the *Army and Navy Quarterly*, October, 1885, page 488.—TRANSLATOR.

the successful availability upon the field of battle is the *conditio sine qua non*, the one consideration, without which the cavalry is not worth the money expended upon it, and without which,—as, certainly, beyond all question, it cannot be relied upon to bring about the achievement of decisive issues on foot,—it must deteriorate to the position of a merely auxiliary arm. And as we, so labor also the others: in France, where even now it is proposed to introduce again the lancers and where the cuirass itself has been again included in the equipment of a portion (six) of the regiments, in which it had been discarded; in Austria, in Italy, everywhere the same principles are being acted upon and a new spirit animates the cavalry; in dispositions and regulations suitable to present demands, it is thought the goal in the fulfilment of the most ardent hopes, is being reached—and this with especial regard to the vastly increased efficiency in results attendant upon the infantry combat of the day; and the opportunity is yearningly looked for, in which it may be vouchsafed to put to the test upon the adversary, whether perfection shall have been attained. And in the mean time the Russian cavalry, which, being the most numerous of all, should be the first to strive to equal these ideals, throws the lance to one side and, taking the point, fixes it in the shape of a bayonet upon the muskets of its troopers, so that they may fight *on foot*, neither cavalrymen, nor foot soldiers, because they no longer have confidence in themselves, to horse. The Cossacks, it is true, are still to be mounted in action, as the lance has been left in their hands; but Cossacks in themselves cannot be imbued with tactically cavaleristic ideas, and time out of mind their employment for the closed attack was not to be thought of. Besides, how long will it be till they also shall have lost their old historical weapon? The idea has already been advanced, to rob them of it, for of course it is useless in fighting on foot.

Fighting on foot is to-day to constitute the most notable method of fighting for the cavalry. What it has lost in utility when mounted, it is to regain through so much the greater achievements with the firearm. On foot, it is to shun no adversary, whether in attack, or defense; it is even to attack positions held by the hostile infantry and to drive out the latter at the point of the bayonet. Now it may be granted that a thoroughly excellent cavalry, upon occasion, *when it is imperative*, must not, as a matter of course, recoil dismayed before the duty of capturing and occupying points and defiles, etc., which are defended by infantry. But can it be thence construed that this is intended to apply to the more important conflicts, with the masses of the inimical infantry ranged in line of battle? Having advanced before the front of armies, shall the cavalry, after it has driven back the enemy's horse and comes upon the latter's infantry, attack this also; or shall they go so far as to dismount in battle and, forming battalions, proceed to advance in steady and continuous *fusillade*, shoulder to shoulder with the infantry, against the enemy's lines? The Russians require this. Dismounted cavalry cannot count upon success against infantry, except through its artillery, or through surprise, or through great numerical superiority, and in those cases only where relatively weak bodies of infantry are concerned. With the instant, where the hostile cavalry has disappeared from the scene and ours has encountered the main forces of the adversary, its duties as an offensive arm cease, and these duties, in order to maintain until the approach of our own main body, that which has been accomplished and won, become distinctively defensive. Of a further pushing forward, there can momentarily be no longer any question; one keeps up with the enemy and touches, and feels, and observes, and reports, but nothing more; with force nothing further is to be done, and least of all on foot. To oppose dismounted masses of cavalry to infantry, is already in itself an error for one reason alone,—quite independently of all considerations having to do with their inferiority in appropriate qualities,—in that the cavalry, in view of its diminished numbers, as well as its peculiar situation, must suffer inordinate loss in face of the tremendous advantage possessed by the infantry. For the losses sustained are aggravated by the enormous number of horses and horse-holders, which must inevitably trammel and impress an unwieldy character upon the squadrons to such a degree that their combatant power may well be reduced to a minimum.

The Russians should certainly know this. Or are they of opinion that their 155,000 men make them independent of considerations of this sort? They will acknowledge the reverse, if their cavalry shall really carry out what is required of it. It does not suffice that it shall not avoid a conflict with the infantry, but it must even court the opportunity to bring one on, by seeking out the flank and rear of the latter, dismounting, and then proceeding to the opening of the attack in inverted front,—an order which can never become ominous or prejudicial to it, on account of its horses! And while it would, to be sure, be possible, on occasion, to ride down an infantry disturbed through the threatening of its line of retreat, the fundamental idea is that the contest with fire-arms and the final attack with the bayonet, if less expeditious, lead more surely and readily to the object to be attained, and that the mounted attack should be the exception, not the rule. That the last will actually be the case, we are quite prepared to believe.

A body of troops educated to fight as infantry, will only brace itself to a mounted charge with reluctance. The fight on foot appears to it the least dangerous. But let us now imagine one, two, or three cavalry divisions advancing against infantry in position. Can they in any case look for success? We are of the opinion, that a body of infantry, which can be brought to yield through the appearance of dismounted cavalry, should be forthwith transformed into garrison troops, and, to speak with Frederick the Great, should be shorn of hat-trimmings in disgrace, unless, indeed, the cavalry be tenfold superior to it in skirmishers. To give way before the cutting and thrusting of the squadrons, which attack it in flank or rear before it has time for reflection or to assume formations requisite for defense, may be honorable for the infantry; but to be vanquished in the fight by these squadrons, *when they dismount is simply disgraceful*. It is one of those great lies which Napoleon I., not only as man and politician, but also occasionally as a soldier, did not hesitate to hurl into the world, that 3000 dragoons on foot, grow into 2000 infantrymen. The 3000 dragoons are *reduced* to 2000, as it is, as a third must act as horse-holders; and then these remaining 2000 are still only dragoons, and in the true signification of the word, *i.e.* cavalrymen,—not infantrymen, by far.

In many ways, the Russian takes after and affects the Frenchman. What is new exercises upon him an irresistible charm; animated because of apparent progress, he does away with and demolishes old time-honored institutions and labors upon the erection of new ones, until the consciousness is brought home to him that he has built upon sand and that his hopes and fantasies have led him astray. So it is with his social and political relations, and so it is in the army. Once already had he wandered into the same crooked by-paths. But the experience which should have been gained with those dragoon corps of Nicholas I., was fruitless. To-day the cavalry divisions are to be a sort of universal arm. Infantry with the musket and bayonet, cavalry with the horse, they are strongly supplied with artillery, that they may be the better adapted, and in heightened degree, to energetic combat, whether in the conflicts aiming at distinctively decisive results, or otherwise. Indeed, latterly it has been thought that they should not even be deprived of the valuable support of pioneers, that eventually they may be enabled to make available the various means of aid of field fortification. To one of the cavalry divisions (the fourth), a squadron of mounted sappers was assigned over a year ago, and it may well be premised that this example will shortly be followed in the case of the others.

The crucial test as to the efficiency of an arm must ever be independence in every respect. But as this is unquestionably correct, it must have its limits, like every other general rule. Mounted sappers, a handful to a division, for peculiarly technical work on railways, telegraphs, bridges, etc., can render excellent service;—in undue proportions, they become a species of ballast and lead to ideas, which should have and can have nothing in common with the efficient activity of the cavalry divisions. Artillery is essential to secure a proper standard for the combatant power of cavalry; without artillery, the latter must fare detrimentally in all those enterprises devolving upon it, which require thoroughness and that independence which may enable it to sustain prolonged contests; two batteries to a division of four regiments are, however, too much of a good thing. That when at hand in such proportions they would in many cases afford the cavalry the opportunity to dismount to fight on foot, would be no misfortune; but they will as frequently operate to embarrass and interfere with distinctively cavaleristic action and bring about a weakening of the offensive power of cavalry, in consequence of the necessity of detaching from the latter, suitable supports:—if we mistake not, the Russian *règlement* designates two squadrons, as the force to be invariably employed for this purpose. Where the artillery is too strong, it inevitably becomes, in the nature of things, the chief arm, and the *rôle* of the others assumes a subordinate character, being confined to rendering support and affording cover. Detachments of one battalion with one battery, where the infantry is charged with the performance of an independent duty peculiar to this arm, are tactically not to be thought of; detachments of four cavalry regiments with two batteries, only where certain conditions are satisfied. But these latter detachments can least of all be of advantage, where it is proposed to fight on foot, for these four regiments have no skirmishers; and this would be true, even though no mounted reserve or especial assignment of a supporting body for the artillery, were necessary. It is true, it appears to be intended to raise the standard of the cavalry regiments of the guard, and army to six squadrons,[12] but until this change shall have been accomplished, we cannot regard the prevailing relation between the two arms as a favorable one.

The reports of General Gurko,[13] upon the latest strategical cavalry manœuvres, speak of the peculiar and, from a cavaleristic stand-point, the deplorable fact, that on the last day of manœuvre both the contend-

---

[12] Most of the regiments of Cossacks now number six sotnias.

[13] V., for example, the before-mentioned paper of A. von Drygalski, as also No. 34 and succeeding numbers of the first year of the German *Heeres Zeitung*.

ing parties, upon encountering one another at Ananjew, dismounted to fight on foot, without apparently having made even the faintest endeavor to attain a decision through a mounted attack. This is one of those sickly misconceptions, of a false system of greater and lesser tactics, consequent upon unsound views, which have often heretofore been brought to the light of day, when, having in mind a perfectly correct idea, one has allowed one's self to be carried away to illogical conclusions, which lie beyond the domain of the possible.

But if, with all their predisposition towards fighting on foot, the Russians shall some day attack us, in obedience to an irresistible impulse, or because they shall be led by officers, who have yet remained cavalrymen;—when their united forces of all arms, reënforced by their second and third categories, shall come surging towards us!? Then there will come to pass cavalry battles, such as the world has not heretofore seen; then it must be demonstrated, that not the masses alone can achieve decisive results, but, on the contrary, the spirit which animates them! Victory is not secured by superiority in numbers, but by horsemanlike thoroughness, by the insight, the keenness, the aptitude, the military eye, of the leader. In Russia, our system of instruction is derided, our riding-school training is declared to be exaggerated, our three-file tactics calculated for the place of exercise alone, and the opinion is seriously entertained that their Cossacks and dragoons would soon settle with men like ourselves, *i.e.* with *manège* riders drilled like machines. For our part we cannot relinquish the belief that with our organization, our *règlement*, our instruction, but, above all, with the inherent spirit of our arm, we have taken better counsel than the Russians.

Herewith we have in contemplation the Russian cavalry as it is at the present day; not as it may become in the future, in the event the crooked road, whereupon it has suffered itself to be betrayed, shall be further followed. It is not enough that the traditions handed down from the time of the greatest fame of the cavalry have been broken with; tendencies are exerting their powerful influence in Russia, that would go far beyond the present aspect as we have depicted it, and which, if they prevail, would impose upon the Russian cavalry an exterior that would vividly call to mind the hordes of a Dshingis Khan.

## A RUSSIAN CRITICISM UPON "THE ACTUAL AND OSTENSIBLE CONDITION OF THE RUSSIAN CAVALRY."

(Translated from the *Jahrbücher für die Deutsche Armee and Marine* by STANISLAUS REMAK, late First Lieutenant Fifth U. S. Artillery.)

THE paper by Rittmeister von Dewall, contained in the "*Jahrbücher*," entitled, "THE ACTUAL AND OSTENSIBLE CONDITION OF THE RUSSIAN CAVALRY," has, as was to have been expected, called forth a number of adverse comments in the Russian military periodicals. Considering the rather unfavorable verdict which Rittmeister von Dewall has rendered upon the Russian cavalry, it is not matter of surprise that over there in the great Eastern empire his critical opinions are not relished, and that at times there can be observed a disposition to deal with them in a spirit of no great leniency. The severity, as we should rather say, which his observations have encountered, is the more noticeable, in view of the fact that simultaneously with and embodied in the criticism of the work of von Dewall, appears also that of a more flattering verdict pronounced by another writer. This is a paper published at about the same time as that of Rittmeister von Dewall, by the Austrian Colonel von Walter-Walthoffen, in the "*Organ der militär-wissenschaftlichen Vereine*," 1884, vol. xxvii., No. 1, entitled "The Russian cavalry in its latest phase of development, compared with the Austrian," in which, basing his views upon personal observation and detailed studies from original sources, the author reaches a conclusion differing materially from the verdict of Rittmeister von Dewall and calculated to place the Russian cavalry in a far better light. To this fact, of the expression at almost one and the same time of two such opposite opinions from the pens of professional men, is no doubt especially to be attributed the determination manifested on the part of the Russians, thoroughly to controvert the views of von Dewall.

In the following pages we give the Russian utterances with the greatest fidelity and correctness, consistent with the occasional incorporation in our text of the views of Colonel von Walter-Walthoffen, refraining at the same time from any expression whatever of our own opinions. With the presentation of the observations made by the one or the other of the contending parties, it is, therefore, under no circumstances to be understood that we share them. We may say, rather, that we are far from coinciding in all particulars either with the views of Rittmeister von Dewall, or with the Russian strictures thereon, but have preferred, without comment, to afford a neutral ground whereon the opposing critical contentions may appear and be heard.

The "*Wajennyi Sbornik*" (May, 1884), introduces its remarks upon the work of Rittmeister von Dewall, with the words: "Mr. von Dewall is not acquainted with the Russian cavalry from personal inspection and judges it upon hearsay and the sources which he may have conveniently found at hand; none the less his criticism is very severe and the conclusions to which he gives expression are not favorable to our mounted troops. Fundamentally cognizant only of its organization and numerical strength, Mr. von Dewall derives from the one circumstance—the transformation of our hussars and ulans into dragoons—an opinion upon our cavalry and compares the type of our cavalryman, thus fashioned in his contemplation, with that of the German, naturally according to the latter all preference." In contradistinction to this course, reference is then made to that of Colonel von Walter-Walthoffen, who had, year in, year out, closely followed the activity of the Russian cavalry, not only from personal observation, but also by a careful study of all the printed comments which had appeared, from which, as a matter of course, it becomes evident "that no absolutely groundless accusations or assertions are to be found in his article. And if, here and there, he be in error, he aims in every instance to be impartial and shows a disposition in many respects, to do us full justice." Thus much we premise as to the manner of characterizing the two authors, of whom the last-named discerns in the Russian cavalry a "dangerous adversary" of the Austrian.

As a starting-point for the supervening observations, the Russian criticism selects the article of Rittmeister von Dewall, adding the views of Colonel von Walter-Walthoffen and those entertained at home, "as in the severe style employed in the former, everything happening with us appears to be subordinated to the desire to dwell with especial prominence upon certain individual characteristics." We cannot here continually repeat the text of Rittmeister von Dewall's article, but must confine ourselves to giving the numbers of the pages in referring to especial portions of it. With regard to the introductory remarks up to page 462,[1] the Russian author says that Colonel von Walter-Walthoffen sees no sign of a decay of the cavaleristic element

---

[1] The pages here cited are those of the translation of the original article, in the *Army and Navy Quarterly*, (October, 1885).—TRANSLATOR.

in the distribution of the Cossacks to the regular cavalry divisions, but that, on the contrary, the Russian cavalry had in consequence become better adapted to field service and that the Cossacks had moreover thereby lost something of their irregular character, whether to their advantage or detriment could only be learned through the experience of war. But the dragoons have,—so says von Walter-Walthoffen as opposed to von Dewall—"always rendered better mounted service than the remaining cavalry, and to this circumstance is also in part to be attributed the remodeling of the entire Russian horse into dragoons." His own opinion is expressed by the Russian, Baron E. RAUSCH VON TRAUBENBERG, in these words: "As a matter of fact, the dragoons have never been surpassed by the hussars and ulans in a cavaleristic sense. But the recently accomplished transformation is to be explained by the duties devolving upon the mounted organizations of the present day; not by the assumption that it is proposed to assail the essential spirit of cavalry or practically to give it up as a distinct arm."

To the polemics of von Dewall, on pages 472–473, with regard to manège and field exercise, as also upon the utility of the Russian cavalry horse of to-day, von Traubenberg prefixes the view of von Walter-Walthoffen upon these points, tending to show that while manège riding had somewhat deteriorated in Russia, in consequence of the diminished term of service, there had undoubtedly been brought about an improvement in field exercise, to which the distribution of the Cossacks to the regular cavalry divisions and the great percentage of horses of the steppes, unsuited to the purposes of manège riding, had notably contributed. The rapidity of the gaits is stated to be not so great in Russia, as in Germany and in Austria; but the method, adopted in Russia, of habituating the horse to labor, had been shown to be fully expedient, practicable and satisfactory in results and in every way worthy of imitation. Von Traubenberg states as his own opinion, that the type of the horse of the steppes, principally available for the mounts of the Russian cavalry, is by no means as von Dewall has fancied it. The race had become conspicuously nobler, the growth of the horse greater, and the whole build had undergone so material a change that an eye not well-practised would experience difficulty in at once detecting the horse of Cossack blood in the remounts; indeed, these horses are not infrequently assigned even to the regiments of cuirassiers, which, for a prototype of this race, would be impossible. The care taken in this matter is evident from the appropriate regulations, in accordance with which "the manège gallop and side-steps are required and also exercised in practice, as proof of which the various provisions as to the instruction of the officers, non-commissioned officers and men, therein contained, may be referred to. Star-gazers and runaways undermine the reputation of a chief of squadron, and every possible effort is made to diminish their number." "The view of von Dewall, that manège riding forms the basis for field exercise, is thoroughly correct, and this fact has by no means been lost sight of by us. The horse is only sent to the front and into the field, when he has gone through a complete course of training on the snaffle and curb. He takes the gallop, makes side-steps,—is therefore under the control of the rider. Beyond doubt this training formerly went much further, but this was only possible, because the cavalryman served longer and because, at the same time, the ideas then entertained as to the service of this arm differed from those which now prevail." The closed attack upon the field of battle is to-day no longer the only duty devolving upon the cavalry, and for that reason "as soon as the horse shall be in the power of his rider, the exercises of the riding-hall must give way to field exercise, for the manège is intended to be one of the means, but not the sole object of instruction." Accordingly these things, in addition to other branches of instruction, are practised during the winter, "with the advent of spring, however, the occupations assume a different character—and *terrain* exercise ensues, whereby we employ the term in its most comprehensive sense." Disposing of the strictures of von Dewall as to the method of saddling with the answer that the imperfections of the present cavalry saddle had also been fully appreciated in Russia, and that a new model is in contemplation, von Traubenberg proceeds to the examination of the remarks of von Dewall on pages 476–480, with regard to "mounted infantry," and the decadence of the cavaleristic spirit in Russia on account of the predilection towards an "infanterization" of their bodies of horse. Although von Traubenberg is of opinion that von Dewall goes too far in his complaints against the Russians, and that these are certainly unfounded if they rest solely upon allegations of the favor in which fighting on foot is held; he yet believes that such complaints must inevitably lead every thinking cavalryman to ask himself the question, whether such a tendency may not actually exist, and further whether an outside observer may not judge more correctly than one who is himself directly on the spot, a necessarily passive participant, powerless to withstand the stress of revolutionizing change, and perhaps by his very surroundings precluded from dispassionate investigation. Von Traubenberg regards this self-testing as the more necessary, inasmuch as von Walter-Walthoffen also advances the views of the Prussian Rittmeister, if in far milder form. The latter is stated to have reached the identical conclusion, that the regulations for the fighting of cavalry on foot go too far and partake too much of the regulations for infantry, and " in consequence a tendency to the too general development of fighting on foot is brought about to the prejudice of distinctively cavaleristic instruction. In many cases (as also in the last Turkish war), fighting on foot is resorted to, where this is not imperatively necessary. By a comparison of the Austrian regulations with the Russian, it will be perceived that the Austrians have fallen into the opposite error, while the Prussians hold the golden mean." Further elucidating his thought, von Walter-Walthoffen says : " Thus the Austrian cavalry has remained far behind the Russian in the matter of fighting on foot, while the German may readily enter upon such a contest with the latter ; the Austrians should here tread in the footsteps of the Germans." The question as to whether Russia is moving within appropriate bounds in this respect, or not, von Traubenberg refrains from deciding; but he strenuously combats the view that the Russian cavalry can be regarded as " mounted infantry," and for himself individually denies both the applicability of the parallel, by which it is likened unto the " American cavalry," as well as the intimation that the latter is held forth as a pattern, the more as in Europe one has to do with regular cavalry.[2]

---

[2] In contradistinction to the rather severe judgment of Rittmeister von Dewall upon the activity of the American cavalry, it may interest the American professional reader to learn that in a recent paper in the " *Jahrbücher für die deutsche Armee und Marine,*" (July, 1885), entitled " Recent developments in the Russian cavalry," by A. VON DRYGALSKI, (an acknowledged authority upon the subject, with regard to which he has published a number of communications), reference is made to a scientific gathering of Russian military men, at one of whose meetings the importance of greater enterprise in partisan warfare, as carried out in the American war, was urged and at which the fact, then alleged, that the Americans had copied their raids from the Russians, was apparently dwelt upon with especial satisfaction. These scientific military gatherings have been instituted at St. Petersburg by the officers of the general staff, there stationed, and are participated in by the Grand Dukes. On the evening in question, after a discourse by Lieutenant Colonel Baron " R. v. T." (RAUSCH VON TRAUBENBERG) upon " The views of recent German military writers upon the *rôle* and activity of modern cavalry," Colonel SSUCHOTIN, Professor in the Academy of the general staff, a recognized authority on cavalry, at the solicitation of the Grand Duke Nicholas (the senior), made some remarks, in which occurred the reference above mentioned and in which he " emphatically declared his opinion, that the Russian cavalry, as regarded the peculiarity of its organization, education, instruction, armament, equipment and readiness to fight, mounted as well as on foot, had vastly outstripped the other European armies ; and though, at first, the Russian reforms in this respect had engendered doubt, they had now called forth the desire to imitate them." After referring to the especial availability of partisan enterprises and raids in hindering the mobilization and concen-

The opinion intimated by von Dewall, that the Russians in depriving the Cossacks of their lances, had robbed themselves of the last remains of their cavalry, von Traubenberg is not disposed to share. "The lance is emphatically not an absolute condition demanding to be satisfied, in the armament and equipment of the cavalryman; in the fatherland of Seydlitz it is carried only by the ulans, but does that signify that the remaining bodies of horse are contaminated by a spirit tending to give them the predominant attributes of infantry? In any case, the use of the lance is confined within narrow limits. Its defenders principally advance in their favor, always the one argument only: the moral effect upon the infantry. And while this undoubtedly becomes desirable in the closed attack, it must be remembered that the Cossacks would be employed for such duty on comparatively rare occasions, so that the lance is not really necessary to them; on the contrary, it is frequently quite detrimental in this method of fighting; and, finally, it should be remarked that many of the Cossack Woiskos, as those of the Terek, the Kuban and others, never have had the lance, nor have it now."

With regard to the second part of the work of von Dewall,—as to the conjectures upon the manner in which the Russian cavalry may propose to carry out its strategical activity,—the Russian author complains that here von Dewall again starts with the erroneous assumption that instruction with a view to fighting on foot is dignified as of primary importance and that for this reason the cavalry divisions had been so plentifully supplied with artillery. The concluding paragraph on page 483 of the work of Dewall containing the reference to the hordes of Dshingis Khan, draws forth the remark: "this severe tirade shows on the one hand little knowledge as to the Russian arrangements; then, on the other, it sounds unduly inspirited by a patriotic sentiment, which is little calculated to further the behests of a calm weighing and inquiry as to the subject-matter; the views expressed, demand, moreover, logical demonstration." Premising that the cavalry of to-day has a double duty to fulfil, namely a strategical and a tactical one, von Traubenberg says as to the first of these services devolving upon it, that this necessitates a lengthy separation of the cavalry, dispatched

---

tration of the enemy, latterly so notably accelerated, Colonel SSUCHOTIN insists that "the cavalry must, however, be able to fight equally well, whether mounted or on foot, nor regard a ride of 400 versts as anything extraordinary." The comprehensive discussion of the subject of partisan warfare, as treated, among other writers, by F. GERSCHELMANN, in the "*Wajennyi Sbornik,*" 1884 and 1885, is stated to be in the same vein.—TRANSLATOR.

to great distances, from the other troops, and makes it dependent upon itself and its own resources. To be enabled to carry out this *rôle*, the cavalry must possess a relative degree of independence and, for this reason, instructed by the experiences of the later wars, all the great European powers had armed their bodies of horsemen either with carbines or with muskets, to enable them in individual cases to act without the support of infantry and, here and there, even to take the place of the latter. The assignment of horse artillery to the Russian cavalry divisions is based upon the presumption as to the requirements of the latter in mounted conflicts and is perfectly consistent with the organization of the regiments into four squadrons and still more so in the case of those having six; to base the strength of the artillery upon the number of men dismounted to fight on foot, had least of all been sought after. It must also be superadded that the Russian horse artillery is preëminent for remarkable mobility, decision, and intrepidity and can, therefore, never become a burden to the cavalry.

Remonstrating against the disposition of von Dewall, to allow neither traditions nor the true spirit of the arm to the Russian cavalry, von Traubenberg—remarking that its past achievements had probably not been less glorious than those of the cavalry of the descendants of Seydlitz and of Zieten—states that "the rare instances advanced by the author in support of his adverse comments upon the arrangements for dismounting, have reference to manœuvres, and do not, therefore, really require serious contradiction at the present time. The sabre has not been consigned to oblivion by the dragoons; they are ever prepared for attack with this weapon."

Colonel von Walter-Walthoffen diverges in his views from those of Rittmeister von Dewall. The cavalry divisions have, as stated, the same duties assigned to them in Austria as in Russia. Yet there, there is no fixed distribution of cavalry to the infantry division, which rather has cavalry assigned to it as necessity may arise, and thus it happens, according to the opinion of von Walter-Walthoffen, that the employment of the cavalry in Russia is not always a correct one. The reserve cavalry (the stronger masses of troops), which comprehends all the available cavalry divisions with their artillery, has the definitive problem before it, to hinder the breaking through the line of battle by the enemy, as also to afford time to the troops to occupy new positions; but, besides, it is to execute the last decisive stroke against the unsuccessful antagonist, or, in the event of disorder among the home troops, to rescue and hew them out of such ominous predicament. Here and there the reserve cavalry can also be employed in operations against the flank and rear of the adversary, even on foot ; and it indeed seems as if great weight were accorded to active enterprises of this sort, and as if it were contemplated frequently to resort to them. As to the above expression of von Walter-Walthoffen's views with regard to the duties devolving upon the various Russian bodies of cavalry, von Traubenberg remarks : " Although Mr. von Walter-Walthoffen has studied the official instructions, relating to the active employment of our horsemen, he falls into the same error as Mr. von Dewall in reference to the operations of great masses of cavalry against the flank and rear of the enemy. Without investigating the sources in which the two German writers have searched, we merely observe that such a proceeding is nowhere officially recommended with us, and that therefore, where it may be resorted to, the reason must be sought for in the individual judgment of the commander as to the necessities of the situation." Theoretically developing this question, von Traubenberg reaches the conclusion that " the valuable peculiarity of cavalry—its rapidity—must be taken advantage of, but nevertheless, a methodical attack on foot must not be thought of where the division has shrunken to dimensions approximating two battalions, for then, as a matter of course, even relatively equal excellence being pre-supposed, it can prove no match for the infantry, and we also act accordingly."

In so far as the Russian article has reference to that of Rittmeister von Dewall, we should here have come to an end. But owing to the fact (because, as we believe, our communication thus gains in interest) that we have also drawn the views of Colonel von Walter-Walthoffen within the sphere of our observation, let it be permitted to repeat here the concluding verdict which the latter renders upon the Russian cavalry. He says : " In general we find in the Russian cavalry and especially in the Cossacks, a very earnest, enduring, mobile, untiring, and shrewd adversary. The standard of the mental training and culture of the officers becomes heightened with each year, and the number of those officers who have enjoyed the opportunities for suitable preparation and study grows apace." " Thanks to the recent transformations," we read further, " the Russian cavalry has become peculiar to itself and there is shown in it a greater tendency towards activity on foot than in the cavalry of the other great powers. It cannot be denied that the distribution of Cossacks to the regular cavalry has called forth, or at least developed, a greater mobility and greater aptitude for outpost service and the service of *reconnaissance*, while, in consequence, on the other hand, an exceedingly favorable influence is also exercised upon the Cossacks.

"In the changes introduced into the regulations, the idea of a greater capacity for manœuvre of the cavalry, adapted to recent demands as to its tactical employment, has been carried out. The organization of the Cossacks after the manner of the dragoons and their incorporation into the regular cavalry divisions, materially increase the strength of the cavalry.

"With regard to the theoretical and practical occupations of the officers, the strenuous efforts made to prepare them thoroughly for the severe duties of service before them, are noteworthy. The view entertained by many that the re-organization of the Russian cavalry has transformed it into 'mounted infantry,' is absolutely groundless. The cavaleristic element has emphatically not been lost there. On the contrary the last campaign has shown, that not only in the regular, but also in the irregular, Russian horse, there existed a spirit of enterprise, which became manifest and led to the best results, whenever the leaders understood how to awaken it and make it available.

"Though it be true that the Russian cavalry had then to do only with an inimical cavalry of no great excellence; yet if in the future, it shall be called upon to take the field against active and enduring bodies of horse, well organized, armed, equipped and instructed, it will be demonstrated whether the practical application of the tendency to assign greater importance to fighting on foot than heretofore, has been prejudicial to cavaleristic peculiarities, or not."

Connecting the close of our communications with the beginning, *i.e.*, with the Russian criticism upon the work of Rittmeister von Dewall, it should be added that von Traubenberg designates the author as an officer of esteem in his domain, who has a right to speak with authority, and who, though not free from prejudice against the Russian cavalry, has yet developed such an abundance of interesting observations upon the importance and activity of the cavalry, as to entitle him to recognition as conspicuously conversant with and a lover of his arm.

# THE MORAL ELEMENT IN MILITARY DISCIPLINE.

[We make the following extract from a lecture entitled "Drill or Education?" delivered before the Military Science Society of Vienna by Lieutenant Field-Marshal the Archduke John. It was translated from the German for the Journal of the Royal United Service Institution by Captain W. A. H. Hare, R.E., D.A.Q.M.G.]

A DISTINGUISHED general once said to me that when he was commanding a Hungarian regiment in the Italian campaign he was asked whether he could rely on his men, and he felt he could answer that they would certainly do their duty for the sake of their colonel. And this proved to be true. The affection of men for their commanding officer can do great things, but it must be more than mere sympathy, it must be an affection amounting to a devotion of the most completely confiding and self-sacrificing nature. To be able to gain an affection *of this kind*, however, is not the gift of all, for a good disposition and study are not sufficient; popularity-hunting will never do it. We must have a fellow-feeling for our subordinates, and then only can we gain their hearts. But to display this fellow-feeling only will do no good. You will never win the hearts of men unless your heart is really with them. Unfeeling men are to be avoided just as those hypocrites who are cunning enough to feign a fellow-feeling. They are left in the lurch the moment the game they are playing is laid bare, and they are then the more hateful as we feel they have deceived us. Ordinary individuals have far greater instinctive powers of discernment in these matters than most people give them credit for.

It might be urged by those who object to these principles that it would never do if a regiment would only follow Colonel A and not Colonel B. And it would certainly never do ; but the other kinds of moral motive-power which I have alluded to, insure troops doing their duty under any leader. If, however, our aims are higher than this, nothing but personal influence can attain them. Rustow is perfectly right in saying "the influence of a commanding officer does not arise from chance or accident. He who can get more from his men than can his opponent from his, is always at an advantage."

An Austrian author, describing the habit of discipline in the observation of certain forms as the only means at our disposal, says literally, " It is a myth that in the rapid conversion of our human material so-called beloved leaders arise, round whom men rally with devotion in the hour of battle." Now, to those who know troops by personal contact, and have a fellow-feeling for them, there is, thank goodness, no myth about it whatever. Affection is a thing quickly acquired, but habit is a matter of time. If the rapid conversion of our human material is dangerous to one of these, then I should say that habit is most likely to suffer in this respect. The filling up of the ranks with the reserves, the marches for concentration, and the first, though perhaps ever so small, engagement, are enough to make a commander liked or disliked by his men. Ay, it only requires a moment or so in the hour of danger for a really first-rate man to gain the affection of his inferiors.

One of the most important conditions, and at the same time a useful lever for morally improving the soldier, is *the relation that exists between officer and man.*

This relation is in certain armies based on tradition. Based on conditions that have still something patriarchal about them, and the social standing of the subaltern officers, it is in Russia far more direct and intimate than in other countries, and is, perhaps, too familiar. The Prussian officer, as we all know, having a social standing of the first rank in the country, moves in the best society in consequence, and being represented with his men by excellent non-commissioned officers, is brought far less in contact with them, in fact, his relations with them are almost of a purely duty nature. With us the relation varies very much in the different branches of the service according as the officer lives more or less in close contact with the men.

But on the whole we might observe that, having due regard to the peculiarities of the majority of nationalities in our army, the relation might with advantage be a closer one in the infantry.

The soldier should, in fact, be looked on as a man, and what is more, be made to feel as a man. The officer need not be always on duty from his point of view. Without causing any undue familiarity he can, by daily intercourse with his men, get opportunities, while fully maintaining his position, of showing himself in the light of a sympathizing fellow-creature instead of the mere superior, in caring for their interests and doing all in his power for their material welfare.

If the bonds between officer and man be closely drawn, the former ought never to find it difficult to arouse, without the use of empty phrases, in a way that suits the individual character of the man, such qualities as love for king and country, pride in himself as a soldier, ambition, *amour propre*, a soldier-like feeling of obedience from self-conviction, and a feeling of *camaraderie* and attachment to his regiment. No stone should be left unturned to raise the tone and feeling of the soldier. We can well afford in this to be a little indulgent in insignificant matters; we must not think it serious if regimental feeling goes so far as to make the soldier look down upon other regiments; give the soldier if possible recreation at the right time; put up with his light-heartedness, and even turn it to account,— *and above all things take care not to get into the habit of continually finding fault*, rather bestow praise, even if it is only half due. Approbation is better than blame; it is the indispensable forerunner of *amour propre*, attachment, and cheerful labor. Constant finding fault produces, by the blunting effect it has on the feeling, the most difficult evil to get rid of—apathy.

The officer should have all those moral qualities we look for in the soldier in a higher degree. We have to produce military characters, independent, cheerfully energetic, and thoroughly conscientious men. Though many may look on converting soldiers into machines as a preparation for our next war, the intelligent man will look for it more by fostering their *individuality* and *initiative*. For the shorter the time the fight lasts, the greater is the necessity for seizing opportunities without waiting for orders. The more murderous the fire, the more questionable is the possibility of giving orders, and the more frequent the loss in commanding officers, whose regiments, however, cannot stop in critical moments to have the command taken over. The greater the friction, the more is it desirable to have, instead of a machine-like army, a living organism, the parts of which can act independently in the spirit of the general desire.

It would appear, therefore, all the more desirable that the higher leader should, instead of making his subordinate officers go in leading-strings, direct them intellectually, and so fashion their ideas that he may confine himself to ordering what is only absolutely necessary, and leave the remainder to the initiative of his subordinates, feeling sure that though they may not act strictly in accordance with his orders, they are certain to act in accordance with his intentions. This, again, requires the relations between senior and junior officers to be of the closest kind; to communicate our own ideas and convey our own ways of thinking to others is only possible with close personal contact. There are some colonels and generals who keep almost quite aloof from their officers; very often this arises from an unfounded fear on their part that close contact with juniors is likely to affect their dignity. But the man who is firm in the saddle as a member of the military hierachy feels no necessity for surrounding his person with obstacles to approach, which after all afford a very poor protection to the authority belonging to the *rank* only and not to the *person*, against the skepticism of juniors. A colonel or a general should have the courage to be a friend and comrade off duty.

But when the increased demand for independent and self-relying officers has been alluded to, it has been sometimes met with the question whether independence did not already exist, and only required to be tolerated? No! unfortunately it must be cultivated, for there are too many of our juniors whose minds are dull and without desire, who are only too glad to be relieved of all responsibility by the guardian of inactivity; and the lethargy which is the consequence lasts long after the original cause has been removed. Let every one be given the full free scope allowed by the spirit of the regulations, and let us trust to the responsible spontaneous action of our juniors. We must satisfy ourselves beforehand, however, by the strictest tests, that what is required is likely to be forthcoming, and distinguish between the criminal presumption of the impostor and the proved and consequently esteemed conscientiousness of the reliable man.

Everything that the junior does *cannot always be improved on*. Many an error in execution or even in resolution may be overlooked in order that power of resolve and self-reliance may not be interfered with. We should never let ourselves be influenced by temper or passion, and never color the meaning of others. The eye-servant who tries to curry favor should never be encouraged, nor should the honest man, who, rather than try to ingratiate himself, makes himself perhaps disagreeable, be snubbed. This is the way to produce military characters, otherwise we shall only produce slaves, who in the choice of "to be" or "not to be" purchase the "to be" with the surrender of their individuality, at first, perhaps, against the grain, but gradually with their moral emasculation appeased.

The officer must be naturally inspired by an ideal conception of his profession. He will thus be proof against the attacks of materialism, and encouraged to face the trying duties of his calling.

Let the officer remember that if he can oppose a living dam to the flood of the

---

## CROSBY'S VITALIZED PHOSPHITES,
Composed of the Nerve-giving Principles of the Ox-Brain and the Embryo of the Wheat and Oat,

For fifteen years has been a standard preparation with all physicians who treat nervous or mental disorders. Physicians alone have used more than a million packages, curing nervous disorders, loss of mental or bodily power, restoring lost functions, refreshing the memory, renewing vitality.

It aids wonderfully in the mental and bodily development of children.

In nervous debility it gives sweet sleep and invigorates and recruits the exhausted mental and bodily powers.

It is used by Bismark, Gladstone, and other brain workers.

For Sale by Druggists, or mail, $1.00.

F. CROSBY CO., 56 West 25th St., New York.

disorganizing tendencies of our days, these will break helplessly on the soundness of his strength of character. Let him acquire a pride in himself from the thought of the meritorious work he has done in yearly instilling into the minds of the one hundred thousand men or so that annually join in the colors, a higher moral tone, a love of justice and order, and feeling and character,—in fact, the blessings of civilization which they take with them to their distant homes, to there produce further benefits. The officer thus fulfills in peace a mission just as noble in itself as is his bloody work in war. Let our officers be firmly convinced that in days when opposite disuniting efforts are tending to undermine the monarchy, it is the officers' duty to strengthen to their utmost the bonds that unite it, by instilling into the minds of the thousands that come from all parts of our wide empire a feeling of unity in the whole Fatherland, and the desire to raise the national colors high above the petty strife of faction and party, remembering the noble words of the poet, "Austria is in the camp."

Let the officer fully understand his position; let him raise himself above the ordinary level of moral courage, so as to be, in the closest sense of the term, the *soul* of his men, and lead them to victory. But the soldier, if the call or even the example of the officer is to have any effect, must be susceptible and attached to him.

"Rubbish," I hear again the opponents of these ideas exclaim with a cold scornful sneer. Well, may they never be taught by disaster that troops that are drilled only and not educated will fail them in the hour of trial; may they never have to feel in the bitter hour of defeat what a difference there is between possessing and not possessing the affection—this supposed myth—of their men.

And now enough!

In view of the possibility of the monarchy having, at some not very distant date, to engage in a serious conflict, the traditional patriotism of the Austrian army must and can imperatively call upon every man belonging to it, no matter what his station be, to take the most complete *loyal faith* as his sole guide, and follow the line which most surely leads to success.

There can be only *one right* way, for there is only one kind of truth. But it is difficult sometimes to find and recognize it; hence different views, different faiths.

Supported as I am in my belief when I think of the many high-minded and great men whose wise and reforming doctrines have led me to my present conviction, and when I call to mind how often many excellent troops of our army, though undrilled, have shown the highest discipline in the dark days of misfortune, and by their spirit and moral strength have given the most unmistakable proofs of the greatest devotion, I will preserve unimpaired *a belief in men, a belief in my ideal, and a belief in the way in which it is attained.*

The meaning of this belief is contained in the—

ANSWER TO THE TITLE OF THIS LECTURE.

*Let us not merely drill, let us educate.*

# INDEX.

|  | PAGE |
|---|---|
| ACTUAL AND OSTENSIBLE CONDITION OF THE RUSSIAN CAVALRY (THE). By H. von Dewall. Translated from the *Jahrbücher für die Deutsche Armee und Marine* by Stanislaus Remak, late First Lieutenant Fifth U. S. Artillery | 460 |
| AMERICAN HUMORIST (A FORGOTTEN). By Mrs. Launt Thompson | 36 |
| BALLOONS. By M. J. Jamin, of the Academy of Sciences. Translated from the *Revue des Deux Mondes* by Jas. Duval Rodney | 168 |
| BOOKS RECEIVED | 128 |
| BRITISH NAVY (THE). By Sir E. J. Reed, M.P. | 17 |
| DOES GERMANY NEED A NAVY? By Karl Jacob | 381 |
| ELECTRIC LIGHT ON BOARD THE FRENCH ARMORED SHIP "RICHELIEU" (THE). From *Mittheilungen aus dem Gebiete des Seewesens*, by Lieutenant W. H. Bechler, U.S.N. | 316 |
| ELECTRICITY AS APPLIED TO NAVAL PURPOSES. By Lieutenant W. A. Chisholm-Batten, R.N. | 385 |
| END OF A GREAT NAVY (THE). By Vice-Admiral Jurien de la Gravière. Translated from the *Revue des Deux Mondes* by Jas. Duval Rodney | 74 |
| EUROPEAN CAVALRY. By Colonel Keith Fraser | 1 |
| FRANCE AND CHINA | 222 |
| FRENCH RAILWAY CORPS (THE). Translated from the *Avenir Militaire* and *Journal Officiel* for the *Journal of the Royal United Service Institution* by Captain W. A. H. Hare, R.E., D.A.Q.M.G. | 373 |
| FUNCTIONS OF CAVALRY IN MODERN WAR (THE). By Major Graves, Twentieth Hussars | 328, 405 |
| GENERAL GORDON'S LIFE AND LETTERS | 345 |
| GENERAL LEBRUN AND THE TWELFTH FRENCH CORPS AT SEDAN. Translated from the *Jahrbücher für die Deutsche Armee und Marine* by Stanislaus Remak, late First Lieutenant Fifth U. S. Artillery | 301 |
| GERMAN MILITARY PUNISHMENT. By C. J. L'Estrange | 193, 274 |
| HUMANITY AND WAR. Translated from the *Jahrbücher für die Deutsche Armee und Marine* by Stanislaus Remak, late First Lieutenant Fifth U. S. Artillery | 129 |
| LITERATURE (THE) OF THE THIRTY YEARS' WAR. By J. Watts de Peyster, Brevet Major-General S.N.Y. | 422 |
| LONDON LETTER (OUR). By C. Sleeman | 118 |
| MACHINE GUNS IN THE FIELD. By Captain the Right Hon. Lord Charles W. Beresford, R.N. | 257 |

# INDEX.

|  | PAGE |
|---|---|
| MODERN CRUISERS. By Naval Constructor Theodore Albrecht, Austrian Imperial Navy. Translated from the German by Lieutenant W. H. Beehler, U.S.N. | 209 |
| MORAL ELEMENT (THE) IN MILITARY DISCIPLINE. Translated from the German by Captain W. A. H. Hare, R.E., D.A.Q.M.G. | 493 |
| PRESENT POSITION OF TACTICS IN ENGLAND (THE). By Colonel W. W. Knollys | 55 |
| RUSSIAN CRITICISM (A) UPON "THE ACTUAL AND OSTENSIBLE CONDITION OF THE RUSSIAN CAVALRY." Translated from the *Jahrbücher für die Deutsche Armee und Marine* by Stanislaus Remak, late First Lieutenant Fifth U. S. Artillery | 484 |
| SHAM SIEGES. Translated from the *Jahrbücher für die Deutsche Armee und Marine* by Professor A. A. Benton, M.A. | 202 |
| SOME CHANGES IN TACTICS CAUSED BY THE INCREASING POWER OF MODERN FIRE (ON). By Captain W. H. James, P.S.C., late R.E. | 155 |
| TORPEDO-BOAT WARFARE. By O. Sleeman | 237, 284 |
| TORPEDOES ON SHIPBOARD AND IN BOATS. By C. Chabaud-Arnault, Capitaine de Frègate, M.F. Translated from the *Revue Maritime et Coloniale* by Wm. Bainbridge-Hoff, Commander U.S.N. | 91 |
| WOLSELEY'S (LORD) PLAN OF OPERATIONS | 253 |

## FROM FOUR TO SIXTY-FOUR.

A visitor to a school examination in Athens or Rome on a day in the year A. D. 1 might have heard the question asked by the teacher, "How many elements are there in nature?" and the scholar's answer, as found in the books, would have been, "Four —earth, air, fire, and water." That answer was as far as science had reached at that time, but diligent research, prosecuted in the intervening ages, has given to the scholar of to-day a different answer. A visitor to a school in London or Paris or Philadelphia would hear the same question replied to by a modern scholar with "Sixty-four!" Though there are no more elements to-day than ever, we are getting acquainted with them. One of the most interesting discoveries made in modern times by delvers into the mysteries of nature is that of "Compound Oxygen." Drs. Starkey & Palen, of Philadelphia, the physicians who have been for years treating their patients with this remedy, are in constant receipt of letters full of grateful acknowledgment of benefits received from its use. A few recent testimonies are the following:

"MOUNT PLEASANT, PA., August 4, 1885.
"DRS. STARKEY & PALEN: *Dear Sirs,*—I take great pleasure in stating that my wife derived great benefit from the use of your 'Compound Oxygen.' She had not known a well moment for several years until my attention was called to your Treatment through your advertisement in *The Scottsdale Tribune* about two months ago. In that time it has brought new life to her system.
"Very truly yours, REV. L. R. BEACOM,
"*Pastor Mt Pleasant M. E. Church, Pittsburgh Conference.*"

The following is an extract from an English patient's letter in answer to an inquiry from a lady:

"MADAM,—Instead of being a trouble, it would at any time give me pleasure could I in any way assist a fellow-sufferer from asthma in getting the least relief, as I well know what the feelings are.
"On the 16th of January, 1883, about three o'clock in the morning, I was first attacked with the disease. Next morning, at the same hour, I had a second attack, and I thought I was going to die. On the third morning I learned from my physician the name of my ailment. In spite of all the attention and care of which he and his assistants were capable, I continued to get worse until I was not able to lie down or have one minute's sleep for four days or nights. I then tried patent medicines, various kinds, too numerous to mention; in fact, I tried everything that I thought would benefit me, but the benefit was only of short duration. What I suffered I cannot describe, neither do I want to think about it. In July last I heard of the Compound Oxygen. I wrote to Mr. Garner for a supply. I began inhaling at once, and continued according to directions. *In a fortnight I was able to lie down in bed and sleep well—what I had not been able to do since my first attack—and I am still getting stronger now.* I cannot say I am free from asthma, for I find a little of it at times. But it does not prevent my sleeping well, and I am able to eat without feeling the least pain from indigestion; I am still continuing the use of the Oxygen, but not so often; and intend continuing for some time, as I cannot expect after so much suffering to be well all at once, but am better now than I ever expected to be again in this life, and am thankful beyond measure.
"JAMES MOORE, *Superintendent of Police,*
"*Blandford, Dorsetshire, England.*"

For more than half a century the author of the following letter has been a minister in the Methodist Episcopal Church, and, though eighty-four years old, his face and voice are known to more people than any other man living in Philadelphia, for he maintains the vigor and energy of those younger by a score of years, constantly using his preserved strength in going about doing good:

"TO DRS. STARKEY & PALEN: *Dear Sirs,*—I had thought of publishing something in relation to your life-giving remedies. Compound Oxygen stops my cough instantly. A swallow of my Oxygenupia will stop the irritation (if the water has been more than a month in my house). So much it has done for an old man in his eighty-fourth year A young man might be cured permanently of all such irritation. I recommend Compound Oxygen to all who suffer from throat diseases. Yours truly,
"A ATWOOD, 809 North Seventeenth Street,
"PHILADELPHIA, June 2, 1885."

A patient at Olmsted, Ill., writes:
"I find that the inhaling of the Oxygen is a great remedy for catarrh. It has cured my little boy and helped me.
"Last summer I sent to you for your Home Treatment. I suffered with catarrhal sore throat After using the Oxygen for three months I entirely recovered."

The following is from an editor in Iowa:
"OFFICE OF THE 'STAR-CLIPPER,'
"THAER, IOWA, May 1, 1885.
"MESSRS. STARKEY & PALEN: *Dear Sirs,*—It affords me pleasure to freely offer testimony as to the merits of your Compound Oxygen Treatment. My mother, a lady over sixty years old, was induced by a friend to try it, and a marked improvement is noticed in her health. *The Treatment seems to build up the system, which helps a patient afflicted with almost any disease.* My mother had had head-ache for many years; this has been almost cured. *She has had a cough for twenty years; this has been greatly helped.* And in other ways the Treatment has been a benefit to her. *The principle of the Compound Oxygen is sensible; it is natural, and I believe the Treatment is something that would renew the health of thousands of the suffering and debilitated overworked people of America.*
"ELMER E. TAYLOR, Editor *Star-Clipper.*"

Dadabhoy Byranjee is a gentleman of Bombay, India, who has for some years been living in London. For several months he was on a visit to America, and one of the principal objects of the visit was a search for health. Learning of Compound Oxygen, he used, in New York, the Home Treatment with good effect, and then in Philadelphia took the Office Treatment. Before leaving for London he did us the kindness of the following letter:

"CONTINENTAL HOTEL,
"NEW YORK, May 11, 1885.
"DRS. STARKEY & PALEN: *Dear Sirs,*—Before leaving New York for London, I desire to express my sense of gratitude to you for the benefit I have derived from the use of your Compound Oxygen Gas. I have been suffering for the last five years from chronic bronchitis, contracted in Bombay. During this long space of time I tried a great number of remedies, but failed to get rid of it altogether. In September last I came to New York, when my attention was drawn to your Compound Oxygen Gas. I forthwith commenced the Treatment under the guidance of Dr. Turner, in charge of your depot here, and, I am glad to say, with very gratifying results. I feel I am fully fifty per cent. better now than I was before I began the Treatment Considering the obstinate character of the complaint and the long number of years it has had its hold upon me, I have every reason to be satisfied with the progress I have made toward recovery through the beneficent action of your gas, and am fully persuaded that by persevering with the use of this valuable remedy I shall be able to shake it off before long.
"I remain, dear sirs, faithfully yours,
"D. BYRANJEE."

"However difficult it may be to declare just what this new 'Compound Oxygen' is, it is not difficult to be convinced that the good it is doing mankind can scarcely be estimated. We do not propose here to go into a detailed account of individual cases, but the fact remains undisputed that it has cured thousands of cases of many of the ills that flesh is heir to when all other remedies have failed. Any one who wishes to look into this matter further can do so by simply addressing a postal to Starkey & Palen, 1529 Arch Street, Philadelphia, Pa., asking for *The Compound Oxygen Treatment,* and a book of about two hundred pages will be mailed free of expense. In addition to this the book also gives many hygienic hints worth the time and trouble of reading."—*Christian at Work, New York.*

### NOW READY.
# THE HAZEN COURT-MARTIAL.

The Responsibility for the Disaster to the Franklin Bay Polar Expedition Definitely Established, With Proposed Reforms in the Law and Practice of Courts-Martial.

By T. J. MACKEY, Counsel for Brig.-Gen. W. B. Hazen, Chief Signal Officer, Washington.

Octavo. Cloth Extra. 364 pages. Price, $2.50.

### RECENTLY PUBLISHED.

#### OPERATIONS OF THE ARMY UNDER BUELL.

From June 10 to October 30, 1862, and the Buell Commission. By JAMES B. FRY (retired), Brevet Major-General, U.S.A.; Chief of Staff to General Buell from November 15, 1861, to October 30, 1862. With Portrait of General Buell, and Map of the Campaign. 12mo. Cloth. $1.25.

**ALSO, BY THE SAME AUTHOR.**

#### McDOWELL AND TYLER IN THE CAMPAIGN OF BULL RUN, 1861.

Illustrated with Maps. 12mo. Cloth. 75 cents.

#### THE ATTACK AND DEFENCE OF COAST FORTIFICATIONS.

By Captain EDWARD MAGUIRE, Corps of Engineers, U.S.A. With Map and numerous Illustrations. 8vo. Red cloth. $2.50.

#### THE THEORY OF DEFLECTIONS,

And of Latitudes and Departures, with Special Application to Curvilinear Surveys for Alignments of Railway Tracks. By ISAAC W. SMITH, C.E., Member of American Society of Civil Engineers. Illustrated. 16mo. Morocco tucks. $3.00.

#### A TREATISE ON THE ADJUSTMENT OF OBSERVATIONS.

With Applications to Geodetic Work, and other Measures of Precision. By T. W. WRIGHT, B.A., late Assistant Engineer U. S. Lake Survey. Illustrated. 8vo. $4.00.

#### MAGNETO-ELECTRIC AND DYNAMO-ELECTRIC MACHINES.

Their Construction and Practical Application to Electric Lighting, and the Transmission of Power. By Dr. H. SCHELLEN. Translated by N. S. KEITH and PERCY NEYMANN. With large Additions and Notes Relating to American Machines by N. S. KEITH. Vol. I. With 353 Illustrations. 8vo. $5.00. Volume II. *in preparation*.

#### TEXT-BOOK OF SEAMANSHIP.

The Equipping and Handling of Vessels under Sail or Steam. For the Use of the U. S. Naval Academy. By Commodore S. B. LUCE, U. S. Navy. Revised and Enlarged by Lieutenant AARON WARD, U. S. Navy. Royal 8vo. 670 pages. With 131 Full-page Plates. $10.00.

#### ELECTRICAL APPLIANCES OF THE PRESENT DAY.

Being a Report of the Paris Electrical Exhibition of 1881. By Major D. P. HEAP, Corps of Engineers, U.S.A.; Honorary Commissioner to the Exhibition, and Military Delegate to the Congress of Electricians. 8vo. With 250 Illustrations. Cloth. $2.00.

### IN PRESS.

#### HYDRAULIC MINING IN CALIFORNIA.

By AUGUSTUS J. BOWIE, Jr. Illustrated.

**D. VAN NOSTRAND, PUBLISHER,**
23 Murray and 27 Warren Streets, New York.

*⁎* Copies of above books sent free by mail on receipt of price.

## ANGLO-SWISS MILK.
**Milkmaid Brand. CONDENSED**
Economical and convenient **for all kitchen purposes.** **Better for babies** than uncondensed milk. Sold everywhere.
**ANGLO-SWISS CONDENSED MILK CO. 86 Hudson St. N. Y. P. O. Box 3773.**

No more striking evidence of the growth of the business in condensed milk can be given than in the statement of the Anglo-Swiss Condensed Milk Company, that "The annual production of condensed milk is estimated at 60,000,000 cans, manufactured by eleven different firms in Europe and America, of which the above-named company manufacture 40,000,000; that is to say, the Anglo-Swiss Condensed Milk Company supply two-thirds of the world's entire demand, and the other ten firms the remaining third." This great house has its parent establishment in Cham, Switzerland, with branches in England and America, and it is claimed that this immense growth is due entirely to the superior and uniform purity of their productions, coupled with the low prices at which they are sold.

## ANGLO-SWISS MILK FOOD,
**For Children PAST Teething.**
Write us for testimonials of the medical profession regarding it.
**ANGLO-SWISS CONDENSED MILK CO.**
P. O. Box 3773.     86 HUDSON STREET, NEW-YORK.

Decided superiority is claimed for the Anglo-Swiss Milk Food in comparison with any other farinaceous Food for infants. No so-called Milk Food consists entirely of milk; all are partly composed of cereal products, involving, when not properly prepared, the presence of an injurious amount of starch, which the highest authorities agree in condemning for young children. The Anglo-Swiss Condensed Milk Company overcomes this objectionable feature of Milk Food as usually supplied, by meeting an essential requirement in the method of preparing it, so that when gradually heated with water, according to the directions for use, the starch contained in the materials used is converted, in a satisfactory degree, into soluble and easily-digestible dextrine and sugar.

The Anglo-Swiss Milk Food has been found to meet these essential conditions to the satisfaction of physicians and others who have taken the pains to examine it, and we invite critical examination of it in comparison with any other Food.

# ARMY AND NAVY CLOTHING MADE TO ORDER.

*J. A. Hoyt & Co.*
*Season of 1884-5.*
*10th. & Chestnut Sts.*
*Philadelphia*

The finest BOYS' CLOTHING of our own make and fine MERCHANT TAILORING.
LADIES' HABITS AND OVER GARMENTS MADE TO ORDER.

**DO YOU WANT A DOG?** If so, send for DOG BUYERS' GUIDE, containing colored plates, 100 engravings of different breeds, prices they are worth, and where to buy them. Also, cuts of Dog Furnishing Goods of all kinds. Directions for Training Dogs and Breeding Ferrets. Mailed for 15 cts.
ASSOCIATED FANCIERS,
237 S. 8th St.    Philad'

**BOOK OF CAGE BIRDS**, 100 pages, 150 illustrations, beautiful colored plate. Treatment and breeding of all kinds cage birds, for pleasure AND PROFIT. Diseases and their cure. How to build and stock an Aviary. All about Parrots. Prices of all kinds birds, cages, etc. Mailed for 15 cents.
ASSOCIATED FANCIERS,
237 So. Eight Street, Philadelphia.

**DEMOCRATIC SOUVENIR** — "VICTORY AND REFORM."

On heavy plate paper, 22 x 28 inches. Universally acknowledged to be the best and truest lithographic portraits of **President Cleveland** and **Vice-President Hendricks** (with Jefferson, Jackson, Tilden, and McClellan) ever published. All Military and Naval Officers, Postmasters, and **every good Democrat** should embellish their offices and their parlors with this appropriate souvenir and standard masterpiece of art. Write to the undersigned for sample; mailed to any reader of THE ARMY AND NAVY QUARTERLY for 50 cents in stamps or postal note; three for $1; seven for $2, safely tubed. No free copies. Confidential terms to those who after first order desire to become agents. Rare chance to make money. Address **Souvenir Publishing Co., 41 Park Row, N. Y.**
☛ Cash (by registered letter, money order, or draft) MUST accompany all orders.

# "The Philadelphia Call."

## THE BRIGHTEST OF THE HUMOROUS PAPERS.

*FULL OF INNOCENT FUN AND JOKES.*

## BETTER THAN QUININE, GINGER, OR BITTERS.

For Sale by All Newsdealers.

FIVE CENTS A COPY.   ISSUED SATURDAY.

**SPECIMEN COPIES MAILED FREE.**

Address   ROBERT S. DAVIS,
Proprietor of THE CALL,   PHILADELPHIA, PENN.

# DR. DYE'S ELECTRO-VOLTAIC BELT

AND OTHER

## ELECTRIC APPLIANCES

ARE ALSO A SURE CURE FOR

### *RHEUMATISM, NEURALGIA, PARALYSIS,*

AND MANY OTHER DISEASES.

Thousands of Testimonials verify their Great Curative Powers.

REMEMBER THAT THIRTY DAYS' TRIAL IS ALLOWED.

Do not delay in writing at once for Illustrated Pamphlet and full particulars to the

**VOLTAIC BELT CO.,**

Marshall, Mich.

## TO THE
# Officers of the Army.

Last summer, at the request of Captain Rogers, U.S.A., representing the Quartermaster-General, we designed and made a model overcoat, which, having been submitted to a board of officers, and approved by Lieutenant-General Sheridan, has been adopted for the use of officers in the army of the United States. We are prepared to furnish this coat complete for $75, and without the hood, which is not essential except in very cold climates, for $68, and being the original designers of the garment, are able to guarantee perfect conformity with the model. Rules for self-measurement will be furnished on application. Correspondence invited.

## GLEASON & CO.,
### SUCCESSORS TO HOYT & GLEASON,
### 1517 CHESTNUT STREET,
#### PHILADELPHIA, PA.

# NEW AND INTERESTING NOVELS
## PUBLISHED BY J. B. LIPPINCOTT COMPANY,
715 and 717 Market Street, Philadelphia.

### FOR LILIAS.
AUTHORIZED EDITION.

A Novel. By ROSA N. CAREY, author of "Barbara Heathcote's Trial," "Not Like Other Girls," "Nellie's Memories," etc. 16mo. Paper cover. 25 cents. Attractively bound in cloth, ink and gold ornaments. 75 cents.

Miss Carey is the author of several deservedly popular novels, among which "Not Like Other Girls" will rank with the best works of fiction. Her books are fresh, sweet stories of girl-life, full of genuine feeling, hearty and home-like, with nothing but good in them. "For Lilias" will be found to sustain the high reputation of the talented authoress.

### A MODEL WIFE.
A Novel. By G. I. CERVUS, author of "White Feathers." 12mo. Extra cloth. $1.00.

A very entertaining story of life in and about New York City. The narrative throughout displays an extraordinary knowledge of human nature, and abounds with such descriptions and incidents as will interest the reader, and doubtless secure for the volume a hearty welcome.

### THE LADY WITH THE RUBIES.
A Novel. From the German of E. MARLITT. Translated by Mrs. A. L. WISTER. 12mo. Extra cloth. $1.25.

"An exceptionally interesting story, abounding in action and incident, the plot well constructed and skilfully wrought out. Marlitt has produced a story of great beauty and power, and Mrs. Wister has given to the English reader not only a grammatically accurate translation, but has caught and infused into it the spirit of the refined genius of the author."—*Baltimore Evening News.*

### BARBARA HEATHCOTE'S TRIAL.
AUTHORIZED EDITION.

A Novel. By ROSA NOUCHETTE CAREY, author of "Robert Ord's Atonement," "Nellie's Memories," etc. 16mo. Paper cover. 25 cents. Attractively bound in cloth, ink and gold ornaments. 75 cents.

"Well worth reading. The pure, fresh, natural atmosphere in which the reader finds himself is in itself a charm. The book is one that can inspire only pure fancies and earnest thoughts, and, as such, deserves to be read and appreciated."—*Charleston News and Courier.*

### "O TENDER DOLORES."
AUTHORIZED EDITION.

A Novel. By the "DUCHESS," author of "Doris," "Phyllis," etc. 12mo. Paper cover. 25 cents. Attractively bound in cloth, ink and gold ornaments. 75 cents.

"Like all from her pen it is a love-story, with every charm of freshness and naturalness. Sentimental without exaggeration, vivid, absorbing, and romantic, all within the bounds of probability."—*Philadelphia Saturday Evening Post.*

### A MAIDEN ALL FORLORN,
AND OTHER STORIES. By the "DUCHESS," author of "O Tender Dolores," "Phyllis," "Mrs. Geoffrey," etc. 12mo. Paper cover. 25 cents. Attractively bound in cloth, ink and gold ornaments. 75 cents.

"Unusually good. There is not, in short, one dull page."—*London Morning Post.*

### ONE OF THE DUANES.
By ALICE KING HAMILTON. 12mo. Extra cloth. $1.25.

"Adds another to the few really good army novels that have been published during the last few years. It is good for its spirited style; for its bright and life-like pictures of social life at the distant military post, where the officers' wives and daughters form the aristocracy and society leaders; for its artistic character sketching; and for the deeply absorbing interest of the story that runs easily and consistently through the whole."—*Boston Home Journal.*

### TROUBLED WATERS.
A PROBLEM OF TO-DAY. A Novel. By BEVERLEY ELLISON WARNER. 12mo. Extra cloth. $1.25.

"An essay in much the same field as 'The Bread-Winners;' it is a far more agreeable book than that."—*Boston Literary World.*

"Is an original and deeply interesting story, written with the grace of style that betrays the cultivated author, and touching upon great problems in a way to suggest neither the absurd idealist, nor the unnecessary alarmist, nor the man with a special theory. It is long since we have had a better story of its kind."—*New York Critic.*

For Sale by all Booksellers, or will be sent by Mail, Postage Prepaid, on Receipt of Price by the Publishers.

# CARPETING.

## WILTONS, AXMINSTERS, MOQUETTES, VELVETS, BODY BRUSSELS, TAPESTRY BRUSSELS, AND INGRAINS, AND MATTINGS.

Being manufacturers, retail buyers can save intermediate profits by dealing with us. Special bargains always to be found in our large stock at prices 20 per cent. below market value. We guarantee every Carpet of our own make.

## J. & J. DOBSON,
**MANUFACTURERS,**

809, 811, and 813 Chestnut Street, Philadelphia.

# SEEDS
### FOR
# POST GARDENS.

Profitable Gardening depends first of all upon procuring SEEDS of VITALITY and PURITY. Such can be had from OUR ESTABLISHMENT. We ever have been the oldest and most extensive

## SEED GROWERS AND SEED MERCHANTS
### IN THE UNITED STATES.

We cordially invite all interested to visit and critically inspect our SEED FARMS, feeling confident that the areas, varied soils and climates, systems of cultivation, drying houses, steam machinery, implements and appurtenances generally, will demonstrate our ability to produce larger, more varied, and better stock than any other party in the Seed Trade. We have always been by far

## The Largest Producers of Garden Seeds in America.

Our farms do not exist upon paper, but can be found by any inquirer; and in the selection of stocks and systems of culture we have as a firm the advantages of very NEARLY A CENTURY OF EXPERIENCE. Our farms are situated at

BRISTOL, Bucks Co., Pa.    MANITOWOC, Manitowoc Co., Wis.
BURLINGTON, Burlington Co., N.J.    MONASKON, Lancaster Co., Va.

The whole comprising a total of *1574 Acres*, owned, occupied, and cultivated by ourselves. Upon these lands we have applied in a single season $20,000 worth of purchased fertilizers, a fact which exhibits the magnitude of our operations.

### THE STOCK SEEDS

from which all our crops are grown on all the farms are produced on Bloomsdale, the Pennsylvania farm, and under the daily scrutiny of the proprietors, are thoroughly culled of all departures from the true types, and produce crops of such purity of strain as to warrant us in declaring that *none are Superior and few Equal!*

Commanders of Government Posts who favor us with their orders can rely upon being supplied upon most liberal terms.

### *HORTICULTURAL REQUISITES.*

Post Farmers, Gardeners, or Florists desiring Tools or Appliances for the Field, Garden, or Hot House, will, upon application to us, be promptly furnished with Prices which, upon examination, will be found as low as those of other dealers.

## BOOKS--250 DISTINCT PUBLICATIONS

upon the subjects of the Breeding and Management of Horses, Cattle, Sheep, Swine, Poultry, Bees, and upon the Culture of Cotton, Tobacco, Flax, Roses, and Bedding Plants; upon Irrigation, Drainage, Horticultural Architecture, Forestry—everything that a Farmer or Gardener is interested in—*at Publishers' Prices*—Postage Paid.

Send for our *Catalogues of Books, Bulbous Roots, Seeds, Tools, Garden Ornaments.* We publish Catalogues of Seeds in English, German, Swedish, and Spanish.

These Catalogues will be furnished gratuitously upon application.

## DAVID LANDRETH & SONS,
### Seed Growers,
### PHILADELPHIA.

STANDARD HOUSEHOLD REMEDIES.

# DR. D. JAYNE'S FAMILY MEDICINES

Are prepared with great care, expressly for Family Use, and are so admirably calculated to preserve health and remove disease, that no family should be without them. They consist of

**Jayne's Expectorant,** for Colds, Coughs, Asthma, Consumption, and all Pulmonary and Bronchial Affections. It promotes expectoration and allays inflammation.

**Jayne's Tonic Vermifuge,** for Worms, Dyspepsia, Piles, General Debility, etc. An excellent Tonic for Children, and a beneficial remedy in many of the ailments of the young.

**Jayne's Carminative Balsam,** for Bowel and Summer Complaints, Colics, Cramp, Cholera, etc. A certain cure for Diarrhœa, Cholera Morbus, and Inflammation of the Bowels.

**Jayne's Alterative,** of established efficacy in Purifying the Blood, and for curing Scrofula, Goitre, Dropsy, Salt Rheum, Epilepsy, Cancers, and Diseases of the Skin and Bones.

**Jayne's Ague Mixture,** for the cure of Fever and Ague, Intermittent and Remittent Fevers, etc. These distressing complaints are very generally eradicated by this remedy when taken strictly as directed.

**Jayne's Liniment or Counter Irritant,** for Sprains, Bruises, Soreness in the Bones or Muscles, Rheumatism, and useful in all cases where an external application is required.

**Jayne's Sanative Pills,** a valuable Purgative, and a certain cure for all Bilious Affections, Liver Complaints, Costiveness, Dyspepsia, and Sick Headache.

**Jayne's Hair Tonic,** for the Preservation, Beauty, Growth, and Restoration of the Hair. A pleasant dressing for the hair, and a useful toilet article.

**Jayne's Specific for Tape Worm,** a certain, safe, and prompt remedy.

In settlements and localities where the attendance of a physician cannot be readily obtained, families will find these remedies of great service. The directions which accompany them are in plain, unprofessional language, easily understood by all; and in addition, Jayne's Medical Almanac and Guide to Health, to be had gratis of all agents, contains besides a reliable Calendar, a Catalogue of Diseases, *the symptoms by which they may be known,* together with advice as to the proper remedies to be used. **All of Dr. D. Jayne & Son's Family Medicines are sold by Druggists everywhere.**

**NEW WORK BY ADMIRAL PORTER.**

# The Adventures of Harry Marline;

### OR, NOTES FROM AN AMERICAN MIDSHIPMAN'S LUCKY BAG.

By ADMIRAL PORTER, Author of "Allan Dare and Robert le Diable," etc.

With Illustrations. 8vo. 378 Pages. Paper. Price, $1.00.

A book of rollicking and stirring adventures. The picture of the midshipmen in the olden times will delight our middies of the present day.

For sale by all Booksellers, or will be sent by mail, postpaid, on receipt of price.

**D. APPLETON & CO., Publishers,**

*1, 3, and 5 Bond Street, New York.*

---

# THE GRANT CAMPAIGNS,

As told in three volumes selected from the series "Campaigns of the Civil War," which the Cincinnati *Commercial* calls

"*The ablest and most striking account of the late war that has yet been written. Choosing the flower of military authors, the publishers have assigned to each the task of writing the history of the events he knew most about. Thus, both accuracy and a life-like freshness have been secured.*"

*Three Volumes. 12mo. $1.00 each.*

### THE VIRGINIA CAMPAIGN OF '64 AND '65. THE ARMY OF THE POTOMAC AND THE ARMY OF THE JAMES.

By ANDREW A. HUMPHREYS, Brigadier-General and Bvt. Major-General, U. S. Army.

### FROM FORT HENRY TO CORINTH.

By the Hon. M. F. FORCE, Justice of the Superior Court, Cincinnati; late Brigadier-General and Bvt. Major-General, U.S.V.

### THE MISSISSIPPI.

By FRANCIS VINTON GREENE, Lieutenant of Engineers, U. S. Army.

For sale by all Booksellers, or sent, postpaid, on receipt of price by

**CHARLES SCRIBNER'S SONS, Publishers.**

# GIVEN AWAY!

EVERY YEARLY SUBSCRIBER TO THE

## "HEARTHSTONE,"

AT THREE DOLLARS PER YEAR,

IS PRESENTED WITH EITHER

**WEBSTER'S PRACTICAL DICTIONARY,
DR. FOOTE'S PLAIN HOME TALKS,
OUR WESTERN BORDER,** by McKnight,
OR **NAVAL BATTLES,** by Dr. Shippen, U. S. Navy.

The last two volumes retail at $3 each.
☞ Send your name on a postal card, and full particulars will be sent you. Address

## HEARTHSTONE PUBLISHING CO.,

*268 and 270 South Ninth Street,*

PHILADELPHIA, PA.

THOMAS B. HAGSTOZ. JAMES BURDICK.

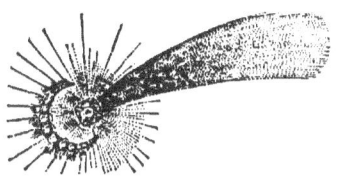

# T. B. HAGSTOZ & CO.,

SUCCESSORS TO

MORGAN & HEADLY,

The only house in Philadelphia making a specialty of

## Diamonds and Precious Stones.

ALSO WHOLESALE DEALERS IN

*Jewelry, Watches, and Optical Goods.*

Mutual Life Insurance Company Building,

TENTH AND CHESTNUT STS.,

**PHILADELPHIA.**

## CIRCULATION, 100,000.

# THE
# PHILADELPHIA RECORD

### THE GREAT DAILY OF THE KEYSTONE STATE.

Issued every day, including Sunday, it forms an uninterrupted and unrivaled channel of communication, with a constituency of readers which is not excelled in any quarter in number, intelligence, or amplitude of means.

In addition to exceptionally full reports of occurrences,—local, domestic, and foreign,—the "Record" gives especial prominence to agricultural, scientific, sporting, and dramatic notes and events, household knowledge, fashions, etc.

Fearless editorials on all important topics are features of the paper.

*A VALUABLE PAPER FOR ANY LOCALITY.*

ADDRESS

## THE PHILADELPHIA RECORD,
917 and 919 Chestnut Street, Philadelphia, Pa.

## How Consumption Comes.

You feel under par. You are heavy and draggy. Your appetite fails. You are off in color. You are weak and short of breath after exertion. Your skin is clammy at times; at other times feverish. You cough dryly. Your rest is broken. You are annoyed with night sweats. You lose flesh, worry, get nervous, fail more and more.

### A CRITICAL PERIOD.

This is the period when tubercles are forming in the lungs. Your lungs are a magazine. A spark, like a cold, may inflame them and ripen the dreaded tubercles. Then you have consumption.

### BREAK IT UP.

Can you do it? Beyond a doubt. Go right to the root of the trouble, which is not in the lungs, but in the stomach, the liver. The active principle of Mandrake, as found in Dr. Schenck's Mandrake Pills, is nature's remedy for that condition of stomach and liver which precedes Consumption and invites it. Cleanse the system thoroughly. Change the entire secretions. Set the organs in healthy action. To help nutrition and bring about good, rich blood, use the Seaweed Tonic, which promotes appetite, favors assimilation of food, and enriches the blood.

### IN CASE OF NEGLECT.

But if you have allowed the tubercles to get into the lungs, then the previous treatment must be assisted by Dr. Schenck's Pulmonic Syrup, which ripens the tubercles and helps the lungs to throw the ripened matter off. It cleanses and heals the sore spots by its action on the blood, and works a perfect cure. Dr. Schenck's remedies for Consumption are made to co-operate to one end, and thus save precious time and the vital forces as well. No other treatment has such a worldwide reputation. It has stood the test of over half a century, and its cures are numbered by the tens of thousands.

## Dr. Schenck's
### WORLD-RENOWNED REMEDIES.
Standards for over Half a Century. Proved on every Continent. Accepted in every family. Praised on every Trial.

**DR. SCHENCK'S MANDRAKE PILLS**

Cure indigestion, sour stomach, heartburn, flatulency, colic, and all diseases of the stomach; costiveness, inflammation, diarrhœa, piles, and diseases of the bowels; congestion, biliousness, jaundice, nausea, headache, giddiness, nervousness, wandering pains, chills and fevers, malaria, liver complaint, blood poisoning, and all diseases arising from a gorged and sluggish liver. They clean the mucous coats, reduce gorged or congested conditions, break up stubborn complications, restore free, healthy action to the organs, and give the system a chance to recover tone and strength.

**DR. SCHENCK'S PULMONIC SYRUP**

Is recognized everywhere as the best known remedy for colds, congestions, and inflammations in the throat, pipes, and lungs, and all diseases of the chest or other parts where matter has to be ripened and thrown off. It is an invaluable part of Dr. Schenck's celebrated treatment of Consumption of the Lungs, which has been used in the largest special practice in the United States, if not in the world, for over fifty years, and which has resulted in so many permanent cures.

### A NEW AND EXCELLENT BOOK.

Dr. Schenck has just published a useful and interesting work on the Lungs, the Liver, and the Stomach. It treats of the function of these great organs, and of their diseases and their cures. It ought to be in the hands of every one, but especially in the hands of sufferers from Dyspepsia, Liver Complaint, and Lung affections. Sent free.

## DR. SCHENCK'S MEDICINES,
### Pulmonic Syrup, Seaweed Tonic, and Mandrake Pills,

are sold by all Druggists, and full directions for their use are printed on the wrappers of every package. Address all communications to DR. J. H. SCHENCK & SON, Philadelphia, Pa.

# Penn Mutual Life
## INSURANCE COMPANY OF PHILADELPHIA.

PURELY MUTUAL. —•—!——;—•—Incorporated 1847.

### ONE OF THE OLDEST, STRONGEST, AND BEST.

Cash Assets, January 1, 1885 - - - - - $9,663,884.26.
Surplus over all Liabilities - - - - - - 1,812,360.34.

**THE PENN MUTUAL** issues all approved forms of Life and Endowment Policies, surplus being available in reduction of the SECOND and succeeding payments. Such returns of surplus have reduced the average cost of insurance much below the figures of many first-class competitors. Its **Non-Forfeiture** and **Extension** systems, voluntarily adopted, are the most liberal extant, full reserve being applied at lapse to extension of original sum insured, or to the purchase of **Paid-up Insurance**, as may be desired.

### ALL POLICIES NOW ISSUED CONTAIN THE FOLLOWING:

"*After three years from the date hereof, the only conditions which shall be binding upon the lawful holder of this Policy are, that the premiums shall be paid at the times and place and in the manner herein stipulated, and that the provisions of this Policy as to the age, residence, travel, and employments of the insured shall be observed, and that in all other respects, if this policy matures after the expiration of said three years, it shall be indisputable.*"

As an *investment, or Accumulated Surplus, Policies present the advantages of Endowment and other forms at a less rate of premium.*

Officers of the Army and Navy may pay premiums in monthly installments if desired, and are not required to pay any extra premium for "climate risk" while in the service.

S. O. HUEY, President.

H. M. NEEDLES, Vice-President.  H. O. BROWN, Secretary.

# HORSFORD'S ACID PHOSPHATE
[LIQUID]

## FOR DYSPEPSIA,

*Mental and Physical Exhaustion, Diminished Vitality,*

### NERVOUSNESS, ETC.

Prepared according to the directions of Prof. E. N. Horsford, of Cambridge, Mass.

A preparation of the Phosphates of Lime, Magnesia, Potash, and Iron, with Phosphoric Acid, in such form as to be readily assimilated by the system.

As FOOD for an EXHAUSTED BRAIN, in LIVER and KIDNEY TROUBLE, in SEASICKNESS and SICK HEADACHE, in WAKE-FULNESS, INDIGESTION, and CONSTIPATION, in INE-BRIETY, DESPONDENCY, and CASES of IMPAIRED NERVE FUNCTION, it has become a necessity in a large number of households throughout the world.

**Universally recommended and prescribed by physicians of all schools.**

**Its action will harmonize with such stimulants as are necessary to take.**

**It is the best tonic known, furnishing sustenance to both brain and body.**

It makes a delicious drink with water and sugar only,
AND IS
### INVIGORATING, STRENGTHENING,
### HEALTHFUL, REFRESHING.

Prices reasonable. Pamphlet giving further particulars mailed free.

MANUFACTURED BY THE

### RUMFORD CHEMICAL WORKS, PROVIDENCE, R. I.

*BEWARE OF IMITATIONS.*

# TORSTENSON:

"A HERO OF THE SEVENTEENTH CENTURY."

## Torstenson before Vienna;

OR,

THE SWEDES IN AUSTRIA,

In 1645—1646.

WITH A

### BIOGRAPHICAL SKETCH

OF

### FIELD-MARSHAL GENERALISSIMUS LEONARD TORSTENSON.

" Om denna lifeltens ara
Europa hapen an hat evigt vittne bara."

SVENSKA FRIHERRN.

BY

J. WATTS DE PEYSTER, LL.D., A.M.

BREV. MAJ.-GEN., S. N. Y.

New York:

CHARLES H. LUDWIG, PRINTER, 10 & 12 READE STREET.

1885.

# LIST OF PUBLICATIONS.

## J. Watts de Peyster:
### LL. D.

Master of Arts, Columbia College, of New York, 1872.—Hon. Mem. Clarendon Hist. Soc., Edinburgh, Scotland; of the New Brunswick Hist. Soc., St. John, Canada; of the Hist. Soc. of Minnesota, Montana, New Jersey, &c.; Life Mem. Royal Hist. Soc. of Great Britain, London, Eng.; Mem. Maatschappij Nederlandsche, Letterkunde, Leyden, Holland, &c., &c.—Colonel N. Y. S. I , 1846, assigned to command of 22d Regimental District, M. F. S. N. Y., 1849, Brigadier General for "*meritorious conduct*" to command of 22d Regimental District, M. F. S. N. Y., 1849, Brigadier General for "*important service*" [first appointment—in N.Y. State—to that rank, hitherto elective], 1851, M. F. S. N. Y.—Adjutant General, S. N. Y., 1855.—Brevet Major-General, S. N. Y., for "*meritorious services.*" by "Special Act" or "Concurrent Resolution," N. Y. State Legislature, April, 1866 [first and only General officer receiving such an honor (the highest) from S. N. Y., and the only officer thus brevetted (Major-General) in the United States.]

### AUTHOR OF

REPORTS—1st. On the Organizations of the National Guards and Municipal Military Institutions of Europe, and the Artillery and Arms best adapted to the State Service, 1852. (Reprinted by order of the N. Y. State Legislature, Senate Documents, No. 74, March 26, 1853.) 2d. Organizations of the English and Swiss Militia, the French, Swiss, and Prussian Fire Departments. Suggestions for the Organization of the N. Y. Militia, &c. 1853.

Life of (the Swedish Field Marshal) Leonard Torstenson (rewarded with three splendid Silver Medals, &c., by H. R. M. Oscar I., King of Sweden). 1855.—Thirty Years War, and Military Services of Field-Marshal Generalissimo Leonard Torstenson (Series), N. Y. Weekly Mail, 1873 ; A Hero of the XVII. Century (Torstenson).—The Volunteer, Weekly Mag., Vol. I., No. I., 1869.—The Career of the celebrated Condottiere Fra Moreale, Weekly Mail, 1873.—Frederic the Great. (Series.) Weekly Mail, 1873.—Eulogy of Torstenson, 4to., 1872.

The Dutch at the North Pole, and the Dutch in Maine. 1857.

Appendix to the Dutch at the North Pole, &c. 1858.

Ho, for the North Pole! 1860.—"Littell's Living Age."—The Dutch Battle of the Baltic. 1858.

The Invincible Armada. (Series.) 1860.—Examples of Intrepidity, as illustrated by the Exploits and Deaths of the Dutch Admirals. (Series.) 1860-1. Military Gazette.

Gems from Dutch History. (Series.) 1855.—A Tale of Leipsic, Peabody's Parlor Mag., 1832.

Carausius, the Dutch Augustus, and Emperor of Britain and the Menapii. 1858.

The Ancient, Mediæval and Modern Netherlanders. 1859.

Address to the Officers of the New York State Troops. 1858.

Life of Lieut.-Gen. (famous "Dutch Vauban"—styled the "Prince of Engineers") Menno, Baron Cohorn. (Series.) 1860.—Military Lessons. (Series.) 1861-3.—Winter Campaigns. 1862.

Practical Strategy, as illustrated by the Life and Achievements of a Master of the Art, the Austrian Field-Marshal, Traun. 1863.—Personal and Military History of Major-General Philip Kearny, 512 pp., 8vo. 1869.—Secession in Switzerland and the United States compared; being the Annual Address, delivered 20th October, 1863, before the Vermont State Historical Society, in the Hall of Representatives, Capitol, Montpelier. 1864.

Incidents connected with the War in Italy. (Series.) 1859.

Mortality among Generals. (Series.) 1861.—The Battle of King's Mountain. (Series.) 1861-2, 1880. Oriskany, 1878—Monmouth, 1878—Rhode Island, 1878.

Facts or Ideas Indispensable to the Comprehension of War; Notions on Strategy and Tactics. (Series.) 1861-2. Eclaireur, Military Journal. (Edited.) 1854-8.—In Memoriam. (Edited.) 1st, 1857; 2d, 1862.

The Bible in Prison. 1853.—A Discourse on the Tendency of High Church Doctrines. 1855.

A Night with Charles XII. of Sweden. A Nice Young Man. Parlor Dramas. 1860-1.

Aculco, Oriskany, and Miscellaneous Poems. 1860.

Genealogical References of Old Colonial Families, &c. 1851.

Biographical Notices of the de Peyster Family, in connection with the Colonial History of New York. 1861.—Biographies of the Watts, de Peyster, Reade, and Leake Families, in connection with Trinity Churchyard. 1862.—Military (1776-1779) Transactions of Major, afterwards Colonel 8th or King's Foot, B. A., Arent Schuyler de Peyster and Narrative of the Maritime Discoveries of his namesake and nephew, Capt. Arent Schuyler de Peyster. 1869.—Local Memorials relating to the de Peyster and Watts and affiliated families. 1881.—In Memoriam, Frederic de Peyster, Esq., LL.D., Prest. N. Y. Historical Society, St. Nicholas Society, St. Nicholas Club, &c., &c. 1882.

(*Continued on third page of cover.*)

From the Original presented to Gen. J. Watts de Peyster, by Col. Count Eric de Lewenhaupt, Privy Secretary to H. R. M. Oscar I., King of Sweden, in 1850.

## LEONARD TORSTENSON.

(The Lion-strong Son of the Stone of the Thunder God.)

Field Marshal-Generalissimo of the Swedish Armies in Germany,

Governor-General of Pomerania,

Hereditary Lord of Reisa, Fürstenau and Reisigkh, Baron of Wiersta (Wörestadh) and Count of Ortala,

&c., &c.

BORN 17TH AUGUST, 1603.    DIED 7TH APRIL, 1651.

# TORSTENSON BEFORE VIENNA.

DIE

## SCHWEDEN IN OESTERREICH

MDCXLV.–MDCXLVI.

EIN BEITRAG

ZUR

GESCHICHTE DES DREISSIGJAHRIGEN KRIEGES

VON

JOSEPH FEIL.

A TRANSLATION, WITH NOTES,

BY

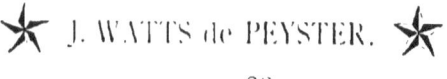 J. WATTS de PEYSTER.

JUNE, 1885.

NEW YORK:
CHARLES H. LUDWIG, PRINTER, 10 & 12 READE STREET.
1885.

J. WATTS DE PEYSTER,
A.M., LL.D.

LIFE MEMBER OF THE ROYAL HISTORICAL SOCIETY OF GREAT BRITAIN.
MEMBER OF THE NETHERLANDS LITERARY ASSOCIATION, LEYDEN, HOLLAND
HONORARY MEMBER OF NEW JERSEY, MINNESOTA, MONTANA AND
NEW BRUNSWICK (CANADA) HISTORICAL SOCIETIES,
THIRD ARMY CORPS UNION,
&c., &c., &c.

AUTHOR OF THE "LIFE OF FIELD-MARSHAL LEONARD TORSTENSON, SWEDISH
GENERALISSIMO," "HISTORY OF THE THIRTY YEARS' WAR,"
&c., &c., &c.

# TORSTENSON.

## Feil's "Die Schweden in Oesterreich."

Page 379. NOTE.—It was not until the time of the Emperor ALBERT II. [previously Duke of Austria, long before] [March, 1438—October, 1439] that Vienna was connected with the further side of the river by bridges. Shortly before his death, 4th July, 1439, he had determined to build such, at his own and the city's expense, over all the islands between the two banks, supported by a fixed toll, yet crossing by them was not made compulsory, since it was still allowed to cross by water from the old landing places (Hormayer's "Wien," iii. c. 57-58, from the Town Records). Then the Emperor Frederick III. allowed, 13th May, 1440, that the Viennese, who had already been at considerable expense for furnishing timber, &c., might apply the income from the tolls, first of all to a preliminary covering of the cost of building the bridge. He himself, 29th August, 1440, and King Ladislaus, 26th May, 1453, confirmed the above pledge of the Emperor Albert II. (The documents in reference to this in the Town Archives, printed in Weschel's "Leopoldstadt," Vienna, 1824, Urk. Books No. VIII., IX. and X., pp. 11, 12 and 14.) Thus were these bridges built—the first in Austria [proper]; for that at Krems was not built until 1463-1464, that at Linz, 1497 (Hormayer's "Wien," viii. p. 48).

Care was taken at once, to protect the newly erected bridges by entrenchments [bridge-heads]: one such for the middle bridge, a second thrown up on the so-called Neubruche (fresh land) and the third the *Wolfs-schanze* (Fortalicium in lupe proper pontem), are found already mentioned in the year 1484, when Matthias Corvinus appeared before Vienna for the second time (Dr. *Tichtels'* "Contemporaneous Diary," in RAUCH, *Script. Rer. Aust.*, II. 544, 545). On the 18th Dec. 1540, the city of Vienna undertook all receipts and expenditures for the Long Danube Bridge on its own account (*Hormayer's* "Wien," IV. a. 217-218), Wolfgang *Schmalzl's* "Panegyric on the City of Vienna," 1547, 1548 and 1849, published at Vienna in 8vo., also copied in *Hor-*

*mayer's* "Wien," VII., Urk. Buch No. ccxxiii.) gives exactly the length of these different bridges. The WOLFSBRIDGE 260 paces, Schritte, 520 feet, has 13 Joche (supports); the next in length 160 paces, Schritte, 320 feet and 8 Joche (supports); the Longbridge, 500 paces, Schritte, 1000 feet and 30 Joche (supports); finally the Schlachtbrucke, 96 paces, Schritte, 192 feet and 5 Joche (supports). The direction which the bridge then took, more westerly than at present, can be exactly made out from old plans and drawings, such as that on the copperplate of LAZEN'S "Topography," which contains Vienna, first and original edition 1561; also on a woodcut in the description of the public entrance of the Emperor Maximilian II., after being crowned at Frankfort, which appeared in 1563. (The title of this already very scarce publication (piece of printing) is cited in "*Vogel and Gruber's* Spec. Bibliotheca Aust.," II., 636; also in *Schirmer's* " Wien seit 6 Jahrhunderten," Vienna 1847. II., 289, in which last the book is more particularly described. Further in *Vischer's* " Topography of Lower Austria," 1672 (in the to this appended general view of Vienna from the south, there is clearly depicted, with the drawing of the Kahlenberg, the star fort (Stern-schanze) beyond the Wolfs-au). Also in the well-known large picture which represents the Turkish siege of the year 1683. Of this (picture) the chief part with the view of Vienna on a smaller scale is appended to *Dr. N. Hocke's* description of this siege, published in Vienna, 1685, and in a copy of the picture (last-named) appended to *Gensau's* " History of Vienna," IV., 160. The above-mentioned woodcut of the year 1563 shows the road through the Schotten-au (at present Brigitten-au) as being probably on account of the clay soil a corduroy road (Holztreppel Weg) raised on piles. To the right of the drawbridge lay a shooting-box, SCHISHUTT, and further in the same direction IEGER-haus (Jagerhaus) at about the end of the now-a-day *Jager Zeile*. At the beginning of the bridge which leads over into the Wolfs-au (on this cut designated simply as WOLF) was a THEBER and to the left of this a SVDELKVCHE, either a cooking place where lard was tried out (wo Fettesausgekocht wird) or more probably a guard kitchen (compare *Frisch's* " Worterbuch," Berlin, 1741, p. 355c and 357c). To the right of the " Thebers " on the bank, a little more remote, on the right corner of the SCHOTEN-AV, several houses are designated and close by them EIS GRUB; about halfway between this and the above-named " IEGERhaus " several buildings are again seen, among them one exceptionally large, with a tower-like addition and a sign GLAS HVT, without doubt a glass factory, which gave to the present *Jager-zeile* its former name of " Venediger-Au " (Venetian meadow), erected in 1486 by Nicholaus Walch, the first

Venetian-glass blower (*Sclager's* Wk. Sk., V. 11). The learned English doctor of medicine, Edward Browne, whose travels through the Netherlands, Germany, &c., were printed at Nuremberg, in 1686, and who (as may be seen on p. 196) was in Vienna, 1672-'73, says, on leaving the city, 1673, p. 271 :

"*I was obliged to pass over the great Vienna bridge which crosses the broad Danube, and to pass the chapel of St. Bridget which is built with eight corners. This bridge is a great, solid and strong work, and stands on four supports (Joche), which are overlaid with from two to three thousand cross-beams, upon which lie the flooring (Ober-zimmer holzer), over which one rides and walks, as bridges are generally built in Germany.*—(Author has omitted the stretchers.—Tr.) *At Ratisbon there is a beautiful stone bridge over the Danube and thence down to Vienna there are several others—wooden ones—but from Vienna down to Greek-Weissenburg, or Belgrade (Alba Græca), I could see none other than bridges of boats.*"

It was not until 1688-1698 that the road with the connecting bridges, from Vienna across the Danube, obtained the direction which it now follows (*Bergenstamm's* " Gesch. des unteren Werds " —Islands), [Leopoldstadt] Vienna, 1812, p. 40, also in *Hormayer's* " Wien," IV., b. 221-222, and Weschel, I., c. 315). An atlas prepared under the supervision of the Oberst-Jagermeister, Count Julius Hardegg, for the use of the Emperor Charles VI., in 1726, "Atlas der kaiserlichen Wild-bahnen—game tracks," in Austria and on the Enns (1st part, the Ebersdorfer district, with the Prater and city grounds.) This may now be found in the Imp. Roy. Library (73, D, 12 Atlas o, Tab. LVII.) It shows on the other side of the Brigitten-au as still existing the " Wolf-Schütt " and upon (über) the " alten Stuben," is the so-called " *Louis-Schanze*." perhaps a remainder, or, at least, nearly on the location of the old *Wolfs-schanze*.

(353) This war, sustained essentially by German blood, now [1645] had turned with the full force of its afflictions into Austrian lands. As formerly Thurn, with Bohemian warriors, first alone and then allied with Bethlen Gabor (June and November, 1619), so now the Swede TORSTENSON, with an army chiefly composed of Germans, stood before the gates of Vienna, and it seemed as if Austria, after the sacrifices of seven and twenty years of misfortune, must finally lose her pre-eminence in Germany and her preponderance in Europe.

(355) Field-Marshal Gustavus HORN and General Johannes BANER were, after the death of the king, Gustavus Adolphus [1632], entrusted with the chief command of the Swedish-German armies, the last soon alone, when Horn (taken prisoner at Nordlingen,

27th August, 1633) suffered seven years' captivity. When Baner closed his heroic career in death (10th May, 1641), LEONHARD TORSTENSON, his companion in arms, and next to the fallen king, *the greatest Swedish general of the time*, succeeded him as commander-in-chief. His titles were Leonhard Torstenson, General-Field-Marshal of the Crown of Sweden in Germany, Hereditary Lord of Reisa, Fürstenau and Resigkh. &c. In 1647 he was raised to the dignity of Count of Ortala.

Long imprisonment and multiplied exposures in the field had indeed crippled his body, but not his mind, which surmounted all obstacles from corporeal suffering, and which was animated by undiminished power and acuteness, as he most abundantly proved. He had but just, with great difficulty, obtained a furlough from military service in the spring of 1641, when the government appointed him, *as the best proved of their generals*, to the chief command in Germany. This he, not without giving well grounded reasons for declining it, finally undertook, but could only actually assume in the following autumn. But even then that hereditary malady of the generals of the Thirty Years' War, the gout, afflicted him to such a degree that the report of his death had already spread in the army. Yet he was finally able, at last, by being carried about in a litter, to conduct the war in person. In one course of victory, he, in 1642, pushed across the Elbe into Lusatia, took Gross-Glogau by storm (24th April), conquered Olmutz (5th July) and closed the completely successful campaign of that year by [his victory near by and] occupying Leipsic.

The depreciating idea which the Austrians then entertained of the Swedish army may be gathered from the book of a fugitive Jesuit (Pater Antoni Zeylern). He says the Swedes consist of from 5,000 to 6,000 miserable ragamuffins, to whom 12,000 to 15,000 German rebels have joined themselves. To crown all they are commanded by a sick nobleman (TORSTENSON) (356) and the Master-General of the Ordnance limps about on crutches.

As early as the beginning of 1643 the Reichs-Chancellor urgently advised Torstenson to profit by his victories for *advancing through Bohemia and Moravia to Austria and for transferring the theatre of war to the Danube, as Richelieu and Oxenstiern had always wished Gustavus Adolphus to do.*

This course Torstenson appeared to follow and it was half a victory for the Swedes that Gallas, the noted ruiner of armies, stood opposed to them. Yet Torstenson avoided any battles and moved through Bohemia and Moravia directly upon Austria. Already Gen. Wittenberg raided with his cavalry almost up to

Vienna and caught 800 lately recruited Imperial soldiers and [Helmold, " The Mad or Wild "] Wrangel in the beginning of July, with 3,000 cavalry, stood for a long time threateningly posted before the Vienna bridge. On this occasion 100 Wallachians went over to the Swedes with the words: *"Pro verbo Dei et pro Patria suscipimus hæc omnia"* inscribed on their colors, and although the imperial pardon was offered them declined to return.

(357) Just then the Danish war suddenly called Torstenson from that theatre of action, to which he did not return until the beginning of 1645, after overthrowing Gallas in Jutland, but now he was firmly determined to attack the emperor in the heart of his own lands.

This year marks the culmination of Torstenson's glory as a commander, but for Austria herself it was the most deplorable in the course of the whole war, the miseries of which she had now to feel in full measure.

When Torstenson returned from Denmark, the emperor himself had hastened to Prague for the purpose of raising a new army. Of the 5,000 men thus obtained, he gave the command to Hatzfeld. Field-Marshal Goetz joined him; and finally the Elector of Bavaria had sent to their aid 3,000 men under the bold swordsman, Jean de Werth. These forces met Torstenson at Jankau, three [German, about 15 English] miles from Tabor in Bohemia. " Help, Lord Jesus Christ," was the battle-cry of the Swedes; "Sancta Maria" that of the Imperialists. Misunderstandings among the three Imperial generals and unfavorable ground between hills and ponds of water soon [clubbed] brought them into a bad condition. Still, victory wavered. Torstenson's wife had already been captured by the Imperialists when these latter forgot the pursuit of the enemy in a premature pursuit of booty and were soon annihilated by Torstenson's [charge of cavalry led by himself, and by his] superior artillery.

(358) The victory of the Swedes was perfect and decisive. Torstenson had by it opened the way to Vienna; his talent as a commander had filled his own men with new confidence and had imbued the enemy with fear. After the dead had been buried Torstenson caused a thanksgiving festival to be held on the bloody field, under the thunder of his victorious artillery, and at once marched with the Swedish army toward Austria.

(360) The " Quartier Direktorium " at Vienna, &c., were just doing someting to alleviate what sufferings that part of Germany was experiencing from the war, when the terrifying news of the battle of Janikau and the advance of the Swedes toward Austria reached Vienna and demanded sacrifices far greater and those most urgently.

The Emperor Ferdinand III. was just then in Prague, while the Empress Maria Anna, born Infanta of Spain, was at Linz. How uncertain the communication between Prague and Vienna had become, even in the beginning of March, is shown by the circumstance that two gold chains, sent from Vienna to the emperor at Prague by the ordinary post, 1st March, 1645, fell into the hands of the enemy. * * *

Escorted by a number of cavalry under the Imperial Colonel Truckmüller * * the emperor left Prague on the 8th of March, about two P. M., leaving all valuables there behind him. He took with him only his crown and 100,000 ducats for defraying the expenses of the army. Travelling throughout the night he arrived about nine o'clock on the morning of the 9th at Pilsen, and the same day took up the court-quarters at Haid, at the foot of the Böhmer-wald. * * *

(361) After completing these arrangements the emperor proceeded on his journey and took his next night quarters at Witschau in Bavaria. On the 13th of March, before three P. M., he arrived, riding a little black horse, exhausted and dispirited, at Ratisbon. * * * It was supposed he would rest at Ratisbon for some days, but one courier followed another with discouraging news that the Swedes were directing their march on Austria and the French advancing on Nuremberg and Neuhausel. On this the emperor left Ratisbon the next day (14th) about two P. M., after dinner, to continue his journey by water and in the greatest haste. * *

(362) The emperor had left Linz immediately on receiving news of the mishap at Jankau, on the 13th, and had already reached Vienna on the 14th March.

(363) On arriving at Vienna the emperor at once took measures for defence, &c., and for this it was already high time, for the next day Swedish raiders were across the Austrian frontier. Torstenson, then encamped at Iglau, had given permission to the 23-year-old Cornet Rutger von *Ascheberg*, afterward made a count and raised to the dignity of governor-general and field marshal, to pursue the flying Imperialists with 130 troopers. In the night of the 15*th of March he had crossed the Austrian borders, the first of the Swedes to do so.* This is in the vicinity of *Retz*. In a village close by was quartered the dwindled remainder of the Imperial regiments Piccolomini, Pompejo and Bassompierre, reduced in the last battle to 450 men. These worn out and sunk in deep sleep [Paoli's Tavern, 1778. Hackensack, 1779, Am. Revotlution] were surprised by Ascheberg after he had already set fire to the village in several places. Terribly shocked, each of them thought only of his personal safety.

Still, only a small number succeeded in concealing themselves in the neighboring vineyards. All the others were killed or taken prisoners, among them a lieutenant-colonel, a major, 5 captains, 5 lieutenants, 9 cornets, 113 rank and file — altogether 134 men. actually four more than the Swedes numbered. Besides 4 standards, 285 horses, all the led horses of General Pompejo, and much other booty, fell into the hands of the young risk-his-neck, who at once returned to the main body. * *

(264) On the 19th of March, the day after Torstenson had broken camp at Iglau, which he took by stratagem and put under contribution, the emperor with his court and high nobles, escorted by two hundred musketeers, arrived, by way of Linz * * * in Vienna, to the great comfort of the anxious Viennese. It was not to reach safety, but to give it, that the emperor had come. * * Only the ignorance or the party malice of later historians would torture this pure action on Ferdinand's part into a flight to Vienna, or, still more falsely, into a flight from that city. * *

(365) That *Torstenson*, with the forces then at his command, even when fortified by the intoxication of a surprising victory, was not in a condition to carry through his *coup de main* on Austria, the wise Swede, even now, saw clearly [and what was best to be done?] The bare effect of a surprise, however powerful at the moment of the first terror, ensures no lasting success. It was above all important for him to secure the assistance of Ragoczy. This person, Prince of Transylvania by election of the representatives, was bound to acknowledge both the Emperor and the Porte as his superior lords, claimant of Hungary, self-seeking and vacillating, had, after antecedent preliminaries in direct communication with Torstenson, dated Weissenburg, 6th May, and Tobitschau, 20th July, 1643, finally, with the approval of the Porte and of the crown of Sweden, 16th September, 1643, concluded an alliance with Torstenson against the emperor, by the mediation of France, and had liberty from the Sultan to make open war. Trusting for a favorable result to his negotiations with the Porte for the possession of Upper Hungary under a yearly tribute, he had soon made hostile advances against the emperor. But being beaten by the Imperial Lieutenant-Field-Marshal, John Christopher, Count von Puchhaim, at Tirnau, in September, 1644, Ragoczy vacillated as to his further proceedings and repeatedly entered into peace negotiations with the Imperialists. But scarcely had the latter left Tirnau than Ragoczy again showed himself hostile, and Swedish and French envoys with promises of French gold soon brought him again in sympathy with Torsten-

son's successful and victorious course. When, therefore, the emperor, after the defeat at Jankau, arrived at Vienna, his first endeavors were directed to, if possible, resuming the peace negotiations with Ragoczy and on the other hand to treat with the Porte, through Lupul, Prince of Moldavia, that Ragoczy might be held back from proceeding further in the alliance with Sweden and France against the emperor. That Ragoczy was at least again brought to a state of indecision and Count Czaky, on the 28th March, 1645, could bring from Tirnau to Vienna the preliminaries of a fresh *Peace-Necociation*. *The successful result of these precautions was the sole cause which stopped Torstenson's victorious career in Austria and that rescued Vienna from the Swedes.*

(267) Torstenson on his return from Jutland found only Olmutz and Gross Glogau still in possession of the Swedes, and had, after his victory at Janikau, marched the main body of his army towards Olmutz, which had been for nine months beleaguered by the Imperial General, Count von Waldstein. When, however, Lieut. Colonel John Walter, whom Torstenson sent forward, reached the town, he discovered that Waldstein had already withdrawn and Torstenson found it only necessary to strengthen the Swedish garrison. After the retreat of Waldstein the Swedes had thrown themselves with hurrahs onto the works of the Imperialists to destroy them. *They then raided the whole surrounding region* for supplies and published throughout Moravia that all places which would send their quota to Olmutz should be free from any plundering and have safe-guards furnished them. Since, however, only few places answered this summons, the Swedes robbed what came to hand, plundered the cloister *Wellehrad*, and the towns Neutitschein, Kremsier, &c., and demolished the Maria-chapel on the Holy-mount (called also Marienberg), near Olmutz. Olmutz was occupied by the Swedes from June 16th, 1642, to July 12th, 1650—eight years.

(367) Meanwhile General Wittenberg was despatched to *Iglau* with 200 cavalry and 2,000 infantry, and arrived before its walls 11th March, P. M. * * The attempt of the citizens at defence amounted to little. * * The Swedes put a garrison into the town under Colonel Osterling, fortified it with walls and ditches, and leveled the suburbs. The booty was more than 2,000 horses, cloth to the amount of several thousand Reichsthalers. *Torstenson* now removed his headquarters to *Iglau* and was, much against his will, forced to remain there several days by reason of his sickness being aggravated. He demanded from Iglau a contribution of 60,000 Reichsthalers. . . . . . All captured Imperial generals and colonels were forwarded to Iglau.

It was not until the 19th of March that *Torstenson* could break up from Iglau, in order to advance to Znaim, leaving four regiments and 40 field pieces at the former place. Znaim was bravely defended by the Imperial Colonel Welisch with 200 men, but unsuccessfully, against the superior force of the enemy. The Swedes took the town by storm at the second attempt. . . . From here he marched straight for the Danube. The 23d of March his headquarters were at Schratten-thal, not far from Retz, around which town the main body of the army encamped. . . Both Horn and Drosendorf surrendered on being summoned, and Retz after a brief resistance.

1. On the 24th March Torstenson had pressed forward to the Danube near Krems—that river the insuperable limit to his course of victory.

2. As before mentioned the Swedes had already occupied the heights commanding Krems and Stein. The next day (25th March, the festival of the Annunciation) they descended to the Danube and occupied part of the Capucine cloister *Und*, situated between the two towns, where they acted in hostile style. When they, however, at once made use of the chapel of "Maria-Bründel," which had an image honored as miracle-working since 1643, for their horses' stable, Torstenson, it is said, was so enraged that he had the soldiers at once driven out by Colonel Copy and an ensign's (Fahndrick's) guard posted there as safeguard. [This seems somewhat doubtful, since Torstenson had no superstitious scruples.]

The garrison proper of *Stein* consisted of only 100 men, commanded by a captain. The citizens able to bear arms joined them, full of spirit, but the most determined courage could not long withstand the superior numbers of the Swedes, intoxicated with victory. Even on the second day, March 26th, Stein was taken by storm. The whole garrison, with their captain, and all arms-bearing citizens, fell victims to the first rage of the enemy as they entered. The town was gutted. It is said that only five citizens were left alive. The captain commanding was killed with his own weapons, the clergyman was mortally wounded and the burgomaster stripped to his shirt. Revolting cruelties were enacted—happily, in such measure, without a second example in all the remaining course of the Swedish inroad. The neighboring village of *Loiben* was plundered and ravaged, 1000 eimers of wine poured out, three householders shot, several cudgelled to death, and a total loss of 6,460 florins occasioned. The town of Stein and the Berg-Schloss (hill-citadel) within were at once garrisoned by the Swedes.

(369-70) The bombardment of Krems now went on more

earnestly. It was commanded by Colonel *Ranfft*, a man in bad repute with the Swedes, because it was said that, being taken at the battle of Leipzig and paroled on his word of honor, he did not again present himself. Although he had only 300 infantry at his disposal Ranfft was determined to make a stubborn (courageous) defense.. The terraces and the loose-vineyard-ground of the hills above Krems made it impossible to bring heavy artillery up them and the enemy attempted to command and bombard the town with light pieces. For three days and four nights it shook under the hostile artillery. Things seemed to have come to the last extremity. Men, women and children fell at the feet of Colonel Ranfft, beseeching him to surrender, but he refused. Finally Krems was surrendered andtaking possession of it had commenced, when a drunken peasant fired a shot (cannon ?) which killed the Swedish Lieut.-Col. Essen and several privates, and mortally wounded Troop-Sergeant-Major of cavalry Suanto Bielck, the last much regretted by Torstenson. Upon this supposed breach of faith the enraged Swedes recommenced firing, but Col. Ranfft at last exculpated himself and appeased the enemy.

(371) During the siege of Krems Torstenson had his headquarters in *Weilderhof*, near Nieder-Rohrendorf, scarcely an hour's (eine Stunde) [2½ English miles] travel from Krems.

(572) After the Swedes had actually taken possession of Krems they showed, to the joyful surprise of the anxious citizens, many honorable traits. The clergy, it is true, were obliged to bind themselves in writing that they would have no interchange of letters with the Imperialists, and that they would point out all (church ? ) property which had been brought to Kremsfrom other points (*alle dahin geflüchteten Güter*). In exchange a sufficient safeguard was at once furnished, at their urgent request, to the Jesuit college (then the Piarist Cloister on the hill). Several Swedish soldiers who were guilty of plundering and ill-treatment suffered the punishment of running the gauntlet. ☞ Such traits in a victorious enemy an impartial historian should not pass unmentioned.

That the Swedes often, and, as it were, designedly, were forced into severer measures, is shown, among other proofs, by the following instance. Not far from where the Damp empties into the Danube, about five miles from Krems, already in V.U.M.B., is the castle of *Grafen-egg*. It then belonged to the Imperial privy councillor and grand court steward, John Baptist, Count Werda von Werdenberg. One of his daughters, Anna Camilla, was married to the noted soldier, subsequently Imperial Field-Marshal, Freiherr von Enkevoirt. Already during the negotiations for the surrender of Krems Torstenson had despatched a Quartermaster-General, *Conrad*, to the castle. Enkevoirt, who was a prisoner of war, but, as were all other prisoners of rank, was treated with all consideration by Torstenson, had begged the latter to spare this castle of his father-in-law and to place there a safeguard. This Torstenson assured him of, and also promised that place should not be occupied by the Swedes. When Quartermaster (General) Conrad with the safety-guard arrived at the castle, the second-captain (Kapitain-Lieutenant) in charge, commanding 27 infantry and a number of armed peasants, refused to admit them. When seriously asked if he would surrender, he jeered the enemy from the castle walls, asking if the Swedes took him for a coward or a sneak that they thought he would so easily surrender. Thereupon the Swedes came up close to the castle ditch and renewed their demand for surrender, sending a drummer into the castle to negotiate. He was received with boastful scorn. "The Swedes must indeed be very hungry," cried the captain to him, " if they think so easily to win such a castle. One may easily take partridges, but not such a castle." At the same time he sent two partridges with their wings chopped off, a jug of wine and a glass with the bottom out into the Swedish encampment. So scornfully treated the Swedes resorted to harsher measures, and after the capture of Krems they appeared with two 12-pdrs. (halbe Karthaunen) before the castle. Once more they gave an amicable summons; then again the commandant, with impudent mockery, called out to the Swedes, " You must be extraordinarily hungry if you have already devoured the partridges. Wait a little till the young hares come. I will send you some of them." Then the patience of the besiegers gave way and they commenced battering (cannonading) the castle door. However, when the commandant was hit by a musket (Rohr) ball in the shoulder and there was no surgeon to bind the wound, miserable cowardice took the place of impudent bragging, and he humbly offered to come to terms. This was not, however, agreed to. He was, on the contrary, advised to take to prayer and prepare for death. After a short respite two sergeants performed the duty, and two shots made the loose mouth forever dumb. The next day the body was hung up, for a warning, at the castle gate. The Swedes stormed fiercely into the castle, and in the first rush hewed down the cook and his assistants. The remainder of the garrison and inhabitants of the castle were made prisoners. After this Torstenson took up his quarters in Grafenwörth, close by, as did also the Landgrave of Hesse at *Spitz*.

(373) But by Torstenson's plan the principal line of his operations did not lie in that direction, but as soon as he had secured

his rear he at once marched straight upon Vienna. He aimed especially at the decisive advantage of securing the bank of the Danube. From Weissen-Kirchen, Spitz and Wosendorf, which places the Swedes occupied on the 25th of March, he conquered the whole Wachau at one blow.

The castle of Durnstein, on the other hand, was taken by storm on the 26th of March and the little town set on fire.

Thus in possession of the left bank of the Danube, from Krems to Persenbe(u)rg, the Swedes attempted the crossing of the river at various points, but they were in every case driven back by the Imperial troops on the south side—particularly by the Puchheimer troops at Mautern, and further up towards Linz by those of Gallas. For the purpose of crossing, the Swedes had, in connection with a block-house on a neighboring flat, worked hard on restoring the injured bridge between Stein and Mautern, indeed a report was already spread in Vienna, by a young Count von Zell, that the Swedes had forced the surrender of the, from its mountain position, fortress-like, cloister of Göbbweiz, and had appeared before Melk (Molk). But this turned out mere report. *The Swedish army has never trod this bank of the Danube as conqueror.* [*The author, of course, means only* NEAR *Vienna.*]

The Imperialists had, happily, withdrawn all large vessels in the vicinity of Krems to the south bank, and the smaller craft at the disposal of the Swedes were not adapted to the transportation of troops. Guarding the river seems to have been performed by the Imperialists, at times, with reckless stringency; for when Count *Kurz*, with some of the Imperial troops collected after the battle of Jankau, wished to cross to the south bank at *Aggstein*, the passage was denied him by the officer there commanding, doubtless through a *misunderstanding* such as even *in those times* took place. Consequently the count with his men and much baggage fell into the hands of the Swedes, who made considerable booty and took prisoners those who were not slain.

(377) However, the abandoned [undefended] Abbey (Stift) of Zwettl, plundered by the Swedes only once, was robbed by the *Imperial* partisans (people) of Königswiesen, Böhmisch-Gratzen, Waidhofen and Rappottenstern six times, and each time a contribution exacted.

While these things were occurring in the upper part of the so-called Waldviertels, Torstenson, with the main body of the army, was continually advancing nearer the heart of Austria. On the morning of the 5th of April he broke camp at *Grafenwörth*, where we last left him, and on the same day fixed his headquarters at *Stockerau*. After that, the Swedes, previous to leaving, had plundered the positions they held during the siege of Krems, on the march the market town of *Hadersdorf* on the Damp, and had set fire to Langenlois. From this latter town almost everyone had fled.

(378) After that *Ober-Säuserdorf*, near the Russbach, had also been laid in ashes. The town of *Korneuburg* and the castle *Dientzenstein*, near to it, were attacked. *Korneuburgh*, *Kreutzenstein* and *Laa* had been already before this provided with Imperial garrisons, which in the two last places were commanded by Col. *Lucas*. A prolonged resistance, or at least the extorting of favorable conditions, was expected, but on the appearance of the Swedes before Korneuburg, Lucas without the slightest resistance surrendered the castle of Kreutzenstein and also Korneuburg, 8th April.

When the Swedes took possession of Korneuburg they found a large store of provisions, among which were 20,000 cimer of wine, 5,000 muth of breadstuffs, quantities of oats and a store of salt worth 60,000 florins, and 22 field-pieces. In addition a contribution of 12,000 rix-thalers was demanded.

And now *Torstenson* moved directly on *Vienna* itself. This, the emperor's residence, was connected with the further (north) bank of the Danube, over the various intervening islands, in a different direction than now-a-days. ☞ The road *from* Vienna then took the direction of the present Augarten-street in the *Schotten-au* (now Brigitten-au). It led past the site of the later built Brigitten-Kapelle and the then-existing Custom House, to a bridge, at the further end of which was the *Tabor-au*. From this, then, the so-called *Long Bridge* led into the *Wolfs-au*. Through this a small channel or arm cut its way, over which a shorter bridge was thrown. Finally, on the further bank from the Wolfs-au across (beyond) the fourth bridge, a star fort, the so-called Wolfs-schanze, formed a strong bridge head.

Into this fort a garrison of the Imperial Regiment Fehrenberg had been already thrown on the first news of the advance of the Swedes to the Danube (about the 26th of March). They were not obliged to remain long inactive, for they soon had to drive back straggling Swedish raiders (bummers—Streif-zügler), then also larger bodies of the enemy and again lawless bands of Imperial cavalry routed at Jankau. These were every time driven off with the loss of a few men, yet these skirmishes indicated the necessity of enlarging the fort and throwing in a stronger garrison. At last, on the 9th of April, the Swedish main body appeared before the fort and apparently proposed, by taking it, to open a direct way into the imperial city. Soon the enemy began a heavy cannonading and began to open their approaches. On the other hand the fire was answered with equal fury by the Imperialists until the coming down of night silenced both sides.

(380) Despairing of the success of a further resistance the Imperialists during the night entirely evacuated the fort, burned the smaller buildings within and near it and also burned the bridge behind them. The flames crackled (gushed) brightly upwards and shone with glowing red through the darkness of the night; the burning beams fell crackling and hissing into the stream below. With break of day the Swedes marched into the abandoned fort and immediately threw up strong breastworks facing the bridge. The Imperialists threw up counter fortifications on their bank. [On the island opposite,]

☞ So then *Torstenson* had pressed forward victorious into the heart of the Austrian state and stood threatening before the walls of the palace city of the German emperors. ☜ The hour of decision had come on. If *Ragoczy* united with *Torstenson* for one grand stroke, and by a quick junction reinforces the Swedish line of battle in this decisive moment, *the Northern leader marches a conqueror through the streets of Vienna*, and what human penetration could foresee the whole line of consequences of this event. But Ragoczy's *selfish policy* once more, at the most important instant, hesitated, uncertain from which side the surest advantage would be for himself, and this *contemptible* condition was the instrument by which Providence stemmed the sweeping course of events and this, and as so often for the rescue of Austria, brought in causes on which a miserable, halting faint-heartedness least of all reckoned. That the emperor with a sure glance recognized the point on which the decisive event turned, that he at once comprehended which was the Achilles heel of his opponent; this alone, as already said, saved Vienna—Austria.

(381) If the alarm in the capital increased every hour during the conquering approach of Torstenson, consternation reached its highest pitch now that the enemy stood close in front of the walls of Vienna and the worst might be feared at any instant.

(382–83) As regarded the measures of detail to be taken, it was first of all necessary to bring under control the confused flying from, and pressing into the city. As on the one hand all males from 16 to 60 years of age were forbidden to leave, so, on the other hand, those were sent out who were not able to carry arms. The court in this set the example. While Torstenson was besieging Krems, on the 28th of March the widowed empress Eleonore, Ferdinand II.'s relict, along with the young archdukes (the subsequent King of the Romans, Ferdinand IV., then 11 years old, and Leopold, afterwards as German emperor Leopold I., then 4 years old; also the princess Maria Anna Josephine, afterwards married to

Philip IV. of Spain, then 9 years old, left Vienna as evening came on, in order to travel to Gratz. More than a thousand wagons with fugitives carrying their valuables joined the train. *It is said that several of the court wagons were on this journey plundered by the Imperial soldiery* [as were those of Napoleon III. in 1870 by his own soldiers, and as the rebel cavalry robbed their own people in 1863-'5]. Many persons of high standing, and priests, fled, part of them to Venice, part of them to Saltzburg. Since many entirely abandoned the Austrian states the emperor saw himself finally compelled to forbid going beyond the boundaries under severe punishment. What confusion prevailed in the midst of planless rushing about, and in what an uncomfortable situation the fugitives put themselves and others, may be gathered from the circumstance that some towns, *e. g.* Wr-Neustadt and Gratz, were soon over-peopled and therefore, on account of the exorbitant price of provisions thus occasioned, shut their gates closely against any further arrivals.

(383) The strong-believing emperor, as a stimulating example, ordered, with preliminary concurrence of the Archbishop of Vienna, Frederick Philip, Count of Breuner, a general supplicatory procession. The emperor himself, confessedly an almost fanatical promoter of the honoring (Verehrung) of the most holy Virgin and of the belief in her immaculate conception, had at once, on the advance of the Swedes, made a vow to erect in a public place in Vienna a statue in honor of the holy mother of God. He fulfilled this vow three years after by the erection of one, in what is called "the Hof," which Leopold I., in 1667, replaced by that now existing. At the sounds of the great bell of the Schottenkirche, on the 29th of March, the day of the surrender of Krems, at 7 A. M., the emperor and empress were in this building, which could not hold the assembled multitude. After prayers the image of the Virgin, reputed as miracle-working, was brought out of the chapel by the Benedictines and carried on their shoulders with pomp to the cathedral of St. Stephen. . . . . In zealous prayer the anxious hearts poured themselves out. . . . In the evening the litany was repeated. The holy image remained set out for the like honor (homage) for eight days. On the morning of the ninth day it was carried back to the Schotten cloister with the same homage.

(385) The citizen militia was mustered and the students, called out by an imperial decree, aligned themselves spiritedly with the defenders of the Fatherland. Each faculty (of the university) was put under its separate captain. In short about 5,000 armed men exhibited their skill in handling their weapons before the emperor. The artillery was at once transported to the walls and the

citizens, students and artizans at once occupied the posts of duty assigned to them in the city. With great haste impromptu fortifications were thrown up on the Danube side of the city, the damaged part of the regular fortifications were repaired, especially in the neighborhood of the Kaiserburg and the Burggarten; next a new work was erected at the Neuthor and at the Rothenthurm, which was considered so important that it passed for an advanced work of the whole country. For the purpose of carrying through these works many houses belonging to the civil hospital had to be demolished, for which the institution received compensation on the upper and lower meadow. For digging the ditches not only was the robust portion of the female population called on, but, according to the standing orders for defense, those subject to socage duty within a circle of six miles from Vienna were summoned for a month's service.

As the Swedes held in occupation the whole of the further side of the Danube, had erected several blockhouses, and closely watched the whole length of the stream, the commerce by the river and the supply of provisions by this means were entirely cut off. Especially by reason of the great multitude which came into the city there was soon a sensible rise in the price of all the necessities of life. An order, issued through the public crier (the, at that time, most speedy way of announcing measures of police), had indeed been previously issued, which directed that every one, of high or low rank, should lay up food for one year and that all fugitives from outside, all regular beggars (Bettgewand) and old loafers should be put out of the city. Nevertheless a needy crowd remained who had nothing beyond their daily bread.

(386) Decree that every house, without exception, should furnish within fourteen days one able-bodied man fully armed with musket and pike, under penalty of confiscation of the house.

The environs were ordered to furnish one able-bodied man, with musket, &c., and side-arms, for every 18 to 20 houses. This within 14 days, and especially for the security of the river bank.

As a further provision for strengthening the garrison, all the district and Imperial foresters, with their sharpshooters, jägers and boys, were distributed in the Prater-au, partly for making strong abattis, partly to oppose by their skill in shooting the attempts to cross in small detachments, which were at various times made by the Swedes. These were very useful. After the Swedes had already occupied an island, called the "Kothlocke," with four pieces of artillery, they were so sharply picked off that they were forced to a hasty flight, leaving their cannon behind them.

[This is another valuable proof of the necessity of providing practised marksmen, as was especially shown at the Siege of Sebastopol, the Revolution in Geneva, and during the Slaveholders' Rebellion, in fact in all modern wars.]

(387) Things looked much worse with the regular Imperial regiments, particularly after the disaster of Jankau had torn great gaps in them and scattered the fugitive troops far and wide. Very few regiments had their ordinary complement. No cavalry regiment had more than 60 men. From Prague 400 men marched off who called themselves 20 regiments, and carried one hundred and twenty (company?) colors.

Difficulties in reassembling the scattered troops after the battle of Jankau. Gallas was stationed at Prague and afterwards at Budweis for this purpose. One corps organized, gained great fame in the defence of Brünn under *de Souches* orders; 600 men from Budweis had reached the Danube and crossed it at Mauthausen, in order to occupy (das Viertel ober-Wienerwald). Suddenly they received unexpected counter-orders sending them back into Bohemia.

(388) By this concentration of the fugitive troops and by the enlistments (Werbungen) in progress it was hoped that in a short time the Imperial army in the Hereditary Lands would, exclusive of those Gallas was raising, be brought to a strength of 35,000 men, foot and horse. These and the troops expected from Italy were then to be assembled on the plains about Tuln, in order to resist the Swedes with a respectable force. About the 12th of April Puchheim reached Vienna with three regiments of foot and five of horse; then came 2,000 Hungarians, 13 field-pieces and several of the banners captured from Ragoczy. The troops were sent to Mautern for an effectual defence against the Swedes, who were attempting to throw a bridge across, near Dürnstein, to effect the passage in mass. These troops of Puchheim, as well as some 1,000 which had been brought by Gallas and had crossed at Enns, were now put in quarters along the southern bank, for protecting the river. In addition, a detachment from the troops of Gallas were sent over the river near Melk, for the purpose of reconnoitering, after Torstenson had commenced, beginning with Spitz, to assign contributions on all lordships and market-towns. The Imperial forces received a further reinforcement by 2,000 infantry and 18 pieces of artillery, sent by the Elector of Saxony.

(394) The general-feld-marshall (field-marshal-general) occupied in the field the position of the general-lieutenant (lieutenant-general, *i. e.*, substitute for the Emperor), commander-in-chief, and this either independently or as a subordinate to such

lieutenant-general; but things were in their worst condition when several field-marshals, without a common superior, commanded together. It is universally acknowledged that the confusion which was followed by the loss of the battle of Janikau, is principally to be ascribed to the circumstance that three-field-marshals, Hatzfeld, Götz and John de Werth, were commanding at the same time, and by their separate individual orders crossed, hindered and confused each other.

Under the FIELD-MARSHAL GENERAL stood the "Feldzeugmeister," Grand Master of Ordnance as *General of Infantry*, and the *Wachtmeister-General* [Quartermaster-General?] [Major-General] as *General of Cavalry*. Of such, we have at the time of which we speak, the Count of POMPEJO and Ernst von TRAUN, John Francis BARWIZ, Freiherr von Fernemont, also court councillor and *Colonel* of an infantry regiment, the Spaniard Don FELIX, TRAUDITSCH, ZARADETZKY, and so on. Immediately subordinate to the two general officers (general of infantry and general of cavalry) were the general-field-marshal-lieutenant. As such we find in the Imperial army opposed to the Swedes, Count BRUAY Hannibal, Marquis of GONZAGA, Hans William Freiherr VOGT VON HUNOLDSTEIN, at the same time commandant-general of "Austria below Enns," MERCY, Adrian Freiherr (at a later period) Count von *Enckevoirt*, Count Raymond von *Montecuculi*, and John Christopher Count von *Puchheim*, at the same time vice-president of the court council.

(395) To the general staff belonged also the field-sergeant-colonel (Obrist-Feld-Wachmeister and the Obrist-Kriegs-Commissar) the military commissary colonel, which last was the head of all business for furnishing the troops with provisions, the horses with forage and for moving the trains. The auditor-general was the head of the military law officers and also charged with the ransoming or exchange of prisoners. Every general officer had an *adjutant-general, i. e.* an officer, who, as the mouth-piece of the general, had to communicate or carry out his orders and at the same time to *keep an exact daily record of them*.

The common soldiers (of the cavalry) were called *gemeine Knechte* (gregarii). Arquebusiers and dragoons, *i. e.* light mounted soldiers who, when called on, had to dismount and serve on foot, and were armed with a musket (*arquebus*). The two terms, arquebusiers and dragoons, are identical in meaning we find in 1645, *e.g.* the dragoons [or arquebusiers] of Counts Gallas and Serav.

(396) It should also be noticed that the Imperial regiments of that time were not yet uniformed, a custom first introduced in France under Louis XIII. († 1648) and which Prussia followed

in 1703, Austria not until 1737. Before that time it was the business of each colonel to give the soldiers of his regiment some badge of distinction by which they might be recognized.

(398) The next endeavors of the emperor were directed to secureing the release of the Imperial generals, colonels and other officers, held prisoners by the Swedes. As has been mentioned, Torstenson had caused these officers, including Generals Hatzfeld, Kara-detzky, &c., together with 3,000 common soldiers, to be brought to Iglau. But beside those taken at Jankau there were two other generals, who had been previously captured and were not yet liberated. These were (General-Wachtmeister) General of Cavalry Adrian, Freiherr von ENCKE-VOIRT, and (Master of Ordnance General) General of Infantry, John Francis, Freiherr von FERNEMONT. ENCKEVOIRT had once been released at the end of March, 1641, on the application of Piccolomini, in exchange for the Marquis de Gesures and Mr. d'Aiquebelle, from a prior captivity, he having been taken with John de Werth on the 3d of March, 1638, at Rheinfelden; but he had experienced the same fate on the 3d December, 1644, being taken by Torstenson and Geiss between Wittenberg and Jüterbok. . . . FERNEMONT, (398) on the other hand, had remained in the hands of the Swedes since the battle at Leipsic (2d Nov., 1642), and notwithstanding his repeated applications to the Lower Austria house of delegates that they should at least advance the ransom money, had not yet been redeemed. . . . The demands of the enemy were not inconsiderable—for each colonel, 50,000 Reichsthalers. Mistrust on the part of the Swedes, which arose from a like transaction in 1641, was the reason that the affair was not at once concluded. In regard to some of the higher officers, however, the ransom was soon given and accepted, especially for Hatzfeld and Zaradetzky. It was forwarded to Iglau, and Colonel Ranfft joined his command at Vienna on the 3d of May. Finally, by the mediation of Imperial General-Auditor GROSS with TORSTENSON, it was agreed that all captured colonels and other officers should be freed for 120,000 Reichsthalers. After the money was collected Lieut. Field-Marshal Count Puchheim was charged with delivering it and with the receiving of the prisoners. Clearly that comparatively small ransom was arranged by the reciprocal discharge of Swedish officers in the hands of the Imperialists. Still this arrangement seems to have met with obstacles in its details, for Enkevoirt was released on parole from Leipzig, to go to his estates in Bohemia and Moravia. He received, however, all military honors from the enemy, for he had a "fine" escort and two cannon were fired (losgebrannt) in his honor. ☞ There was, how-

ever, only one opinion as to the honorable way in which
Torstenson's chivalrous sentiments had always been shown in the
treatment of the higher prisoners.

Now that the enemy had penetrated into Austria the emperor's great object must be to give his army a really competent
head and one commanding general-confidence; in short, to appoint as chief a man, who, in commanding respect and in possession of wisdom and force of character was fully equal [if such
were possible] to his great adversary Torstenson. The loss of
Jankau had taught what were the consequences when unity of
command was wanting. Götz had fallen in that battle. Hatzfeld on account of the loss of the battle, as well as by reason of
the ignoble pains he had taken to put the whole blame of this
[loss] on the dead Götz, was not exactly in the bloom of the trust
reposed in him. Gallas had lost one battle after another, was decried as the " destroyer of armies," and was now, in his misfortunes, in the highest degree given to drunkenness.

On the contrary (to these) stood the Archduke Leopold William, now the only brother of the emperor, equally respected as
a prince of the church and as a general, in the 31st year of his
age, in the bloom of his strength and fame; on account of his
uncommon virtues called an " angel " by his father, the emperor
Ferdinand II.; a realized ideal of high refinement in the devoutness and purity of his life, he was, it must be confessed, after the
manner of his time, particularly favorable to the Jesuits, and, of
course, highly esteemed by them. The things, however, which
that order may have used only as a means to earthly ends, were
in the clear fountains of his devotion entirely separated from
such objects, &c., &c. [I do not see that he (Feil) shows him
(Leopold) to have been " Ein Mann, dessen Ansehen, Klugheit
und Kraft einem grossen Gegner wie *Torstenson gegenüber
vollkommen gewachsen wär."*] .

(402) About the 24th April the Archduke Leopold, having been
made commander-in-chief and having made the journey from
Linz by land, with six post horses, arrived in Vienna. It is revolting to notice that the prince on his journey was besieged
[actually attacked] in the vicinity of St. Polten by the assembled
Imperial soldiery with impudent demands for money [pay and
arrears of pay], and had to suffer many unpleasant things. In
such a desperate condition of affairs, such bad conduct had
to be most severely punished for the sake of the example. Of
the five ringleaders arrested, one lieutenant was beheaded, one
captain of cavalry hung and two privates were simply shot.

(403) That the powers plenipotentiary confided to him (Leopold) actually gave him the position of generalissimo is

convincingly shown by the following details. All his arrangements and orders were to be regarded as if the emperor were personally in the field, and unconditional obedience was to be paid him. The administration of military justice, even to life and limb, as concerned the whole Imperial army, from the highest general officer to the lowest soldier, was intrusted to him. He had the power, without consulting the emperor, to do whatever he considered necessary and appropriate for the bringing in of good order and military discipline, &c.

(404) Among the many evidences of the necessity of putting at the head of the Imperial forces a universally honored and a tried man, stood, most prominent of all, the complete ruin of all military discipline. (405) A memorial from the Lower Austria delegates to the Diet of May, 1645, gives a lamentable picture of the times. It is related how the Imperial soldiery, as soon as they had crossed to the country south of the Danube, acted worse than the enemy; that, laying aside all discipline and paying no attention to the appropriate Imperial orders as to subsistence, they had plundered whole villages and market-places, entered castles, robbed churches and driven off cattle. In their quarters, although provisions in kind were furnished them in abundance, they, under all sorts of pretexts, extorted coin, and when it was refused, threatened to fire the places, so that in a range of twelve miles along the Danube, from Tulbing to Amstetten, all the inhabitants had abandoned their houses aud fields and hid themselves in the woods. These in spite of all admonitions and threats from their clerical and secular supervisors, could not be induced to return, and even threatened the lives of the officials sent out to them. Immediately upon a place being abandoned by its inhabitants, not only did the wretches (soldiers) look upon themselves as masters of everything left behind—wine, grain, hay, oats and straw—to do with it as they pleased, but were abandoned enough maliciously to destroy what they could not consume or take away with them. It was just as bad for those peasants who did not abandon their dwellings; they were not only obliged to give up their own property, but compelled by threats of burning their houses and by all kinds of bodily tortures to betray the possessions of others. Every troop that followed another surpassed the preceding one in impudent lawlessness, without the most threatening imperial orders having the slightest effect upon them. Out of simple indifference (unvorsichtigkeit) the market town of Blindenmarkt, not far from Amstetten, was fired. ☞ The impudence of these lawless fellows went so far as, on one occasion oo the empress dowager's

journey from Vienna to Gratz, to actually plunder wagons of the Imperial court, and to attack the person of the Archduke Leopold William, as has already been mentioned.

(414) Torstenson took his headquarters at Stammersdorf. For four days the concentrated Swedish army remained in this threatening position. The terror in Vienna grew with every hour, as they beheld three handsome villages, fired by the enemy, send their bright flames upward and the Swedish artillery began to pour a heavy cannonade upon the city, Vienna. But just as anxiety had reached its highest pitch and every moment the worst seemed impending—it was the 14th April—the enemy suddenly, contrary to all expectations—the believing disposition (gläubige Sinn) of the time saw in it a visible token of the Virgin's intercession—broke up from his strong position and marched (took up his line of march) northward. Only Lieut.-Col. Sebastian Kallow, of the Copy regiment, who was still suffering from wounds received at Jankow, remained with 300 men in the fortifications, while Torstenson moved northward with the main body and the same day took his headquarters at Mistelbach for the purpose of, in some measure, resting out himself and his army, which needed quiet after such severe exertions. The fact was (nämlich) that Ragoczy had delayed bringing the promised reinforcement and Torstenson did not feel himself sufficiently strong with his own army alone to risk a decisive battle. In addition to this his rear was not secured since the strong places on the Moravian boundaries and several fortified castles in the Lower Manhartsberg circle were still in the hands of the Imperialists. His next purpose was, by taking them, to secure his rear and then to await the reinforcements of Ragoczy. In this way, however, he lost the irrecoverable advantage of a surprise, and although he victoriously took one strong place after the other, yet the Imperial forces gradually recovered self-confidence, while he, by the fruitless siege of Brünn, weakened the marrow of his army and by splitting up his forces, in the result, more and more dried up the stream of his heretofore victorious course.

(415) While the Swedes were in position at the bridge over the Danube at Vienna, the Hungarian General-Field-Marshal Ladislaus Barakozi, summoned by an order of the emperor and of the viceroy (Reichs Palatin) of Hungary, had posted himself with 2,000 Hungarian and Polish cavalry on the banks of the March. Here, by means of detached raiding parties, he captured a number of Swedes who were out seeking forage, whom he, in good Magyar fashion, at once decapitated, and then carried away the heads in sacks. Enraged at this piece of cruelty Torstenson sent out Colonel Jordan with some companies against the bar-

barians. These were soon overtaken at Angern, driven across the March, the bridges over the river at their position taken and a number of the monsters killed, among them the Polish Colonel Sebinsky. ☞ Thoroughly frightened the barbarous hordes withdrew and did not again appear. Torstenson immediately caused the pass at Angern to be occupied, to secure himself, on his own side, from such incursions. While he remained with the main body at Mistelbach he sent out separate parties to master the strong places in the Lower Manhartsberger Viertel and in Moravia. Major General Mortaigne * * * took the frontier town of Laa and the market town of Falkenstein by a *coup de main* and captured many cannon.

(416) At last, on the 27th April, Torstenson broke up from Mistelbach and took his headquarters at Hohenau. Here he had the army drawn up in battle array and celebrated a thanksgiving for the victory won at Jankau and for his so far successful course, upon which the troops were put into regular quarters.

Torstenson had also, in the circle above Manhartsberge (im Viertel ober dem Manhartsberge), with some slight exceptions, *e.g.* Feldsberg, captured the most important places and had made himself master of Lower Austria beyond the Danube. He now undertook the siege of the town of Brünn with the castle (am Spielberg). On the 3d of May the advance guard appeared before the walls of the town. The heroic defence of this town and of its castle, under the courageous and inflexible de Souches, by which the Swede lost irrecoverable time and his best forces fruitlessly, and against which his army was wasted in vain attempts to storm the place and then melted away, infected by the pest caught from Ragoczy's rabble, and sinking under dysentery, was the crisis of Torstenson's up to that time unchecked career of successful war.

Although Torstenson had already subdued all Lower Austria north of the Danube, and, in rear of this, the greater part of Moravia, he thoroughly realized how difficult it would be to maintain possession of this without having given a decisive blow in regard to the capital. As this was only possible in conjunction with Ragoczy, whose ambiguous behavior allowed of no certain reliance, the clearsighted Swede was careful at least to secure himself as far as possible in regard to the declared enemy of his untrustworthy ally, Ragoczy, and at once, by diplomatic means, to bring the Hungarian party, which was under the lead of the viceroy (Reichs-Palatine) Count Nicholas Esterhazy, and still devoted to the emperor, to at least a one-sided neutrality. (417) In his letter to the Palatine, of the 25th April, 1645, from his headquarters at Mistelbach, he, before all else, defends himself from the supposition that he wished to destroy the Christian name and faith. At the same time he endeavors to put what had already happened in a softened light, that is to say, if he had hostilely occupied any part of the kingdom of Hungary as being joined with the Imperial lands, as, according to the laws of war, had been the case with other renowned kingdoms and mighty principalities, it was only the course of the war which had compelled him to do so, and the necessity for following up the Imperial hostile forces who had fallen back across the frontiers of that kingdom. There was no one who more heartily than himself and his Queen wished that Christendom might soon obtain a permanent peace, but if not, he must wish that the opposite should be maintained in a Christian fashion, at least with so much of it as was practised toward the Jews and the like, whom they tolerated. He would not inquire whether Ragoczy could have entered into alliance with Sweden and France, and, in addition, even with the Turks, without the previous knowledge of the Hungarian and Transylvanian; nor would he inquire whether the adherence of the diets to the Palatine was loosening. But he had been assured that Ragoczy had taken up arms for the maintenance of the freedom of the Hungarian diet and could not be prevented from concluding the conventions made, for important reason, with other Christian powers; there was rather every reason, existing to give increasing praise to his conduct, especially since he also was in arms only for mediating the peace finally desired. He left untouched the Palatine's remark regarding the composition of the Hungarian diet, and that the Swedes ought not to form any connections with them, and passed over the threatening resolution of opposing himself to the Swedish arms with the last drop of his (the Palatine's) blood. No one, however, could find fault with himself (Torstenson) if, after the tyrant-like acts of which Barakozi had lately been guilty towards the Swedes, he should aim at making himself safe in the direction of the Hungarian frontier. And this without reference to the not yet forgotten impression made by the effective aid which, since the times of Gustavus Adolphus, the Hungarians, with every demonstration of hostility, had given to the Imperial arms; not only on the frontiers of Hungary, but also in the German empire, in Bohemia, Moravia, Silesia, Saxony, indeed up to the very sea-coast. He, on the contrary, felt confidence that the number of peace-loving patriots was large who would not associate themselves with the Palatine, but rather, when they once understood his (Torstenson's) sentiments, would seek shelter and protection from him; in which case they and all belonging to them should remain in perfect security on their estates, in their dwellings, and in whatever were their oc-

cupations. If, however, the contrary proved to be the fact, the
threats made by the Palatine should not deter him, and no one
ought to wonder if he then acted according to the usages of war.
In conclusion he repeated the wish that sighing Christendom, after
long suffering the direst extremity, should at last obtain a worthy
peace. That these advances from the Swede remained without
effect on the loyalty of spirit of the Palatine, Count Nicholas Esterhazy, towards his king is easily to be supposed and was proved
by the result.

(418) However vigorously and energetically these measures for
collecting an army, &c., on the part of the Austrians, were pressed
forward, the more the scattered forces for rescuing the fatherland
from an arrogant foreign sway were concentrated, it is the more
melancholy to see that even then a detestable party in Austria
itself were secretly brooding over disgraceful treason. One example will suffice for understanding this. In the middle of April
at Weitenegg on the Danube, where, as before mentioned, there
was still an Imperial garrison, although the Swedes had already
subjugated the whole Wach-au district, a man, who was in great
haste to cross the Danube, was arrested as a suspicious character.
On being searched a letter was found concealed in his walking-
stick, in which it was betrayed in detail to the Swedes, when,
where and how they could best gain possession of Vienna.

On further examination the confused man at last confessed
that he had received the letter from the Lutheran [?] Stände. [Is
not this a Papist shift of responsibility on to innocent shoulders?]

The Empress suddenly left Vienna for Gratz. [The author
thinks from a supposed plot to assassinate the eleven-year-old
Archduke Ferdinand Francis by a Frenchman.]

(419) It was a singular coincidence of circumstances that, at the
very moment when the Swedish forces lay before Vienna and held
the city almost in blockade (10th April), the there resident Papal Nuncio, by commission of the Pope, prepared a brief for
setting free a sovereign prince of the German empire, who had
been for eight years a prisoner in Vienna. This was Philip Christopher von Sotern, Elector of Treves, who, driven to extremities
between Spain and the Netherlands, between France and the
Swedish Protestant party, and abandoned by the Emperor and
the League, could find no other recourse than, on the advance of
the Swedes (Dec., 1631), to throw himself into the arms of
France. Papal brief arrived in Vienna 20th March, 1640, under
the thunder of the Swedish artillery.

The 11th of May the released prince left Vienna with a
stately escort and was forwarded on Imperial vessels with abun-
dant supply of provisions to Passau, whence he continued his

journey. The circumstance that a festival should again take place in the just-before terror-stricken Vienna allows us to conclude that here it was supposed that the most threatening danger was, at least for the moment, passed, after the withdrawal of the main body of the Swedes, although the Wolf-schanze was still occupied by a detachment of the enemy. (420) The emperor too allayed the fit of terror which had seized his officials, in the already-mentioned bulletin of the 26th April, with the comforting words that the course of war-events was now in such a way altered that the dangers of war were no longer so great for the city of Vienna and all necessity for removing the government archives away from that city was now at an end. ☞ In fact, the conquering Torstenson behaved, in respect to Vienna, as an honorable enemy, and as at the end of the Thirty Years' War, which, in the long duration of its cruelties had already drawn in and made savage a whole generation, could scarcely have been expected. ☞ He not only opened again the freedom of commerce upon the Danube, under a certain toll, but returned to the subjects (Unterthanen—peasants, countrymen), under moderate conditions, the cattle he had seized. This conduct was answered by responding courtesy on the part of the Viennese, in that, from time to time, Swedes were admitted into the city to purchase what they needed. Indeed, it is related that a valet [chamberlain?] of Torstenson came to Vienna from the Swedish headquarters at Stammersdorf with an Imperial pass, in order to purchase for his master some thousand reichsthaler's worth of saddles and horse furniture, a circumstance which at first startled the Viennese not a little. They, however, willingly, by this little politeness, requited the considerate treatment which Torstenson accorded to the Imperial generals and superior officers captured by him.

☞ Even if it be supposed, from this, that just then Torstenson was not fully in earnest with the siege of Vienna, this occurrence is yet an honorable trait for both sides.

(421) Even before the return of the Archduke Leopold William (he had gone to Pressburg to provide against a reported advance of Ragoczy) preparations had been commenced for reconquering the Wolfs-schanze fort, near Vienna, which was still occupied by the Swedes. As the most effective promoter of this understanding and its successful result we find the name of Colonel Frederic Reich, a name here (in these pages?) for the first time brought into remembrance after two hundred years.

(422) ☞ Colonel Reich was not at the battle of Jankau. He intimates plainly that he was not wanted there. He, without

hesitation, ascribes the loss of the battle by the Imperialists to Torstenson's surpassing talents as a military commander.

(423) Then Imperial troops were crossed over in three vessels, who attempted to storm the breaches made by the artillery in the fort. Kallow [the Swedish commandant] and his men were obliged to retire into the innermost work. Here too the Swedes defended themselves manfully, but the Imperial soldiers (424) [impressed men, deserters, perhaps] who were among them, so soon as they were under view of their countrymen outside, refused to fire or resist any longer and made from the breastworks the signal of voluntary surrender with their hats. Finally, at four o'clock in the afternoon, the fort was taken by storm without the loss of a single man on the Imperialist side. . . .

(424) It was, however, high time that the fort should be taken, for at 8 A. M. on the very next day (31st May, 1645), General Wittenberg, marching from the Hungarian frontier to the relief of the fort, had arrived within a mile of it. He, however, turned about at once on receiving intelligence of what had happened. The fort was at once occupied by a sufficient Imperialist garrison and under the direction of Colonel Reich four redoubts were thrown up for securing an unrestricted commerce on the Danube. The Swedes ascribed the loss of the fort simply to the circumstance that the forty Imperialist soldiers captured by them refused to make any further resistance, as the party who had penetrated the outer works pressed forward and began what they called a "treacherous union" with the Imperialist troops.

(429) The plan for taking Krems by stratagem was foiled by the treachery of a citizen of the town and the Imperialist forces were obliged to withdraw with considerable loss, for Torstenson, on learning of the advance of the Imperialists, immediately detached 1,500 men to its relief. In Krems itself things seemed in an evil condition at this time, in consequence of the hostile occupation. The vineyards in a great measure torn up in making fortifications and trenches, lay, for a great distance around, destroyed, and gave, in this year, not the slightest yield. Many of the best buildings were burned down and ruined, as, for example, the golden Kammer Hof (Exchequer-Court—Exchange), first plundered and then demolished; the rest had been obliged to furnish Swedish quarters and to pay heavy contributions. Lutheran preachers preached in the parish church (St. Vitus') and administered the sacrament in both kinds to many thousand country people from Upper Austria and Bohemia. Meantime not a single citizen of Krems deserted the faith of his fathers. It should, however, be properly noticed the enemy exercised not

the slightest compulsion in matters of faith; on the contrary, they allowed the Catholic service to be held in the Jesuit church without interference. At the same time they prohibited any communication of the captured Imperialist soldiers with the Jesuit college, because the latter had brought themselves under a suspicion of secret correspondence with the former.

(431) The Dominican cloister Imbach (formerly Minnbach), in the neighborhood of Krems, was spared by the enemy, from a most honorable feeling of gratitude. The nuns, indeed, had taken to flight on the approach of the Swedes, and gone to Salzburg, where they were hospitably received, at the Cloister of St. Peter, by Abbot Albert. Three lay-sisters, however, had remained behind, who exchanged their cloister costume for common dress and it so happening that the wife of the Swedish commander (Torstenson's?) was delivered of a child in the cloister, these women tended the lady (Wochnerin) and her offspring with the kindest and most devoted care. As a handsome acknowledgement of this service, so it is said, the cloister remained untouched. . . . In a note (3) there is some account of Torstenson's wife, but it seems probable that the lady here mentioned was the wife Lt.-Col. Hans Lundidh.

(439) At the market town of Gaunersdorf, the inhabitants, alarmed by the approach of the Swedes, attempted to hide themselves in excavations in the ground, of which some may still be seen in the town market-place (im market) and in the parochial court-yard (im Pfarrhofe). In these, it is said, the enemy suffocated many of them with smoke and that others died of hunger. At a place outside the town where an already much weather-beaten built-up pillar stands, at a point where the road turns off to Högersbrunn in the direction of Mistelbach, it is said that fifty inhabitants of Gaunersdorf fell into the hands of the Swedes and were butchered by them in the most horrible manner. The pillar is said to at once mark the place of this occurrence and that where the unfortunates were buried. Thus much is certain—the market-town of Gaunersdorf was in this year fired by the Swedes and burnt to the ground.

(441) In the beginning of June the Generalissimo Archduke Leopold had gone to the shrine [of the black Virgin] at Mariazell in Steyermark, to obtain fresh strength of soul for the approaching decisive crisis of the war, and to beg of the Disposer of our lots, victory for the forces entrusted to his leadership. While Torstenson, with half of the forces at his disposal, continued in front of Brünn and pushed the siege with energy, but fruitlessly, Gallas marched on the 10th of June from Vienna to join the troops as-

sembled in Bohemia, with the purpose of making an unexpected diversion which might draw him off from the blockade of Brünn. There were already 14,000 men assembled at Schuttenhofen and thither Gallas proceeded by way of Budweis. The archduke was to join him with an additional 8,000 men who had already crossed the Danube. On the other hand the two Ragoczys, father and son, were advancing with some thousands of Hungarian horsemen to strengthen Torstenson's forces, but [Imperial Marshal] Puchheim followed from Hungary, close upon the two Ragoczys, to watch their proceedings. Notwithstanding this the young Ragoczy, after he had joined Torstenson at Brunn, sent out raiding parties in various directions ; 1,000 Hungarians made a dash as far as the bridges of Vienna, here fell upon some subjects of Count Hoyos who were about to cross over to Vienna, detached from their wagons 136 horses and knocked out the bottoms of many casks of wine.

(442) Yet it was not allotted to the Emperor to remain longer in his capital for, as it were, to fill full the measure of tribulation for that year (1645) the destructive epidemic-pest (Pest-Seuche) brought by the hordes of Ragoczy from Hungary into Austria, broke out in the month of July with great severity. In Vienna itself from 30 to 40 fell a sacrifice to it daily. On account of it, the Vienna High-school was, after the autumn vacation, not reopened for that year. Throughout the city all measures were taken to prevent the spread of the disease, especially by the Imperial orders of the 28th July, 19th August, and 20th November, 1645; the Infection-Regulations of the year 1644 were strictly enforced. The police regulations taken in Vienna and issued through the public crier, strove to restrain the eating of unripe fruit and to prevent any contamination of the air. Since, at that time, in the absence of our modern sewers, the refuse from the houses was carried by so-called gutters (Rinnsäle) into the main channels which ran in the middle of the streets and lanes, it was ordained that every house-holder should cause these gutters to be washed out three or four times a day. The fruit and poultry market was removed outside the city, the leather cutters and saddlers were no longer allowed, as before, to keep the skins required by their business in the city. The butchers and wine shops were obliged to cleanse the air of their stalls and cellars with Kronawet-rauch from the hurtful exhalations. The physician, Dr. Strasser, was charged with issuing passes for those who wished to be removed from the infected houses to the Spittal-au (hospital mead or meadow), whence, however, they were not allowed to return to the city for forty days. He it was, too, who, at a later period, issued bills of health to those who wished to

visit the Imperial residence at St. Pölten. In addition, it was ordered that people should not run against each other in the streets, (?) and that no one should show horror (! ?) when passing the lazarettos (pest hospitals). Every sick person who did not wish to go to the hospitals was at liberty to remain at his house, but secluded and in his own way (nach ihrer Gelegenheit—convenience) pass through his sickness and medical treatment. Fearful were the ravages of this devastating disease. In many houses of both Wienerwalder-Kreise all were dead. They remained deserted, and willingly would the owners have rented them for nothing, if they could only have procured tenants (Stift Leute). The Emperor remained (until past the middle of August) as long in Vienna as it was possible to do so, without extreme danger to the safety of himself and of his family.

(443) The Emperor wrote to Brünn that the Archduke was doing his best to march to their relief. For the Emperor did not yet know that on the day before, after a sixteen weeks' siege, during which it had held out through the heroic bravery of its citizens, its students, and of the garrison under the skillful command of Colonel de Souches, Brunn had been freed from the enemy and won the crown of undying military renown and unchangeable loyalty. For Torstenson, whose troops were infected with the pest from the wild hordes of Ragoczy to such an extent that two regiments had almost entirely died of it, while the rest were suffering from diarrhoea brought on by the immoderate eating of fruit, could the less cherish any hope of a successful result; that, at the very time, the peace negotiations commenced by the Emperor with Ragoczy had come to a favorable conclusion. It was a happy coincidence of circumstances, after a long period of dark trouble, that on the very day when the siege of Brunn was fully abandoned, i. e. the 24th of August, the, at last successful, closing of a treaty with Ragoczy (on the 22d of August) was proclaimed amid the cheers of thousands, and that a Te Deum could be performed at Vienna for this important event.

(444) The Emperor with the Archduke Leopold journeyed to Linz, whence the Emperor, as King of Hungary, under date of the 16th of September, issued the important edict which, under the name of the Linz Pacification, and at the demand of Ragoczy, secured to the Protestants of Hungary the free exercise of their religion.

Torstenson, for his part, after raising the siege of Brunn and after preliminarily forwarding his wife, with the other females and a considerable amount of treasure, to Olmutz, under escort of Colonel Paikul, had marched with his main body to Mistelbach. Here he allowed his troops some days of repose and sent off, under date of the 30th of August, a detailed report in which he gave the reasons for retiring from Brunn and an account of Ragoczy's falling off from the Swedish cause. Here also he held councils of war as to the plans for further operations. The decision was to march directly upon the Austrians and offer them battle. In case they would not accept it, then to cross the Danube and so make the south bank also a part of the theatre of operations. . . . From Mistelbach Torstenson sent Major General Wittenberg with 3,000 cavalry to the Vienna bridges, but this raid had no success and cost the Swedes 40 men, who were brought prisoners into Vienna.

On the other hand the Swede gave loose in the northern districts to his discontent, at the fruitless siege of Brunn and at Ragoczy's want of faith, by plundering everything in the region of Nikolsburg and by burning thirty market places, advancing his troops to Austerlitz and Feldsberg, and scorching and burning up to within two [8 or 10 English] miles of Krems. Then he fixed his camp at Mistelbach and marched, towards the middle of September, with the principal part of his forces to Stockerau, after he had, with a wide swath, wasted the country toward Hungary. While here he most energetically pushed forward increasing the fortifications of Kornenburg, which city he raised to the rank of an actual fortress, so that the town previously defended by walls, after Torstenson had given the labor of 600 men for fourteen days in constructing ravelins, was fully capable of withstanding a long siege and for keeping the country, for a wide circle around it, under contribution. To this end the Swedish Colonel Copy was made commandant, 900 men thrown in as garrison and the place provisioned for a year and supplied with artillery and ammunition.

(446) The Archduke had, with sixteen Imperialist regiments (only, however, 5,378 men) successfully hastened to the assistance of the Bavarians against the advancing French. The remaining Imperial troops, under Puchheim and Gallas, although severely troubled by the pest and by diarrhœa, watched with great strictness the right bank of the Danube, and had thrown up not less than fifty one forts in the direction of Lanz. Since all the crossing points of the Danube were thus shut against communication, Torstenson did not receive intelligence of the march of the Archduke until eight days after his departure, when it was too late to follow him. Yet if Torstenson had actually broken across the Danube, the high mountains and narrow defiles of Upper Austria would have most materially interfered with the movements of a large army—since, while so strictly guarded by the Imperialists, the crossing of the Danube, unless it were frozen, was ab

solutely impossible for the Swedes, and since they, after such long-continued severe exertions, stood in need of a long rest, Torstenson was obliged to hasten in evacuating the already exhausted district in which he was, before the wet autumn weather had softened the ground and rendered it impassable, for the purpose of securing safe winter quarters at some other point, especially as it was always to be supposed that the Archduke Leopold William might, in conjunction with the Bavarians, at some unexpected moment break out from the mountain passes. After Torstenson, in the beginning of October, had undermined the castle of Kreutzenstein, near Korneuburg, in four places and blown it into the air, he was obliged to content himself, for that year, to strengthen and provision several places already occupied by the Swedes, such as Korneuburg and Krems; but he could only put garrisons into Falkenstein, Staaz, Nikolsburg and Rabensburg, for the purpose of keeping open the free communication between Olmutz and Iglau. This done, he first proceeded to Iglau, to which place he had sent, in advance, 300 wagons loaded with cloth and other military necessities; then he moved into Bohemia in order to here fix in winter quarters his wearied and thinned-out troops. Puchheim and Fernemont here too followed close after him. On crossing the Bohemian frontier, however, the wasting sicknesses afflicting Torstenson's army ceased.

(447) At this time, *i. e.* in the month of October, the Imperialists made a fresh attempt upon Krems, in that they cannonaded it and really gained possession of the two outworks, St. John and Weinzierl; these, however, were unexpectedly retaken in the beginning of November by the Swedish commandant and a fresh closing of the Danube followed. No further advantage was gained by the Imperialists at this time. Krems remained, up to the 6th of May, 1646, in the occupation of the Swedes under Lieut-Colonel Hans Lundidh of the Axel-Lilje regiment. Here the contribution moneys had to be paid and from here the Swedish Commissary-General, Frederic Thilesius, so exercised his work of provisioning the garrison that on occasion it became regular robbery.

(454) In concluding what we have to record in relation to the year 1645 one circumstance, very lamentable in its results, cannot be passed over and which, although it did not happen in Austria proper had, alas, a very near bearing on it. It has been already mentioned that the Swedish Colonel Paikul was commissioned, after the abandoning of the siege of Brunn, to escort the wife of Torstenson, with the other Swedish females, to Olmutz. The thoughtless talk of a Jesuit of that place, named George Pelinza, who, with very ill-timed wit, spoke of a treasure amounting to

many thousands, meaning thereby the costly library of the Jesuit college at Olmutz, awakened Paikul's attention, and he shortly afterward, in company with some officers, visited the library and in fact took much interest in it. And lo! after a few weeks a Swedish librarian appeared, who selected, not only from the library of the Jesuit college, but from the other cloister libraries of Moravia, the choicest printed and manuscript works. From the archives, too, and especially from those of the town-hall at Olmutz, he took the most valuable documents, and sent 100 wagons, loaded with books and manuscripts from all Moravia, to Sweden. (Murray, Guide Book Southern Germany, p. 409, says these books remained till near the close of the 18th Century at Stralsund, packed up in readiness to be conveyed to Sweden. Since then all traces of them are lost.—W. P. W.) The endeavor has been made in later times to clear Torstenson from any connection with this plundering of the libraries and archives of Moravia and Bohemia, and to ascribe the fatherland's loss in this respect to a disagreeable general passion for acquisition on the part of Konigsmark, Wrangel and Paikul, but could Paikul without the knowledge of the commander-in-chief have levied such a war-contribution of literary and archival valuables?

1646.

(455) According to the plan of operations for this year, as formed by Torstenson, the first care of the Swedes was to maintain the army and to effect a junction with the French, and until this was done to attempt nothing of capital importance. This, once carried out, however, then with their united forces they were to drive the enemy over the Danube. But the result was different from the calculations.

Insomuch as our narration of military events confines itself, by our intention, entirely to the events occurring in Lower Austria, this year offers the precise counterpart of the one preceding it. If then the conquering enemy, with crushing footsteps, threatened the very residence of the Emperor, we now, in 1646, see the Swedes (deprived of any hope as to a lasting and effective alliance with Ragoczy and turning their regards towards France as their last anchor of hope) more and more crippled in their enterprise against Austria. On the contrary we see the Imperialist forces growing stronger in returning self-confidence and under a proved leader finally able to eject the enemy from all the strong places occupied by him, so that by the end of August not a single one remained in Lower Austria. At the very commencement of 1646 troops of Puchheim had been assembled on the north side of the Danube near Vienna, with the intention of marching on

Budweis (in conjunction with the regiments Pompejo, Pallavicini, Gonzaga. Ferrara, Rebenstock and Wachenheim, from the south side). As, however, a deep snow covered the country, far and wide, the citizens of Vienna were obliged to provide several hundred wagons with their teams for the purpose of forwarding these Imperialist troops with all speed to Bohemia. There yet remained a proper reserve of troops stationed on the Danube. The Emperor at the time remained constantly at Linz.

(457) With the end of February, 1646, as already stated, the hard-pressed inhabitants of Horn were released from all contributions after the Swedes had entirely evacuated that region.

On their departure there were in the town of Horn only 75 left of 86 houses; in the whole lordship of Horn only a total of 125 still standing. Meantime Ragoczy, in spite of the peace he had concluded with the Emperor in August of the preceding year, had (unterm) 22d February, 1646, attempted treacherously to renew his former alliance with the Swedes and France on the condition that the consent of the Divan should be first obtained by these powers, and the subsidies agreed upon punctually paid. But Ragoczy's faithlessness could no longer win any trust from these powers and the whole proposal came to nothing, especially as, in case of its acceptance, France and Sweden must sacrifice large sums of money. Thus Ragoczy was forced, much against his will, to preserve at least the appearance of being honorable, and to remain in peaceful relations with the Emperor.

In the meantime the new military commandant for Austria (Obrist-Feld-Zeugmeister—Lt.-Colonel of Ordnance? [perhaps equivalent to a General of Division or Corps-Commander]) Count John Christopher von Puchheim, had pushed everything forward with the purpose of entirely driving the enemy out of Lower Austria with the greatest energy; that, what with the continued barricading of the Danube, constantly made raids of the enemy, the severe oppression of large contributions, and the merciless proceedings in collecting the latter, the condition of affairs had become absolutely unbearable for any longer time.

Scarcely had the approaching spring melted the deep snow when the Swedes recommenced their burdensome hostilities in every direction. Count Puchheim had, in the beginning of March, scarcely left his last headquarters at Gross-Enzersdorf on the Danube,when the Swedish raiders at once fired the place, and in consequence the church and large supplies of grain became the prey of the flames. Shortly after, about the 10th of March, 1500 troopers sacked the lordship of Orth and the Swedes in Korneuburg had done the same to Mistelbach and Poysdorf on account of refused contributions.

(459) It happened that nearly at the same time the city of Vienna had to suffer from both water and fire. By reason of the suddenly melted snow from the mountains the river was, in the beginning of March, swollen to an extraordinary height and carried away three [wooden-piers] (Joche) of the Vienna drawbridge and six piers of the Danube Long-bridge, so the work of repairing had to be made with all speed in order to restore the imperiously necessary communication between the two banks of the Danube. On the other hand, on Good Friday, 30th of March, (1646), at eleven o'clock at night, through carelessness of the housekeeper (Haus-meister) fire broke out in the royal castle at Vienna and caused great damage. Fortunately the court was not then at the castle, for the emperor lived continually at Linz, for which place the Imperial War-Counsellor and Forester Schmidt had left with splendid Turkish carpets and other presents of the Bassa of Ofen and carrying the assurance, in the name of the latter, that the military preparations of the Turks in Ofen were entirely against the Venetians. At the same time it was reported from Gratz that the Turks were already making forays into Hungary and plundering and burning one village after another, and, among others, had led off as prisoners many people from the estates of Count Budiani.

(462) SIEGE OF KREMS BY THE IMPERIALISTS.—Already in the beginning of May it was hoped speedily to obtain possession of Krems, when the chancellor of Hungary, Count Veselenyi, on his journey to the Imperial court encampment at Linz, passed through the neighborhood, Count Puchheim did not neglect to show him all the preparations for a vigorous siege, in order that the latter might communicate to the Emperor the secure hope of a happy result. Count Puchheim and Lieutenant Field-Marshal Hunoldstein, personally superintended all the siege operations and passed a great part of their time in the approaches and at the (advanced) posts, so that the rapid progress of the operations might be strenuously maintained. While work was continued without interruption on the mines, the flanks of the bastions in the directions of Stein and Galgenberg, and then in that of the Wachterthörl, were in the most part ruined for the use of the Swedes by mere quarter-charges (Quartier-schlagen?) On the side of the besiegers, from the commander-in-chief down to the common soldier, all were cheerful. Some thought that Lundidh (the Swedish commander) would not let things proceed to extremities, especially as he had his wife and children with him and could not well calculate on the siege being raised. Others, on the contrary, thought it might be considered conclusive, from his activity in counter-works, that Lundidh securely counted on re-

lief. He spared his soldiers in every possible way, but, on the other hand, forced the peasantry to the most exhausting labor and used them, too, for sentry duty and as musketeers. Indeed, he even pushed them, instead of the soldiers, into the most advanced works. What must have been the feelings of these (462), as they were forced to risk their lives in repulsing the forces which were to relieve them from their calamities, may be easily conceived. Lundidh caused also many houses, although no churches, to be completely levelled; as to the others he took off their roofs and heaped sand about (on) them, to keep them from injury by the enemy's artillery. [Did he cover the upper floors with sand?] By a lucky find the besieged had also obtained 160 cwt. (*Zentner*) of powder that had been buried. The Imperialists were meanwhile ready to batter a breach in the walls, the mines only were waiting for completion. Since, however, the Emperor, for the purpose of sparing the common soldiers, expressly commanded that the place should not be stormed until the mines had done their work, the final assault had yet to be delayed for a while. Puchheim therefore pushed forward the work unceasingly, in order to finish the mines as soon as possible, and in order that the besieged might at least be kept continually at their posts and so the sooner become exhausted. At last the work was advanced so far that Puchheim might hope to batter a breach by evening and then the next morning the more conveniently to press upon the Swedes, as they were engaged in repairing it. On all sides courage and determination were predominant. All hoped to reconquer the town for the Emperor within twenty-four hours. General Puchheim was present wherever he was needed and shunned no danger (463) so that the common soldiers could not conceal their anxiety that he should take greater care of his person, lest, by some unlucky chance, the whole undertaking should be endangered and brought into confusion, as indeed only a short time before, Captain Lorenzo, abandoned by his soldiers, had been thrust through by the Swedes and carried into the town.

The siege was continued with activity, and soon one work near the Vienna gate was taken and the Swedish soldiers occupying it were mostly slaughtered. At the same time several towers on the fortifications of the town were battered down. But still no general storming-attack had been undertaken.

Then, just arrived from the Imperial court camp at Linz, and after the recapture of Nikolsburg in Moravia (12th April), Colonel de Souches, the glory-crowned defender of Brünn, joined Puchheim.

The troops destined for conducting the siege were now assigned to three headquarters.

I. In the hamlet of Weinzierl Colonel de Mers had his headquarters with his regiment, in the angle formed below the Vienna gate by the junction of the Krems and the Danube. Here approaches and redoubts were ready, a battery was built and downstream toward the Danube two mortars (*Böller*) were posted. There was also a second grand battery on the hill alongside the road to Langenlois.

II. In the first mill lying in the Krems valley was Colonel Count John Colloredo and in the second mill Hunoldstein, each with their regimental quarters. Their batteries, connected by approaches and redoubts, commanded the town on the north on the Reben-hügel hills, from the " Laimgrube " onward. In advance of these batteries at one point two, at another three mortars were planted.

III. The regiments Ranfft and Traun had, on the other hand, established themselves in Stein. Their approaches and redoubts were between the Capucin cloister Und and the Steiner-gate of Krems.

[" Between *Krems* and *Stein* is a solitary building, once a monastery, now a military hospital, called *Und*, which gave rise to a riddle : ' *Krems* and ( *Und*) *Stein* are three places.' " MURRAY'S "*Southern Germany*," Route 197, Danube (D).]

The principal battery of Colonel Ranfft, consisting of ten field Karthaunen [48 pdrs.], stood on the Galgenberg. Two mortars were in front of the Capucin cloister.

In addition to the above, two small batteries were erected on the island which had been retaken by General Field-Marshal-Lieutenant von Hunoldstein, in order to command the town on the fourth side, *i. e.* that of the water gate on the Danube. This island, which has since been swept away, lay directly opposite to the Danube side of Krems.

Altogether there were then some fifty battery [siege] pieces and Karthaunen and ten mortars in active work against the town. A heavy fire was maintained on both sides. The besiegers, it is true, had soon battered down the battlements of the town-walls and several of the little square fortress-towers, yet they also received much damage from the unceasing fire from the town. It was, therefore, the next object to command the town from the near hill-slopes. Great difficulties had to be contended against in getting up the cannon over the dreadfully cut up clay-ground, and since horses could not be used for the purpose, 800 (464) musketeers were harnessed in order to pull up one piece after the other. [Calculating 800 men at a tractile power of 175 pounds each, they could draw 120,000 pounds, and taking one horse at a tractile power of 1200 pounds, these 800 men exercised the draught force of 100 horses. W. P. W.] After that, wearying as it was, they had thus occupied the heights, the siege guns commanded the whole town, which now, fully overtopped, was exposed to their fire. At the north-east side of the town, at its highest fortified point, there arose a massive (*mächtiger*) round-tower with an outstanding machicoulis gallery (*vorgeschobener Zinnen-Gallerie*), called the "*Lueg ins Land*." Its walls were said to have been of extraordinary strength, according to accounts, probably exaggerated, five to six Klafter (fathoms, 30–40 feet) in thickness. Lundidh had surrounded this tower with double entrenchments, and stored it with great supplies of food and ammunition, intending here to hold out to the uttermost, even if he had to give up the town. This tower was, of course, the principal objective of the besiegers, and Colonel de Souches had, immediately on his arrival, advised the opening of a mine under it. Meantime, a messenger had been captured with dispatches, from which it appeared that the Swedish garrison of Korneuburg proposed, at an early date, to make a diversion in favor of that in Krems. In fact, the garrison of Krems sent some messengers with letters to the commandant of Korneuburg and to the Swedish head-quarters, urgently asking for relief. These letters, hidden in a loaf of bread, reached Korneuburg, but the answer of the commandant of Korneuburg was given to the messenger concealed in a hollow stick. The messenger on the road fell in with some imperial troopers who required that he should show them their way. On his refusing to do so and deporting himself obstinately, the troopers seized the stick and cudgelled him thoroughly with it. The stick broke in two and the letters fell out. When the besiegers ascertained the contents of these letters, the town was bombarded with such renewed energy that directly twelve houses burst into flames. Notwithstanding this, the besieged made a daring sally and dragged back many prisoners into the town. On this, de Souches, who, as has been said, counted very much on the good effects from laying mines, caused such to be laid against the fortifications at three places.

The siege guns, distributed in twelve batteries, had now kept up an almost unceasing fire the whole day and night of the 4th of May, and on the 5th of May, up to 2 P. M. Already two breaches had been established, one near the Vienna-gate, the other, and greater, between the Wächter-gate and the "*Lueg ins Land*." Yet the besieged endeavored, with fiery energy, to remedy the breaches by forming extemporized retrenchments (Abschnitte).

NOTE.—Abschnitte (*Reduit, Retirade, Coupure*) are those parapets and ditches, or with fascines, gabions, sandbags, &c.,

hastily constructed barricades which the besieged erect at any part of the bastions, outworks, &c., which have been thrown down by mines or battering. They thus obtain a fresh breastwork, and hinder the progress (pressing in) of the besieger. For this object, such places are also, according to circumstances, strengthened by palisades, and so-called paltraps, or crows-foots (Wurfeisen, Fussangeln, Chaussetrapes, Murex vel Tribulus ferreus) are thrown about outside. These are irons [caltrops] with, generally, four points, so arranged that, however it falls, one point projects upwards.

[An Abschnitt may be original, not extemporized.—W. P. W.]

(465) When, however, at last, the great square tower at the Vienna-gate gradually fell, the advanced works at that place, as also the ravelin at the Steiner-gate had been set on fire and destroyed, the mighty "*Lueg ins Land*" battered down, and then a great breach made above the Steiner-gate, such as could not be "retrenched;" when, on the part of the besieged, no relief could be well reckoned on—then, at last, they had to abandon all hope of further defense, and negotiations were begun. Puchheim demanded by a drummer a surrender at discretion. The Swedes declared they had rather die than surrender unconditionally. ☞ The heroic demeanor of the Swedes throughout the siege, and their now unmistakable strength of resolution, could not but fill the conqueror with respect—and, at once, hostages were exchanged, and honorable terms were treated of. ☜ Finally, it was agreed that the Swedish commandant, with that part of his troops who had never been in the Imperial service, should march out with flying colors, bag and baggage, arms and armor (*Ober- und Untergewehr*) and with muskets, pikes and sidearms, and should be escorted to the Swedish headquarters at Gross Glogau in Silesia. Consequently, the heroic Lieutenant-Colonel Lundidh, with 150 Swedes, marched, on the 6th of May, out of the town, their brave defense of which during a full month deserves, from a military point of view, the highest, all possible credit. That part of the garrison (250 men) who had formerly been in the Imperial service, remained behind.

(465, 466) NOTE.—1. In the *Theatrum Europæum* (v. 1068) is a neat bird's-eye view. 2. Ground plan (*Situations-plan*) of Krems at its capture, by Franz Pironi. 3. An entirely independent but coinciding ground plan, by Eusebius Mayr.

(466) The Imperial troops at once moved into the town, where they found notable supplies of food and ammunition. Yet, Krems, which had been occupied by the Swedes since the 31st of March, 1645, and through this time had suffered all the evils of a hostile occupation, presented a pitiable appearance. The fortifications were ruined, the houses unroofed, and many of them terribly torn

by shot; 12 of them completely burned down. Including these last, of the 308 houses of the town, 111 must have been torn down, 18 remained uninhabited, and only 179 were in good condition and used as dwellings. 500 florins were paid out as a reward to Puchheim's artillery officers, who had more especially contributed to the recapture of the town. As regarded the war expenses, however, there arose a great contest between the towns of Krems and Stein, since Stein obstinately refused any contribution toward them.

The recapture of Krems was an event of marked moral effect in the scale of Imperial success. After a year filled with lamentable losses, at last once more a token of power on the soil of Lower Austria could not but revive, with fresh vigor, throughout a wide circle, HOPE, long absent or frightened away, into renewed energy.

(476) Torstenson closed, in the autumn of 1646, with the taking of Leitmeritz, his career as military commander in the field; after that he had already, at the commencement of the year, on account of the increase of his sickness, most urgently prayed the Queen [of Sweden] for liberty to lay down his command. Finally, on the 28th April, 1646, the Queen [Christina] filled out the plenary commission for Torstenson's successor, already long before prepared or educated up to the position, Charles Gustavus Wrangel, now Field Marshal [to enjoy the weight of sufficient rank.] ☞ *Still, the latter,* ACCORDING TO HIS INSTRUCTIONS, *undertook nothing of importance, so long as Torstenson remained in Germany, without Torstenson's advice. Those hostile to the Swedes were in exstacies over the departure of the dreaded Commander-in-Chief, Torstenson, and reckoned his removal equivalent to the loss of ten thousand men by the Swedes* [the estimate of David by his people (II. Kings xviii. 3), equivalent, when men of might had grown so scarce, to the elimination of an army. When Tilly, in April, 1631, threw 8,000 to 10,000 chosen veteran troops, horse and foot, into Frankfort-on-the-Oder, General Mitchell, an able military critic (W. 198), remarks that such a force was "an army rather than a garrison." In fact, 8,000 to 10,000 highly disciplined, seasoned soldiers constituted an army throughout the greater part of the Thirty Years' War. Another military writer styled this garrison of Frankfort, "an army corps," a term and organization which does not date back further than 1805, and represents a force usually equal to a respectable army. Gustavus Adolphus landed in Germany with only 13,000 men, and his whole force on German soil scarcely numbered 20,000. With these he had to meet immediately quadruple his strength, old soldiers, in fortresses and fortified

towns and positions. [Gfrorer (529) estimates that Gustavus had 20,000 to meet 160,000.] But, then, the Swedes, officers and men, were without equals and, after Gustavus, the greatest man undoubtedly was TORSTENSON.

☞ Reader, remember, all the praise of Torstenson and the Swedes emanates from the pen of an Austrian, whose country was more thoroughly subjected by Torstenson than by any previous commander. Notwithstanding the influence of natural bias, this author, Feil, is compelled to concede to this enemy the highest possible capacity and superlative courage as a Soldier, and chivalric magnanimity and compassionate generosity as a Man.

---

## A HERO OF THE SEVENTEENTH CENTURY.

"Om denna lifclens ara
Europa hapen an hat evigt vittne bara."
SVENSKA FRIHERRN.

["To (Marshal Leonard Tostenson's) this hero's glory
Europe aghast, e'erlasting witness bears in story."]

From *The Volunteer*, Vol. I., No. 1, 1860. By J. WATTS DE PEYSTER.

---

This is an attempt to portray the character and achievements of one of the most perfect men who have ever illustrated the possibilities of our kind ; great as a soldier, general, specialist, organizer, administrator, diplomatist, patron of the arts—in fact as an exemplar in every direction whither patriotism and duty or intellect led ; a crippled invalid endowed by will-power with all the attributes of strength ; a servant of the state whose abilities made him indispensable to his government and country, ever seeking the repose necessary to his infirmities, yet from youth to prime, when he perished a victim to his maladies, to the absolute necessity of crises and to existing circumstances ; pure as a man ; as remarkable for his virtues, which render the family circle perfectly happy, as for that other higher grade of virtues which elevate the public servant into the restricted class which ordinary humanity recognize as superhuman in their general superiority to the weaknesses and faults of their species. He has been styled "the modern Hannibal," on account of his superlative stratagems or strategy, without having a tinge of that bitterness and littleness which degrades those gifts into mere savage cunning. He possessed every characteristic of a great captain, but, while he exhibited all the qualities which made the noble and extraordinary Carthaginian the grandest exemplar of a patriotic leader, the pilot of a state and consummate commander of men, he was not blemished by a single one of the defects attributed by the jealousy, malice and hatred, engendered by fear of enemies, to that victorious Punic general, recognized in all ages and by the best judges as the most wonderful of military chieftains and civil administrators. Moreover, Torstenson enjoyed the exceptional honor of being able, at a period when time and toleration had divested even extraordinary outrages and crimes of surprise and horror—even after two decades of unrestrained military license and fast and faster developing devilment—(witness Wrangel, Piccolomini, even in 1648)—of exerting an influence sufficient to humanize hitherto inhuman war. As Psalm lxxvi. 10, declares, Torstenson—to whose thoughts the language and admonitions of Scripture was ever present—under God, made it so that " Surely the wrath of man shall praise Thee, *the remainder of wrath* shalt Thou restrain."

The people of the present era, more particularly the people of the United States, are too prone to believe that recent events are in reality greater and grander than those more remote. Thus the fame of Napoleon eclipsed that of Frederic the Great, just as the latter in his day overshadowed the exemplary men through whom modern war had a new birth, and by whom the tactics of the Romans, almost superhuman in their simple efficacy, were adapted to fire-arms; and wings, indeed, were lent to the thunder-bolts of war—artillery. Nor are the seamen of the present day as enterprising as those who lived contemporaneous with the new birth of naval warfare. Had the men who almost attained the North Pole (at all events approached as near, if not nearer to it, than subsequent Arctic navigators) known of the power of steam in the marine engine, the tri-color of Holland would have floated, two centuries ago, from the northern extremity of the axis of this globe. While the sailors of to-day go down to the sea in great ships, the sailors of two centuries since ventured amid the Arctic ice, fought fleet to fleet within the Arctic circle, circumnavigated the globe, had their " River Fights " and their " Bay Fights," founded and subverted empires, in single vessels and in squadrons of " fly-boats " scarcely larger than the tenders of our navy.

We Americans have just witnessed and lived through a great civil war which lasted four years, a "war of emancipation," for the liberation of an inferior colored race from physical slavery, which, in some respects, was the grandest conflict for progress ever brought to a successful termination in so short a period and at so little cost of suffering. Still there was a greater conflict for the emancipation of the white race inaugurated two hundred and sixty-seven years ago (1618-48); which, instead of four years, lasted thirty years. This conflict almost depopulated some of the most thickly peopled districts of Middle Europe, and converted all the lands between the Oder and the Rhine, the Baltic and the Danube, into one blood-soaked battlefield and left it strewed with corpses, ruins and ashes. During these thirty years massacres occurred, perpetrated by veteran soldiers, under the eyes of generals deemed humane for the era, which rivaled the horrors of Fort Pillow and Leavenworth, and wholesale atrocities were permitted which equalled the calculated barbarity of Belle Isle and Andersonville. In one respect, however, the hordes of disciplined savages of the Thirty Years' War exceeded in horrors the partisans of the South during the Slaveholders' Rebellion. As far as regarded the feebler sex and non-combatants, the worst fiends of hell seemed let loose upon the earth, and wholesale rape, refined torture and protracted misery, which, to escape, made death a boon, were of daily occurrence, in multitudinous cases connived at by the most elevated, applied by the most liberal, and employed as measures of war by men who, in their private lives, were as exemplary as can be, consistent with bigotry, politics and statecraft.

Of the three of the four great powers who, in fact, fought out and decided this protracted conflict, the only one which displayed any moderation was Sweden, the champion of free thought, which acted the same part in the bloody drama, 1618-1648, as the Union armies, 1861-1865. The Swede, a foreigner in the land, was an angel of light as compared with the German, demons of darkness towards Germans, or the barbarous tribes enlisted against Germans by the House of Austria, or even to the French, under the rule of a sagacious churchman. Nor did these atrocities terminate with the monster—the Thirty Year's War—which gave them birth. They continued to be tolerated as long as the commanders, who first permitted and their pupils survived. Reversing the order of consideration, to any student of history it will be sufficient to name a few atrocities, which characterize their authors, or those who are responsible for them. The ravage of the Palatinate, in 1674 (repeated in 1693 by his apt scholar, Melac), was the work of Turenne. He converted the most fertile district of Germany into a desert. This was foreign land to France, on the eastern bank of the Rhine, and he coolly justified it on the plea of military expediency. The author of "The Army of the Potomac" dared to couple, in the same sentence, Turenne's fiendish desolation of the Palatinate with Sheridan's justifiable destruction in the Shenandoah Valley. Ignorance can be the only excuse. The action of the Union general, as compared to that of the French marshal, was as the burning of a storehouse to the conflagration of a building filled with helpless innocents. Nor was the cold-blooded Turenne contented with the woe wrought to a foreign enemy. Had he not been overruled by superior authority, his plan was to lay waste the territory on the French side of the Rhine, that, in case of invasion, it would afford neither shelter nor subsistence to a military force. To justify the parallel, Sheridan must have destroyed every town and village in the blooming valley south of the Potomac, have driven the inhabitants into the fields to die of cold and starvation, and have left utter desolation behind him, and then have retired into Maryland, with the desire and the will to convert its flourishing uplands and teeming lowlands into the same lamentable condition to which he had consigned the opposite shore. Notwithstanding, Turenne has been held up as a model of virtue.

The Sack of Magdeburg, 1631, which transmuted a flourishing and happy city into a heap of ruins and cinders, soaked with blood and piled with corpses, rests upon the soul of Tilly, who made it his boast that no such desolation had occurred since the fall of Troy.

The "Pasewalk and Penkum Slaughter," a pandemonium of pillage, violation, murder and indecency, was the vaunted exploit of Goetz, another Imperial commander, and to go on and cite the various woes accumulated upon Germans by Germans, would fill a volume with horrors and would prove acceptable lessons of cruelty to the Indians of the West. No Comanche or Arrapahoe, no Sioux, ever imagined greater refinement or malignity in the infliction of suffering. In the Sack of Piseck, in 1620, by the Austrian Cossacks, the town was swept as clean as that of Beziers, in 1208. Friend and foe fared alike and a populous town became a reeking shambles; the last act after the perpetration of crimes against property and virtue. In many instances human beings were slaughtered for food, comrades fed on comrades, neighbors on neighbors, and even the graves were robbed of their dead to prolong existence in the living. Nor did the judges, with their scaffolds and their instruments of torture, display less energy than the Imperial commanders and their soldiers. Amid this scene of universal and diabolical oppression, as regarded Middle Europe, a succession of heroes commanded the Swedish armies, who, as scientific generals, have never been surpassed, if ever they have been equalled. Taken together, the god-like Gustavus, the truly virtuous Horn, the chivalric Bernard of Saxe-Weimar, Baner, "the second Gustavus," until the Saxon Elector's treachery overthrew his equanimity, and the "inimitable Torstenson," the last, "under Sweden's crown, Sweden's greatest commander," in their joint career of victory, they have never been approached, when results, as contrasted with means, are taken into the calculation and considered in the parallel between them and other commanders. They made genius compensate for inferiority of numbers and the resources of their minds discovered means of supply for their own troops in the midst of an utterly impoverished country, in which more than one army opposed to them perished utterly from the face of the earth, and every antagonist saw his forces depleted by nakedness and famine, consequent indiscipline and multiform disease, inseparable from such conditions.* Compared to Turenne, to Tilly and his coadjutors, to Wallenstein's lieutenants, often to Wallenstein himself, to Bucquoy, Dampierre, Goetz, Holk, Melander in Hesse, and a score of others, these five Swedish leaders were angels. As a model of a Christian commander-in-chief, Gustavus is an example for all time. In the sanctity of his character it is scarcely possible to find his parallel in the records of war. Nor did his favorite pupil, TORSTENSON, fall far short of him in god-like virtues. Gen. von Hardegg justly remarks: "Torstenson possessed, in addition to his great talents as a soldier and a statesman [general, executive and administrator, civil and military, diplomatist, scientist, connoisseur, &c.] a highly cultivated mind, an exquisite heart and a lofty sense of honor. In courage, in spirit of enterprise and perseverance, he towered, in spite of his body shattered by diseases, above all his associates of equal rank. He not only understood how to establish and maintain discipline, but to put an end to the barbarities of the soldiery and absolutely make them humane." To this, Hormayer, the Austrian historiographer, adds, and Feil, as seen page 28 *supra*, corroborates, that even when thundering at the gates of Vienna, after Janikau, Torstenson's " chivalric greatness of soul" (ritterliche Edelmuth), so won for him the esteem of the Emperor, Ferdinand III., that it was acknowledged by elegant courtesies on the part of the sovereign whose armies had just been routed, and whose capital was being insulted with cannon shot. Ferdinand even permitted Torstenson to send officers into Vienna to purchase whatsoever might be agreeable to his wife, Beata de la Gardie, who accompanied her

* The more a critic, competent to judge, investigates the career of McClellan and his immediate following or favorites and successors, and compares their chances and conduct with those of such men as Torstenson, the more convinced he will become that, in respect to the discharge of high offices with which the leader and his friends were invested, all were, in degree, more or less utter failures. Without imputing motives or considering causes, they accomplished so little with the means at their disposal that it would be difficult to find a parallel to such shortcomings, involving the influence of men of military education and experience upon national efforts, in trustworthy records of the operations of war. This opinion may be attributed to prejudice and to political bias, but does not come from these. It is the result of solemn conviction, after a long course of study throughout more than an ordinary lifetime, deep reflection and a careful comparison with the acts of living and dead generals in high commands, at home and abroad, for a period of about three hundred years; that is, since the military renaissance, or the development of modern war. Even when tried by the touchstone of the deeds done by the ruthless chiefs of Napoleon, the narrative of the careers under consideration resembles rather the rambling designs developed by the smoke of lamps or torches, in the hands of explorers, upon the roof of a cavern, than the effects of the sunlight awakening and developing beauty and life.

husband in all his later campaigns, was present in the battles he delivered, and at Janikau was captured by the Bavarians under the renowned trooper Werth, and actually recaptured through a charge led by her heroic crippled husband.

Perhaps, considering the interval of seven years, between their supreme commands, which offered more than ample time for utter deterioration, Torstenson rose to an equal, if not an even more remarkable grandeur of soul, than his master. Gustavus led into the empire an army composed almost entirely of his native Swedes, and of Scotch and English formed under his own eye—religiously educated, thoroughly disciplined. God-fearing men. Torstenson received control of an army, demoralized by eight years of diabolical warfare—mutinous men, commanded, too often, by mutinous, if not traitorous, officers, and yet his dignity, his influence, his " lion-hearted" royalty of demeanor and of mind, his fearless assumption of every possible responsibility, his energy, enabled him to convert that disorganized mass into a perfect machine, and deprived war of the greater part of its terrors as regarded non-combatants.

Only one act inconsistent with his character blemishes the record of his otherwise stainless career, and even this one rests upon only a single authority, equivalent to a paragraph in an illustrated newspaper, which originated, perhaps, in the spite of an army correspondent who had not been treated with the deference he expected or demanded.

The wonderful improvements and executive application of modern artillery, attributed to Gustavus, is more than probably due, in its organized efficiency, to Torstenson. At all events, he so well knew how to dispose of it along his front of battle, that, when the cruelest diseases which flesh is heir to compelled him to lay down his command, the enemy rejoiced, hoping that the Swedish cannon, which had so often "compelled victory," were now silenced, and calculated his withdrawal as equivalent to the diminution of his army by the loss of at least ten thousand men, equal to a modern army corps, or, as estimated at the period in which he shone, to an army, In his combination of tactics and gunnery he contributed as much as his master to the winning of the decisive victory of Leipzig, in 1631, and in his union of engineering and artillery he is credited with a feat, the bridging of the Lech, in 1632, the success of which was entirely owing to his consummate handling of his guns, when field artillery was in its infancy. In this he has left a model which may be imitated, but cannot be surpassed.

As a commander of cavalry, Torstenson—a victim to gravel and to gout, so excruciating that he had to be carried, as a rule,

# PLANS

OF

# NINE OF THE MOST IMPORTANT AND DECISIVE
# BATTLES,

AND OF

## THE ONE MOST FAMOUS SIEGE

OF THE

# THIRTY YEARS WAR,

with his troops in a litter—performed one exploit, which, if he had never achieved another, would place him in the same rank with Frederick's Seydlitz and Ziethen, and as far ahead of Murat as our Sheridan towers above ordinary pretenders to the power of handling large bodies of horse. On the occasion alluded to, he had out-manœuvred General Gallas, intrusted with superior forces for his destruction, forced him, simply by the judicious selection of commanding positions, as Turenne admitted with admiration and astonishment, to evacuate one strong post after another, and finally shut him up in the fortress of Magdeburg. It soon became a question of escape or starvation, and one midnight, 21st November, 1644, the Saxo-Imperial cavalry broke out, got a good start and were off. Advised of the movement by his scouts, Torstenson gathered up his own horse, launched forth in pursuit, and by a circuitous route, through Wittenberg, intercepted them at the village of Niemeck, near (N. W. of) Juterbock, where, on the 23d, he fell upon them, crushed them, and captured the greater part (over four thousand men), together with General Enkefort and several colonels, nor would even the smallest remnant have escaped, had not the Swedish cavalry horses been completely exhausted, having made fifteen German (over sixty, perhaps seventy-five English) miles on "one fodder"—a single feed.

As a general on the field of action, his victories were annihilating. That at Breitenfeld, in 1642, and that of Janikau, in 1645, were more like the Nashville of Thomas, in 1864, than any other battle of our civil war. In both cases an army was eliminated from the war problem by simple practical-strategy. Without a single engagement he rubbed out another army in 1644. In his whole career as generalissimo he made but one failure, the siege of Brunn, and that was not due to any shortcoming on his part, but to the treason of his ally, Racogzy, Prince of Transylvania, and to pestilence imported with the latter's barbarous hordes.* Had this place fallen, the fate of Austria

---

*MILITARY DISEASES.—The most terrible enemy to troops in changing quarters for the field, is disease in different forms, consequent upon a mutation of mode of life, rain or snow, cold, different forms of nourishment, unaccustomed fatigue, deprivation of sleep, &c. The third of the effective troops perish in consequence.

"The King of Prussia lost in the campaign of 1778 more men by sickness and desertion than in three years of campaigns of the preceding Seven Years' War. Dysentery carried of the pick of his soldiers (10,000 it is said). The cause of this malady must be attributed to the bad food and severe weather to which the Prussian armies were subjected in Bohemia. It is curious that the French on board the squadron of D'Ovillers experienced the same disastrous results. "Torstenson before Brunn, Ibid., p. iv. 15, 26, note 42, 44, xxxvii., soldiers' perception, 74,

would have been settled. Austrian authors concede this. The failure was due to the base desertion of an allied contingent; to the over-indulgence of his own troops in unripe fruit, and continued wet weather in a malarious country at the worst season of the year. So fatal had been the malaria that he lost thousands of veterans, the kernel or kidney of the wheat, of the victorious survivors of Janikau, and it is stated that two regiments disappeared from the muster-rolls of his army, " cut off, not almost, but to a single man." As an administrator, as a commissary, as a quartermaster, and in every branch of Logistics, which is the comprehensive art of moving and supplying armies, his success was an enigma to the writers of his own day and is one of the incomprehensible marvels which still puzzle the acutest military critics. The Prince de Ligne, in his "Commentaries," admits the fact. His were the principles of Gustavus Adolphus, as well as of Frederic the Great, that war must be made to sustain war, as they had been those of Hannibal, of Philip of Macedon, of Augustus the first, Emperor of Rome, and of Napoleon Bonaparte.

He fed his men and his horses in the midst of districts swept far and wide by the besom of destruction, and he moved his armies over roads declared impracticable, and his trains and artillery over routes never before traversed by any kind of vehicle. Unequalled in his plan of operations, he could do what neither Frederic nor Napoleon ever did accomplish successfully. In his sick chamber he planned out campaigns which his successors had only to follow to succeed. What Halleck dreamed he was equal to, and utterly failed in doing, with the aid of steamboats, railroads and electric telegraphs, Torstenson accomplished through his single and simple genius. What von Moltke, with all the appliances of every modern science, executed in 1866 and 1870-1, for the humiliation of Austria and France, Torstenson carried out, 1645-1648, through couriers and post-horses. "Inimitable" as a general, and especially in the handling of troops, this invalid, who scarcely knew a respite from pain, who besought his government, as the greatest boon they could accord him, to relieve him from his command and send him a successor, this martyr to disease, surpassed every general, before or since, in the rapidity of his marches. His soldiers styled him " the Lightning," and history has united the epithet inseparably with his name. Like an eagle, crowned with victory, bearing thunderbolts in his talons and destruction in his beak, he flew from one extremity of Middle Europe to the other,

---

note 9, An anonymous Prussian Work, styled "Grand Tactics, particularly a Narrative of the Campaign of 1778 in Bohemia." Potsdam, 1780.

now menacing Vienna, then threatening Copenhagen, and, then again, shaking the Imperial capital with the explosions of his artillery. He realized Pope's promises—in reality Stanton's expression—to "make his headquarters in the saddle." His headquarters were either there or in his litter. He ignored bases of supply and lines of communication; he moved free over the country, as a bird of prey through the air, stooping to the "banquet of swords," as the "serpent destroyer," of South Africa, upon the most venomous reptiles, to slay, to rend, and to enjoy. He lived off the country, he inaugurated the system, according to an organized system (attributed erroneously to Napoleon), of making war supply war. He took by force what he needed, and yet he never lost the love of the people from whom he was forced to take, for he tempered judgment with mercy, and severity with the benignity of a power that chastises to preserve. He rolled his war-cloud upon the toe; his thunder terrified, his lightning scathed, and his winds scattered, and then he assembled his army "in battaglia" and rendered to the God of battles the thanksgiving which he felt were due to Him for triumphs accorded and for blessings vouchsafed.

His march of five hundred miles across Germany, at the worst season of the year, in the autumn of 1643, was an undertaking, in comparison to which Sherman's march from Atlanta to the sea might be set down as a peaceful pedestrian tour or a grand picnic. In this he developed, if he did not originate the idea, of "mounted infantry," for he swept the country of its horses, to transport his foot with the celerity of cavalry. His present of conquered continental Denmark to his crown, as a New Year's offering, was as superior to the Christmas gift of Savannah to our nation, as Sherman's preceding movements in Georgia and succeeding operations in the Carolinas were as inferior to Torstenson's winged expeditions from Moravia to the Ore Sound, and thence back, through regular armies of outnumbering forces, from the Eider across the Ore Mountains to the Danube. Neither Gustavus, nor Frederic, nor Bonaparte, accomplished anything like equal results with the legs of their soldiers, and as to the use of their arms, Breitenfeld can compare with the Leipsic of Gustavus; Jankau with any victory of Frederic, even Rossbach or Leuthen (Lissa), marvels considered by experts as without parallels; Wittstock with Austerlitz or Jena. Finally, Bonaparte's passage of the Alps, at the finest season of the year, with every advantage derivable from means and their scientific application, unresisted, is not worthy to be named in the same sentence with Torstenson's transit over the Ore Mountains, under difficulties incalculably greater, at the rudest season of the year, when the valleys were filled, and the mountains covered with the snows of winter, when the impetuous torrents and rivers, too swift for the cold to curb or to chain their impetuous currents, rolled, freighted with fields and blocks of ice. Thus the Swedes, cut off from base, allies and succor, had to conquer nature in her wildest form, and enemies on every side, as they flew to a victory as important as Marengo, in order to relieve their Genoa (Olmutz) which they succeeded in doing, and Napoleon did not.

Torstenson, in addition to his military superiority, was a friend and patron of the arts and sciences, and his ability as a diplomatist, statesman and civil executive, was in no measure behind that generalship which made all Germany as open to him, as if it had been his ample field for manœuvre. He made every Elector, working in with the Imperial interest, the Empire, Austria, and its capital, Vienna, tremble. Had his ally, Racogzy, been trustworthy Vienna must have fallen, and witnessed in the XVIIth century the triumphal possession of a Swede, as in the the XIXth the victorious entry of the Corsican. He humbled the king of Denmark, before his day the rival of Sweden; he made Poland crouch, he avenged Gustavus, he disarmed two Electors, of Saxony and of Brandenburg, and converted them from more or less bitter enemies into paralyzed neutrals if not absolute friends, and, *in summa*, he filled the measure of Swedish glory (1).

A few anecdotes, selected at large from his biography, will illustrate the character of Torstenson better than the panegyrics which seek to glorify the everyday incidents in the lives of some prominent individuals deemed exceedingly great by the more or less ignorant and prejudiced world at large.

Voltaire remarked that, " in all Europe, he (Conde or d'Enghien) and the Swede Torstenson alone, possessed at the age of twenty years that genius which could well pass for matured experience." This corroborates the opinion of the celebrated Swedish historian, Puffendorf, " He (Gustavus Adolphus), Conde and his own disciple, Torstenson, were the only three generals who, at twenty years of age, showed to the (European) public all the effects of long experience." Octavius Cæsar was another.

Macaulay, in two of his brilliant essays, alludes to " great captains whose precocious and self-taught military skill resembled intuition." He then cites Conde, Clive and Napoleon as examples. With all his ability and marvellous memory Macaulay was evidently ignorant of military history, in that he omitted several more striking examples—Hannibal, Gustavus Adolphus and Torstenson, and the list might be greatly extended. In his essay on Clive, he shows much more knowledge of the subject.

"Nor must we forget that he (Clive) was only twenty-five years old when he approved himself ripe for military command. This is a rare, if not a singular distinction. [Not so.] It is true that Alexander, Conde and Charles XII. won great battles at a still earlier age; but these princes were surrounded by veteran generals of distinguished skill, to whose suggestions must be attributed the victories of the Granicus, of Rocroi and of Narva. Clive, an inexperienced youth, had yet more experience than any of those who served under him. He had to form himself, to form his officers and to form his army. The only man, as far as we recollect [modest], who, at an equally early age, ever gave equal proof of talents for war, was Napoleon Bonaparte."

In the sentence in which he justly ascribes the victories of Alexander, Conde and Charles XII. to the experienced officers by whom they were surrounded, he exactly hits the mark, and it is still more pertinent to the case of Napoleon, who, through a great error—showing how little he knew of the subject under consideration—Macaulay makes an exception, whereas he was an example of the rule cited. If ever a man owed his success to an army which he did not make, and to lieutenants who rose as quickly as he did, it was Napoleon. In the case of Conde, Rocroi was due to Gassion and to Sirot, who had been formed in the school of Gustavus. To institute a comparison between Clive and Torstenson is just. Both were necessities of the moment and the occasion. Both were indispensabilities. Before he was eighteen Torstenson had given ample proof that he had the most comprehensive idea of generalship; at twenty-two or three he had saved a decisive battle—just about the age at which Clive had approved himself ripe for military command;" at twenty-seven he was at the head of the Swedish artillery and already famous; and at twenty-nine, while a prisoner, Gustavus had urged upon Oxenstiern his ransom at any price, "as THE man fit to command THE WHOLE, or ANY army." Again, when Baner died, he bequeathed his army, the sole hope and stay of Sweden, to the bed-ridden cripple, Torstenson, as the only man competent to command it; and that cripple rose from his couch of agony as the sole individual capable of making the end of the Thirty Years' War a certain success for his country. All the precocious generals, so credited, from Lucullus down to the Crown Prince of Prussia, in 1870, were dry-nursed; Torstenson dry-nursed his nurses.

Torstenson's exhibition of instinctive military perception must have occurred during or prior to the Riga campaign, in August–September, 1621, and *may* have happened [although it is not likely] in one of the Russian wars ended by the Peace of Stolbova (Stolba), 27th February, 1617. Torstenson was born 17th August, 1603; in 1618 he became the king's page, or "Squire of the Chamber; in 1621 he was the king's armor-bearer, a position of the highest trust; in 1621, when he came of age, he was girded with a sword, according to the old Swedish custom, on attaining majority worthily; and in 1625 he was cornet and the standard or battle-flag of the royal mounted body-guard was entrusted to him, to which reference will be made in quoting the enthusiastic praise of Gustavus III. before the Royal Swedish Academy. In 1630, when his king invaded Germany, such was his celebrity and capacity, he was already, at 27, according to Puffendorf, Grand-Master of the Artillery, and *at once*, in the Swedish army, made it the arm which it has since become in all the military organizations of the world.

A more recent Swedish historian, Fryxell, in his "Gustavus; Prepared for the Instruction of Youth," presents the anecdote referred to, thus: During an engagement in this Riga campaign 1621, the king dispatched him [Torstenson, his page, acting as aide] with verbal orders to one of his colonels, an officer, even now, in Europe, enjoying a higher command than one of our brigadiers, and 250 years ago holding a still more important relative position, for colonels were sometimes selected to command, not only generals, but armies. As Torstenson rode along he discovered that the enemy had made a change in his dispositions, and that the movement prescribed by the orders he bore would be dangerous to the Swedish troops affected by it. Accordingly, instead of delivering the king's order, he substituted directions of his own in the king's name. When, on his return, he reported to the king, Gustavus bade him ride swiftly back again with new orders based on the enemy's change of position, and charged him with directions exactly equivalent to those which Torstenson himself had given on his own responsibility. Torstenson thereupon begged pardon, and confessed what he had done. Gustavus looked on him and said, smiling, "Torstenson, you are better fitted for a commander than for a page." According to Schiller, Gustavus menaced him with his hand, with these words, "Torstenson, that might have cost you your life; but I see in you a good general." That night he was commanded to sit at the king's side at the supper table and from that hour he enjoyed the king's friendship and particular attention.

In spite of all the enthusiasm of Swedish writers in favor of the performances of their troops on the field of Wallhoff, made famous by the fact that there modern infantry first really asserted itself and its inherent strength against excellent cavalry, it would appear that, after all, it was not the easy victory claimed; and the Swedish horsemen were disordered and had to be rallied by the young hero, Torstenson. If such had not been the case, is it probable Gustavus III., in his " Royal Utterance," his " Eulogy of Torstenson," would have exclaimed. "*Fields of Wallhoff!* you can bear testimony to Torstenson's valor! The enemy driven off, *the soldiery once more gathered around the Life-Banner*, victory given to Gustavus Adolphus. All indications of what Torstenson some day will be. His perspicacity, his valor, lead him soon to the chief command. * * Torstenson returns to his native land, where he has scarcely arrived, when Gustavus Adolphus entrusts him with the chief command of the artillery. A larger field opens up to the hero ; a field on which the eyes of contemporaries and of posterity will be fixed."

Scrutinize the conception, inception and connection of all his battles. They are masterpieces. How superlative his grand tactics at Leipsic, 1642 (2), his manœuvres to give himself full room and entice his adversaries into an arena from which there was no escape, except as ruined fugitives. Is it strange that the medal struck in honor of this victory bore the inscription, " *It is believed, Leipsic, that* NOW *thou knowest the courage of Torstenson.*" With what acuteness he beguiled the crafty Gallas, who was too cunning even for the astute Wallenstein, and with what strategem and strategy he gradually rubbed out the Imperial forces sent under that general to trap or crush him in Holstein, in 1644; with what energy and celerity he pursued the Saxon cavalry and captured or utterly destroyed it at Niemeck (3). The cold-blooded Turenne flames up, for the nonce, into admiration and applause. Then at Janikau (4), what consummate perception of the character of his adversaries and of the ground. That was a battle ! He saw the key-point as a sempstress the eye of her needle, and drew through the thread, doubled and knotted it and sewed up the allies, in spite of the supernatural aid promised the Kaiser in a dream. This battle was a perfect example of the proper application of the Three Arms combined.

Moreover, he never broke his word, and better, he never parleyed when he intended destruction ; with him there was no cruel keeping the promise to the ear and breaking it to the hope. It was *Ein Mann—ein Wort* ("One man, one word"). Sir James Turner, Knight, in his " Pallas Armata," Chap. XXVI., observes, " if accidentally a Garrison have provoked the Besieger to revenge, it will be more gallantly done to refuse all Parley, discharge all Quarter ; and in the fury [of assault] put all to the Sword, than to kill them in cold blood ; yet it is frequently done. *But* TORSTENSON, *the Swedish Felt-Marshal, did* GENEROUSLY, *when* [in 1644] *he resolved to put a Danish garrison of* 600 *men to the Sword,* who were in a sconce of the Duchy of Holstein, *he refused all Parley or Treaty*, and in the Storm killed them, every man."

Torstenson has often been styled "the modern Hannibal," and, as the unequalled Carthaginian fought and labored and diplomatised to detach from Rome the Socii or Allies, which had been conquered by the Romans, and attach them to himself, Torstenson campaigned and strove to separate from the Imperial cause the princes and the states which had been won over or cajoled by the emperor—who in 1618-48 represented Rome—and convert them into allies of the Swedes. Hannibal, in spite of sixteen glorious campaigns and three transcendent victories, failed at last; Torstenson, in less than four campaigns, through three astonishing triumphs on the battlefield, accomplished what he undertook to do and first laid the sure basis of the peace he lived to see concluded with such glory to his country.

His simple, unexpected advent more than once struck terror into his adversaries. Witness, for example: In 1642, the Imperialists had regained the control in Silesia—a province always a bone of contention until Prussia gulped it down for good—and satisfied their gratuitous cruelty. Piccolomini, that wretch, although a sufficiently good soldier to become a necessity to the Imperial and Roman Catholic party, was besieging Glogau and the place was reduced to the greatest extremity. Torstenson had been so weak that he had to bide his time. "No sooner, however, had [Charles Gustavus] Wrangel arrived with reinforcements from Sweden" ["the junction with the vanguard of Wrangel's corps took place 26th August"], *than Torstenson suddenly* [7th September] *appearing in sight of the Austrian camp, created such an alarm, that, forsaking their standards, the soldiers fled to the neighboring hills with disgraceful precipitation.*"

In the summer of 1643 an incident occurred that makes an American regret that we had not had a Torstenson in command of our armies during our great Civil War; a generalissimo such as he, to deal with generals, who, allowed to interpret orders for themselves, or act, through bias, for a particular chief or ring, or to disobey, or permitted themselves to be gobbled, or their quarters beaten up by surprise, or their commands scattered or captured through their negligence.

The circumstances now to be related afford a better idea of Torstenson's line of judgment than even more important operations. Three Swedish regiments of horse, under Colonels Dobitz and Werner, and Lieut.-Colonel Dobitz, or Dubald, had been sent out to collect contributions. They halted for the night (28th July. 1643) at Tribau, in Northern Moravia. Betrayed by a peasant named Schulmann, they were surprised, under favor of extreme darkness, by two troops of Imperial horse, and completely disorganized. All three colonels and a number of officers and privates were made prisoners. When Torstensou learned of this disgrace to his arms, he was supremely indignant and availed himself of the earliest opportunity to get the captured individuals back into his hands. He would not consent to exchange Imperialist officers, his own captives, for them, deeming it too honorable a method of treating their case. *He bought them back with money, not considering them worthy of being placed on the footing of an equal exchange*—since he deemed them worthless, and no equivalent for good and brave officers. As soon as the three colonels were in his power he hung up Colonel Werner "*incontinenter*," and had Lieut.-Col. Dubald drummed out of his lines with the utmost ignominy. The third, Colonel Dobitz, appears to have been mortally wounded, and so escaped degradation. He spared Lieut.-Col. Dubald's life solely on condition that he never would let a single human being know that he had at any time held a commison under or in any way served the Swedish crown. Then, to show the enemy that this mishap was not due to him, nor to the rank and file, Torstenson himself led a flying column into Silesia, in pursuit of Count B(P)uchheim, who had been sent thither with 1,500 troopers. So ably was the movement planned that the Imperialists were in turn surprised and completely routed at Prerau, near Mostenitz. Of Buckheim's personal suite or staff, two were captured ; likewise two of his horses and the Count got off with difficulty on a third charger. It did not do to trifle with Torstenson !

On the 18th April, 1651, Torstenson died, "and left a most excellent odour of his vertues everywhere, yea, even among his very Enemies themselves." His last words were spoken to his queen and sovereign. In the Royal Place of Tombs, in the Church of the Knights, near his leader, tutor, friend and king, with the obsequies of a monarch, he was laid to rest, amid the thunder of the artillery he had made. There his body—racked by the severest pains—which had never known repose when duty summoned, at length found that rest denied in life, and he sleeps his long, last sleep, canopied by the trophies he had won. There, halved with his glory, he lies, surrounded by the great commanders and the statesmen he had surpassed. A century and a quarter after his decease, when Gustavus the Third, great king, brave soldier, able seaman, eloquent orator, astute statesman and graceful writer, founded the Swedish Academy, he proposed the Eulogy of Torstenson as the subject for one of the first prizes for eloquence. Anonymously, the royal servant of the muses contended for the prize, which was awarded to the unknown but able competitor. This eulogy, published long afterwards among the works of Gustavus III., was found, after thirteen years' search, and forwarded to the writer of this biographical sketch. In the career of the hero, the accomplished speaker had a theme worthy his acknowledged ornate, but manly, style. If the American reader thinks that the writer has drawn upon his imagination in picturing Leonard (or Lennart) Torstenson, he would find that Gustavus III., one hundred and twenty-five years after the hero disappeared from mortal eyes, proclaimed that he had fulfilled everything predicted of him by Gustavus Adolphus, recorded by Swedish historians and testified by friend and foe, winning in life the love and reverence of the Swedish people, enshrining his memory in their hearts.

Finally read the "Summing up of Torstenson," by Baron Philip von Chemnitz, in his history of these campaigns, said to have been supervised or even, in part, dictated, by the famous Chancellor Oxenstiern : "When it was manifest that for weeks together he was compelled to keep his bed and that his limbs were so racked with inexpressible pains that he could neither move hands nor feet and was unable either to mount his horse or maintain himself in his saddle, except with difficulty ; and that he could not sign a letter, but had to leave even that duty to his trusted secretary; nevertheless he had with such fortune and renown led the army and had won so many bloody pitched battles and glorious victories over the enemy, had conquered so many cities, strong places and fortresses, and, in short, to sum up briefly, had so well sustained and held erect the most difficult, yea, the more than difficult, the most extensive work on which the whole of Evangelical Christianity was dependent, then unwilling consent was given him to lay all this aside which he had performed to the greatest satisfaction of his Sovereign Queen, and to return to his Fatherland. There he was received by Queen Christina with extraordinary testimonials of royal graciousness and soon after raised, in acknowledgement of his great and faithful service, to the rank of count and rewarded and enfeoffed with the countship of Ortala, the barony of Worestadh, besides other considerable domains.

If the opinion of the philosopher Solon, that no one can be adjudged to be happy before his end is considered, be accepted as correct, it must be acknowledged that our hero has to be regarded as unusually fortunate, since, to the last, he was held in the highest respect and affection, for a reputation won by deeds and unflecked by a single or by the slightest spot, not only by the highest authorities, but by his sovereign and by his peers, or colleagues, and by the councils and representatives of the Swedish realm, but by every one, noble or simple, of high or low condition, until the end of his life, in 1650, when he died, overcome by infirmities resulting from the tortures which gradually, with greater and greater violence, got the mastery of his forces. Alas, he was not indeed old in days, since he had not fulfilled his 48th year, yet in wisdom distinguished in the highest degree among men, the real grey hair among men, and a spotless life full of virtues and renown, is, after the real old age, old in the great virtues or characteristics which constitute a real hero, and old in mighty illustrious deeds worthy of such a hero!

Nor was the appearance of Torstenson unworthy of his deeds. He was one of the handsomest men of his time. Divest him of his military insignia and his face might be drawn as the type of manly amiability and resolution. Such, at first sight, it certainly would appear. Close study, however, would reveal the dignity and determination which characterized the man and invested him with that influence which rendered him as mighty as a king in his own innate regal power. His waving hair fell over a forehead beneath which shone eyes blazing with sagacity. At a time when all affected extravagance of dress, his own was simple, rich but serviceable. Gracious in countenance, graceful in mien and royal in manners, no wonder that he retained the respect and love of soldiers and citizens, native and foreign, of superiors, inferiors and even of the haughty, distant Turk, the bigot Austrian, the crafty Frank, the supple Saxon and the eccentric Queen Regent of Sweden. Such was the "inimitable Torstenson;" as a man, almost stainless; as a subject, without reproach; as a husband, a model; as a general, unsurpassed; competent in every arm and branch of the service; equal to any occasion; a consistent Christian, and, to sum up all, "an ornament to the human race."

---

Notes.—(1.) "But if the designs of Torstenson (according to Schiller [ever unable to forget he is a German and rise to impartial judgment] 336) were not crowned with all the success which they promised at the commencement, they were, nevertheless, productive of the most important consequences to the Swedish party. Denmark had been compelled to a peace [Brandenburg to a convention], Saxony to a truce, the emperor in the deliberations for a peace offered greater concessions, France became more manageable and Sweden itself bolder and more confident in its bearing towards these two crowns. Having thus nobly performed his duty the author of these advantages retired adorned (crowned) with laurels."

(2.) Comparisons have been instituted between the Leipsic of

Gustavus and the Breitenfeld (or second Leipsic) of Torstenson, but the latter, as the Prussian critic justly observes, ☞ " Fate denied to their [Baner and Torstenson's] illustrious monarch and preceptor such victories as Wittstock [in which Torstenson was second in command to Baner], Breitenfeld and Janikau. ☞ Yea there were even single moments of their lives which surpassed all the successes achieved by Gustavus Adolphus;" and, again, ☞ at Janikau, "sometimes on horseback, sometimes in his litter, the generalissimo was in every spot where the occasion rendered his presence requisite; and thus ☞ the last battle which he won was at the same time the finest of his life; perhaps it is the finest of the whole Thirty Years' War." ☞ " We," adds the Prussian critic, "regret to say that it is one of those battles [for the advancement of the science of war] which, up to the present date, have been least studied." ☞

At the second Leipsic the Swedes occupied almost the very position that the Imperialists did, eleven years previous, and if Tilly had displayed the superior capacity of Torstenson, especially in taking advantage of the ground, Gustavus, according to all mortal calculations, must have been defeated. What is more, the Swedes and Saxons, in 1631, united, were superior to their opponents, whereas; in 1642, the Swedes were inferior in numbers. It may be argued in favor of Gustavus that the Saxons, as a body, were quickly run out, but unmilitary critics forget it takes *time* and exhausts *strength* even to slay and pursue, and, as distinguished generals declare, " time at crises cannot be purchased at hardly any too high a price." Moreover Tilly's troops pursued too far and lost inestimable time in plundering, as the Austrians and their allies, there, as often elsewhere, and as Prince Rupert did, more than once, to the ruin of the cause for which they were supposed to be giving their whole honest support.

The imperial account concedes that in "*quantity and quality*" both armies were equal, but allows that the Swedes were inferior in cavalry. The numbers given by Gindely, 20,000 Swedes and 22,000 Imperialists, cannot be correct. Each general had about 10,000 infantry, but the Imperialists must have had nearly double that number of cavalry. Accurate examinations arrive at the following, as the circumstantial results : That, including artillery, Torstenson marshalled about 22,000 men, which is 2,000 above Gindeley's estimate, and, calculating on the same basis, the Allies must have brought into the field between 37,000 and 38,000 men.

It is next to impossible to arrive at any trustworthy results in attempting to calculate the numerical force of the regiments, either of foot or of horse, they varied so greatly. If, however, eleven imperial regiments of infantry comprised, according to their own admission, 10,000 men, this would give about 900 men to the regiment, which would be considerably under their full strength. Swedish infantry regiments, under Gustavus, were not more than half as strong as the imperial; but after his death the Swedes seem to have adopted, why, it is impossible to divine, the organization of the enemy, unless the latter required less tactical instruction than the former, and the Swedes could no longer command practiced soldiers adapted to the tactics of Gustavus. Consequently, applying the same ratio to the cavalry as seems equitable from the known proportions of the infantry, the former were a little below half their full strength. The allies had 35 regiments of horse, besides 8 squadrons of Hungarian, and 6 squadrons of Croat, light cavalry. Some of the regiments were a great deal stronger than others, and one or two even more so. Averaging, however, if each regiment was a little below half its full or effective number, 35 would give, besides allowing at least 100 to each squadron of light cavalry, 17,500 men.

Conceding the correctness of the imperial estimate, that the infantry on both sides was about equal, the 11 Swedish would furnish, like the 11 imperial, 10,000 men. There were 22 regiments of Swedish horse, besides 3 small detachments about equal to another. Calculating again on the imperial basis that each regiment was less than half its full strength, 23 would give 11,500. This would make the Swedish army, assigning 500 for the service of the artillery, amount to 22,000 men, which is 2,000 over Gindely's estimate; but on the same basis the Allies must have had between 37,000 and 38,000 men, allowing them, as in the Swedish case, 500 for the artillery; all of which is very near the conclusion arrived at years ago, before the possession of data sufficient to enable anything like a correct calculation. There is a great deal of justification for the belief that the Allies were more than one-third stronger than the Swedes; but, although the former claimed an equality in " quality " as well as in " quantity," that is, numbers, it is more than probable that the quality was as far inferior to that of the Swedes, especially in the horse, as it was superior in quantity, particularly in mounted troops, as is conceded.

The result of the battle decided the " Quality ;" for the Allies abandoned the field as runaways, leaving upon it, as confessed, about 5,000 dead and wounded, and 5,000 prisoners, beside the whole of their artillery train and baggage (including gold and silver services), of every kind whatsoever. The Swedish list of casualties nowhere appears, but it is mentioned as " some hundreds." This is very likely, because during this terrible war, when cold steel decided the matter, the pursuit of the defeated amounted to a massacre to such an extent that escape depended entirely upon the speed of the horse. If the infantry did not throw down their arms there were no limits to the slaughter, excepting the fatigue of the butchers, or the hopes of doing better than killing, by ransom or exchange.

It is conceded by German writers that not one-third of the Allies ever came together again and others admit that this defeat cost the emperor 20,000 men, consequently the attributing of a superiority of one-third to the Allies will afford no basis for a charge of exaggeration. The imperial archduke and general looked upon his defeat as an almost indelible disgrace, since his vastly superior forces seem to have made him perfectly confident of victory.

(3.) It is a very remarkable thing that no history, however critical or detailed, of the Thirty Years' War, furnishes *accurate returns of the force of the army by which the greatest actions were performed. Torstenson won all his successes against very great odds. A careful examination has been made and its results set forth as to the numbers opposed to each other at Breitenfeld, or Leipsic II., in 1642. In 1643, when Torstenson invaded Denmark, it is impossible that he could have had over 20,000 men, if near as many, since when he returned, in 1645, to again invade Austria, proper, with all his enlistments and reinforcements, he could only muster 16,000 men for his decisive battle. To Torstenson were opposed, in 1644, not only all the available forces of continental Denmark, proper, but Gindely, writing at Prague, with all the facts before him, states that Gallas was sent to the assistance of the Danes with 22,000 men, by the orders of the Emperor, to dispose of Torstenson forever. On his march northward he was reinforced by the divisions of Bruay and Colloredo, which together must have exceeded 5,000 men, and he was finally reinforced by 1,000 Danish horse and 3,500 foot. This makes 31,500 men. Loccenius says that Gallas was reinforced by a contingent of 10,000 Danes, which would give the imperial commander 37,000 men. With whatever force he did control, " all that Gallas accomplished was to do in eight days "—on the authority of Chemnitz—" more damage to those whom he came to assist than the Swedes, their enemies, had done to them in eight months." The Danes, reduced to 2,000, when Gallas, justly styled " the Destroyer of Armies," was forced by Torstenson again to quit Danish soil, abandoned him on their frontier and of his own army not more than from 1,000 to 2,000, according to different accounts, ever got back to Bohemia, whence they started. Thus Torstenson, in 1642, destroyed two imperial armies at Schweidnitz and at Leipsic. In 1643 he raided Austria to the Danube, in spite of all its armies. In 1644 he eliminated a third army; in 1645 a fourth; and he would have captured Vienna but for the defection of an ally whom he had subsidized—an ally who sold his birthright for a mess of pottage and infected the Swedish camp with the plague that swept away thousands of the best veteran troops. Nevertheless the imperialists never recovered the most important conquests which Torstenson had made and it is due to the victories of Torstenson that the negotiations which resulted in the Peace of Westphalia first, and only after them, concreted from Semblance into Substance.

(4.) Torstenson's battle of Janikau, 1645; Kaufmann's battle at Makram, 1875; Sir Hugh Gough's Ferozesha, 1865; Frederic the Great's position at Hochkirch, 1759; are all analogous cases and remarks appropriate to them are applicable to the Austrian position at Leuthen, 1758; Lee's position at Antietam, 1862; Meade's position at Gettysburg, and Lee's position at Williamsport, 1863; and in a lesser degree, but still similar, to David's victory in the Valley of Rephaim, B.C. 1048; Joab's triumph at Medeba, before Rabbah-Ammon B.C. 1037; at Telamone, B.C. 224; at Chalons, A.D. 451; on the Plains of Aiz-Nadin, A.D. 635; of Loudon, at Leignitz, 1760; of Ziethen, at Torgau, 1760; of Stonewall Jackson, at Chancellorsville, 1863.

"After this he (Skobeleff) entered into some very frank criticisms of his own operations. Speaking of *Maiwand*, he said, ' I have never been able to understand that battle. Poor Burrows evidently had no conception of fighting. He made the great mistake of charging Asiatic cavalry. I would never have done so. *My maxim in warfare is this—always fight the enemy with a weapon in which he is deficient.* If he has good cavalry, do not charge him with cavalry; if his discipline is perfect, do not try to beat him in discipline. You have read my instructions to the officers before Geok Tepe. * * * Those instructions were framed with great care and contain my views on the subject. The Asiatic has no idea of manœuvring. Do you know the battle of Makram ? That was a splendid battle and redounds to the glory of Kaufmann. * * * Do you know that our operations at Makram were suggested by Sir Hugh Gough's battle at Ferozesha ? . * * * Briefly, the battle of Makram was as follows: The fort occupied a position on the banks of the Syr Daria, sufficiently close to a chain of mountains for the Khokandese to attempt to bar the Russian advance up the valley, by running out an earthwork towards it, armed with sixty-eight cannon, all pointed towards the invaders; and by continuing the line of defence to the foot of the hills themselves, by stationing in the intervening ground a huge mass of cavalry.

At the back of the fort, the settlement of Makram, with its numerous gardens, was held by infantry; the fort itself was armed with guns and the hills flanking the position were crowded with skirmishers. On the opposite side of the river, the position was rendered unapproachable by swamps. On coming in sight of this barricade, held by 60,000 Khokandese, General Kaufmann reconnoitred the position with his staff. Although he had only a mere handful of troops, he decided to make an attack the next day, to prevent the enemy from overrunning the country.' Skobeleff may as well relate, in his own words, what followed. 'Having surveyed the position, he turned to his staff and said, "Who knows anything about the battle of Ferozesha?" I had read all about it, but waited for the other officers to reply. No one knowing anything about it, I described the battle.' Here he drew a rough sketch of the Punjaub, and said, "As you know, Mr. Marvin, Sir Hugh Gough, the father of the General Gough in Afghanistan during the late war, pitched his camp alongside the enemy's at Ferozesha, without reconnoitering the ground; and when they fired into it, he fought at once and lost several thousand men. ☞ The next day he reconnoitred the position, and *found a hill on the flank, that enfiladed it.* Marching thither, he inflicted a crushing defeat on the enemy with a loss of only eighteen men.' ☞ Turning again to the plan of Makram, he said: '*There was a hill on the left flank, at the rear of the Khokandese position,* which corresponded with that at Ferozesha. It is now called the Peak of Kaufmann. The next day we marched straight in that direction, keeping all the way on elevated ground alongside the mountains, until the enemy's position was outflanked. Then we changed front; turning our back upon the hills and our faces to Makram, and, marching straight towards it, swept the enemy right into the river. The river was quite black with heads. Twenty thousand Khokandese perished. I commanded the cavalry that day. The account of Ferozesha I read originally in French, but more recently in English. Makram was a splendid laurel for Kaufmann.' Schuyler in his 'Turkistan,' gives an account of this battle, in which he erroneously ascribes the turning movement to the suggestion of General Golovatcheff, who carried out the Yomood massacre in Khiva, in 1873, two years earlier. * * * Makram was one of the most decisive battles fought by the Russians in Central Asia. It completely crushed the Khokandese and put an end to all ideas of a Mussulman rising against Russia."—*The Russian Advances Towards India,* pp. 106–110, by CHARLES MARVIN. London, 1882.

(5). Page 62, Battle of Breitenfeld or Leipsic II. The list of prisoners captured by Torstenson at Leipsic, in 1642, shows how many unmilitary dependants were attached to the staffs of generals, especially the Archduke Leopold. Among these useless mouths were two servants, charged with the care of the silver plate (which silver utensils became the prey of the Swedes), one beadle attached to his chapel, one head-falconer, one apparitor or door-keeper, one flower-gardener, one usher, besides others of the same kind. In addition to the gold and silver table services, captured by the Swedes, the Archduke carried with him into the field many precious objects of art and luxury; among these a *Madonna* of great value, by ALBRECHT DÜRER, which Torstenson presented to his own wife, who, like the spouses of Baner, Mercy and other leaders of the time, followed her husband's fortunes in the campaign and battle. This lady was captured, in 1645, among the baggage trains in the fight of Janikau, by the celebrated Bavarian trooper, John von Werth, and released by a charge led by her gallant husband.

In a review of the "Literature of the Thirty Years' War," endeavor was made to indicate the most trustworthy authorities. Since then a number have been received from Europe, of which by far the most valuable, because it carries within itself the testimony of its efforts at impartiality and access to documentary evidence, hitherto inaccessible, inestimable in arriving at conclusions and determining judgments of men and matters under treatment. This work is the "*Geschichte | des | deutschen Reiches | unter der Regierung Ferdinands III., | nach handschriftlichen Quellen, | von M. Koch, | mit Unterstutzung der Kaiserl. Akademie der Wissenschaften.*" In 2 vols., 8vo., Wien, 1866.

In Vol. I., pp. 364–368, Koch presents a very fair and clear narrative of the Battle of Breitenfeld, 2d November, 1642, and admits that the Austrians and Saxons had 16,000 cavalry and 10,000 infantry to 10,000 Swedish horse and the same number of foot. He shows that the Archduke Leopold behaved with exceeding courage. When everything seemed lost, like the veteran Roman consul, Æmilius Paullus, worthy a better fate, he dismounted from his horse and cast in his lot with the still resisting infantry. Two of his lieutenants, Puchheim and Borneval, had trouble to find him, seized him by the arms and dragged him out of the churm of battle by force. The Archduke was most grieved that he had not fallen among the glorious dead and sacrificed his life with them, especially the infantry, "the old, veteran, picked footsoldiery, which millions in money could not replace." Again, Vol. I., 475, he more than justifies the calculation of page 62 of this pamphlet, as to the force which Torstenson led into Holstein;

5,000 infantry, 6,000 cavalry and three regiments of dragoons—a total of between 12,000 and 13,500 men, if as many. The conclusion drawn, that Torstenson did not have over 20,000 was intended to include the flying corps of Konigsmark and all other partisans, who, while under the command of the great Swedish marshal-in-chief, were acting independently as to the immediate supervision of the generalissimo. Koch says (I., 480) that Gallas, including the divisions of Brouay and Colloredo, had 10,000 infantry and 12,000 cavalry; but this estimate does not include the troops under Hatzfeld, who was opposing Konigsmark, nor the "*Schnapphahne*" (Danish Free-Corps or Sharpshooters) nor the Danish regulars which subsequently joined the Imperial commander; neither the Saxon cavalry, with which, at a later date, Gallas was reinforced.

It is curious in this connection to discover, amid many other instances, how history repeats itself. The story goes that it was reported to Lincoln, after the fall of Forts Henry and Donelson, that Grant was in the habit of getting drunk. The President, instead of taking umbrage, or being influenced against Grant on that account, declared that, if he knew what particular kind of whiskey Grant used, even to the excess alleged, he would, if possible, procure a big lot of the same stuff and send a demijohn of it to every general in the service. In the same way as charged against Grant, the most able Baner is said to have been accustomed to get intoxicated and stay drunk for three or four days together. While in this condition, he maintained that he conceived his very best plans of operation. Koch (I., 270, 15) says that Gallas had just the same inordinate addiction to liquor, in common with the Swedish hero, but, instead of deriving inspiration from his indulgence, the little military ability which he possessed at other times entirely evaporated when he was in his cups. Thus the same bright ideas which, it was said (whether truly or falsely), were engendered in Baner and in Grant by wine or by whiskey, were never present with Gallas when in his potations; to which he resorted if perplexed, to such an extent, indeed, that when shut up in Magdeburg by Torstenson, he was accustomed to get drunk three times a day, to drown his worry in the oblivion of debauch.

Koch is the only author examined who dares to bring any charge of want of humanity, in opposition to Feil, another Austrian (see pp. 27–28, *supra*), against Torstenson (II. 75–76). He says, that " when Torstenson could no longer continue the glorious career of his activity, it would appear that his failure before Brunn had a powerful influence upon him. He no longer exhibited the equanimity which until then had characterized him, and, according to a Swedish correspondent (Who?) previously cited, he says ' he goes about like a shadow on the wall,' and suffers on account of this failure [before Brunn], in his head, rather than in his feet, the severest torments of the gout. His previous customary urbanity and self-possession is changed into an indescribable impatience and fury. It is impossible to decide whether he is changed (unjust ascription) on account of the loss of his reputation before Brunn, or through having drawn upon himself for the same reason the disfavor of our Crown of Sweden." Koch does not give the name of this calumniator, who doubtless was some one smarting under some application of Torstenson's discipline, which, it is well known, struck high and low, whoever deserved it, alike. Old Hermann Wrangel might have written just such a letter. The answer to the whole paragraph is the fact that Torstenson was so crippled by the gout in his head and chest he had to seek perfect repose, but, as soon as better, he was supreme in the war-councils of his country and commander, if not in the field, through direction. Moreover, honors flowed in upon him from queen and country and to an extent unsurpassed he held the affection and respect of sovereign, peers and the people.

CONCLUSION.—Bildad, the Shuite (Job, viii. 8, 10, revised version), observes, " For enquire, I pray thee, of the former age, and apply thyself to that which their fathers have searched out. Shall not they teach thee, and tell thee, and utter words out of their heart?" Martin, the noted Walloon critic, furnishes the following paraphrase of these verses, which is very clear : " The events of the past shall they not serve for instruction." Bearing this in mind, although few lessons can be learned from the records of the Thirty Years' War applicable to this age of enormous armies—of nations under arms and in the field—of weight and rapidity of fire, when each regiment is an enormous self-transporting mittrailleuse or Gatling gun; when the main question of supplying such vast aggregations of men and animals, tax the gigantic powers of steam machinery simply for their transportation; nevertheless, the great, nay the greatest, lesson presents itself in every form and force—the effect of single minds upon men and events. Leaving aside campaigns, the battles of that war were won by superlative strategy or rather stratagem—throwing out accidents, which belong to another consideration—than by veteran valor. Macchiavelli was right when he declared, " Men, iron, money and food are the sinews of war;" but, however astute, he was wrong when he added that, " Men and iron are the most necessary, for men and iron find money, while money and food can find neither men nor iron." This assertion might seem true on the face, but reflection will show that it is not so. Gustavus had the best of troops and a more than sufficiency of iron,

Nevertheless the subsidies of France were indispensable to him before he could move to advantage. To acquire the knowledge of the secret governing springs of this, and, in fact, every war, makes the revelations of the literature of the Thirty Years' War so exceedingly valuable. As it was in the case of Gustavus so it was in that of Frederic the Great. To the latter the subsidies of England were as young blood in Prussia's depleted and impoverished veins and the money-aid of the same opulent power acted as stimulating and sustaining food to coalition after coalition against the most recent Attila, Napoleon. Montecuculi, one of the most sagacious of experienced soldiers, when asked what was most necessary to the carrying on of war, answered "Money!" and to a second question, "What next?" replied, "More money!" When pressed with a third inquiry, "What then?" he responded, "Still more money!" Satirical old Butler was right:

"Money, th' only power,
That all mankind bows down before."

What makes the literature of the Thirty Years' War so interesting and valuable to those who hunger and thirst for the fruits of experience and the fountains of wisdom in the Past, for sustenance, body and mind, in the Future, is the fullness of the feast to *healthy* digestion. Men were not more ignorant in any practical line two hundred years ago than now and they were much better read in the Humanities, which contain perfect bonanzas now lost, it would appear, like some of the mines of Peru, only a short period since of apparently inexhaustible richness. If this literature teaches nothing else it confirms Polybius, "What in war is without an objective or fore-plan does not deserve the title of an [military] operation." However, as the same very great writer and philosopher admits, "Fortune is more powerful than the genius of great men," how necessary is it to learn that there have been men who seem to have been able even to control Fortune; and how very superior must have been such a man as Torstenson, who, as Sporchil admits, "may be said to have subjected Fortune to his genius and experience;" justifying the boast of Tamerlane, "We have compelled Fortune herself to watch over the prosperity of our empire." Or, as Dryden reads, in his "Don Sebastian:"

"*In all my wars, good Fortune flew before me;
Sublime I sat in triumph on her wheel!*"

(*List of Publications, continued from second page of cover.*)

ARTICLES published in *United Service Magazine* (equal in matter to 12mo. volumes): Torstenson and the Battle of Janikau, July, 1879; Joshua and the Battle of Beth-horon—Did the Sun and Moon stand still? February, 1880; Hannibal, July, 1880; Gustavus Adolphus, Sept., 1880; Cavalry, I., Sept., 1880; Cavalry, II., Nov., 1880; Cavalry, III., Dec., 1880; Army Catastrophes—Destruction of Pharaoh and his host; how accomplished, &c., &c. February, 1881.—Hannibal's Army of Italy, Mar., 1881; Hannibal's Last Campaign, May, 1881; Infantry, I., June, 1881; Infantry, II., Aug., 1881; Battle of Eutaw Springs, 1781, Sept., 1881; Siege of Yorktown, 1781, Nov. 1881; Infantry, III, April, 1882; Waterloo, July, 1882; Vindication of James Hepburn, Earl of Bothwell, Sept., 1882, Oct., 1882; From the Rapidan to Appomattox Court House, July, 1883.—Burgoyne's Campaign, July-Oct., 1777, and Appendix, Oct., 1883.—Life and Achievements of Field-Marshal Generalissimo Suworrow, November-December, 1883.—Biographical Sketch of Maj.-Gen. Andrew Atkinson Humphreys, U. S. A., March 1884.—Address, Maj.-Gen. A. A. Humphreys, before the Third Army Corps Union, 5th May, 1884. Character and Services of Maj.-Gen. A. A. Humphreys, U. S. A., Manhattan, N. Y., Monthly Magazine, August, 1884.

Suggestions which laid the basis for the present admirable Paid Fire Department in the City of New York, in which, as well as in the Organization of the present Municipal Police of New York City, Gen. de Peyster was a co-laborer with the Hon. Jas. W. Gerard, and G. W. Matsell, for which latter Department he caused to be prepared and presented a Fire Escape, a model of simplicity and inestimable utility. Republished in the *New York Historical Magazine*. Supplement, Vol. IX., 1865. John G. Shea, Editor and Proprietor.

The Pearl of Pearls, or the "Wild Brunswicker" and his "Queen of Hearts:" a novel, founded on facts. 1865.—Mary Stuart: a Study. 1882; James Hepburn, Earl of Bothwell: a Vindication, 1882; Bothwell and Mary Stuart: an Enquiry and a Justification. 1883.—Bothwell, an Historical Drama, 1884.—The Life and Military Services of Sir John Johnson, Bart. 1882.—Notices and Correspondence of Col. A. S. de Peyster and Brig.-Gen. Sir John Johnson, Bart., during and after the American Revolution, 1776, &c. 1884.

State Sovereignty. 1861.—Life and Services of the great Russian Field-Marshal Suworrow. 1882.—La Royale, the Grand Hunt [or Last Campaign of the Army of the Potomac], Nos. I., II., III., IV., V., VI., 1872; VII., 1873; VIII., 1871.—Battles of Fredericksburg, Chancellorsville and Gettysburg, in *Onward*, a monthly, 1869-70.—And Gettysburg and Williamsport, in the *Soldiers' Friend*, a weekly, 1870.—Col. J. Watts de Peyster, Jr., U. S. V., A Threnody. 1874.—Sir John Johnson, Bart.: An Address delivered before the N. Y. Historical Society, 6th Jan., 1880, with two voluminous Appendices of Authorities.

Centennial Sketches of the American Revolution, which appeared in the N. Y. *Times*, and especially in the N. Y. *Evening Mail*, and *Mail* and *Express*. 1776-82.—Decisive Conflicts of the late Civil War or "Slaveholders' Rebellion:" I. Shiloh, Antietam, &c., 1867; II. Murfreesboro to Chattanooga, &c., 1866; III. Gettysburg, 1867; IV. Nashville, 1876.—Biographical notices of Major-Generals Philip Schuyler—Address delivered before the N. Y. Historical Society, 2d Jan., 1877; Geo. H. Thomas, (likewise two Addresses delivered on the same subject before the N. Y. Historical Society, 5th Jan. 1875, and Jan. 1876); also, of Bancroft, Burnside, Crawford, Heintzleman, Hooker, Humphreys, McAllister, Mahone, Meade, Edwards Pierrepont, Pleasanton, Sickles, Tremaine, &c., &c.

The Battles of Monmouth and Capture of Stony Point: a series of voluminous and exhaustive articles published in the *Monmouth Enquirer*, N. J., 1879.—Eclaireur (The), A Military Journal, Vols. II. and III., edited 1854-5.

History of the Third Corps, Army of the Potomac, 1861-65. This title, although not technically, is virtually correct, for in a series of elaborate articles in dailies, weeklies, monthlies, monographs, addresses, &c., everything relating to this Corps, even to smallest details, from 1861 to 1865, was prepared with care, and put in print. These articles appeared in the *Citizen*, and the *Citizen and Round Table;* in *Foley's Volunteer*, and *Soldiers' and Sailors' Half-Dime Tales of the late Rebellion;* in Mayne Reid's magazine *Onward;* in Chaplain Bourne's *Soldiers' Friend;* in "*La Royale or Grand Hunt* [or the Last Campaign] *of the Army of the Potomac*, from Petersburg to Appomattox Court House, April 2-9, 1865," illustrated with engraved likenesses of several of the prominent Generals belonging to the corps, and careful maps and plans; in the life of Major-General Philip Kearny; in the "Third Corps at Gettysburg; General Sickles Vindicated" * * Vol. I., Nos. xi., xii., xiii. *The Volunteer*, in a Speech delivered before the Third Army Corps Union, 5th May, 1875 profusely illustrated with portraits of Generals who commanded, or belonged to that organization, &c. These arranged and condensed would constitute a work of five or six volumes 8vo., such as those prepared by Prof. John W. Draper, entitled the "Civil War in America," but were never given as bound volumes to the public, because the expense was so great that the author, who merely writes for credit and amusement, was unwilling to assume the larger outlay, in addition to what he had already expended on the purchase of authorities, clerk-hire, printing, &c., &c.

# FRANCESCA DA RIMINI.[1]

---

### Dante's Inferno, Canto V., Verses 73-123.[2]

AN ATTEMPT AT A LITERAL TRANSLATION IN BLANK VERSE.

---

"Jerusalem remembered, in the days of her affliction and of her miseries, all her pleasant things that she had in the days of old."
LAMENTATIONS OF JEREMIAH.

"Comfort? Comfort scorn'd of devils! this is Truth the poet sings,
That a *sorrow's crown of sorrow is remembering happier things.*"
TENNYSON'S "*Locksley Hall.*"

DANTE to VIRGIL. —" Poet, gladly
Would I accost those two who float together,
And seem to sweep so buoyant on the wind!"

VIRGIL. To me replying, "Thou shalt see," he said,
"When they draw near; then confidence invite
By that great love that guides them, and they'll come."

DANTE. Soon as the eddy wafts them near to us,
I raise my voice, "Oh, spirits worn with grief,
Approach and speak if answer naught forbid."
As doves incited by desire, with wings
Firm and distended, fly to welcome nest,
Cleave through the air and onward borne by will,

So these, from throng which crowded Dido round,
Approach us through the evil atmosphere.

FRANCESCA. "Oh, mortal creature, gracious and benign,
Who visits us through black, empurpled air,
We, who, with blood [our own] distain'd the earth,
If friendly He, who rules the universe,
Our prayers we'll offer to Him for thy peace,
Seeing thou pitiest our misfortune dire;
Of what it pleases thee to hear and speak,
We will both listen and [in turn] relate,
While yet the wind ceases to interrupt.
The city² where [Francesca], I, was born,
Is seated on the coast where Po descends,
To rest in peace with tributary streams.¹
Love, that instinctive springs in gentle heart,³
Made him a captive with the gracious form,
Of which I was bereft in way still grieves;
Love, which to no one lov'd admits excuse
From loving [in return] fill'd me with such delight,
That e'en now, as thou see'st, it leaves me not.
Love led us to one death. The lowest hell⁶
Awaits the murd'rous hand⁵ that quench'd our lives"—

DANTE. These were the very words address'd to us.
(*To Virgil.*) "Ah, what sweet thoughts, what mutual desire
Brought these two lovers to such woful pass!"

\*   \*   \*   \*

(*To Francesca.*)
Thy torments, oh, Francesca, make me weep
And call forth tears of pity and of grief;
But tell me how, in time of the sweet sighs

And in what manner Love reveal'd to you
Desires, uncertain yet, that fill'd your hearts."
FRANCESCA.   Then she replied, "There is no greater pang
Than to recall the happy times by-gone
In present wretchedness; thy guide knows this;
But if thou dost desire, eagerly, to learn
The earliest germination of our love,
I will't impart, as one who weeps and tells.
One day for pastime, we, together, read
Of Lancelot,[8] and how love enthrall'd him.
We sat alone all innocent of guile:
Oft what we read compell'd our eyes to meet
And made the blood suffuse or quit our cheeks:[9]
One thought it was did both us overcome,
When read we how the smile desiring fondly
For kiss of such a lover [Lancelot]
He [Paolo] who from me shall parted never be.
Kiss'd me upon the mouth[10] all tremblingly:—
The book—the author it was Galeotto—
After *that* kiss we read that day no more."

J. W. DE P.

# NOTES

[1] The same idea is to be found in Boethius—Dante—Chaucer. For an illustration see Bohn's "J. C. Wright's Translation of Dante, Flaxman's Illustrations." Sketch, "The Lovers Punished," p. 23.

This episode of Francesca da Rimini has been translated by a number of English poets; among these, last and greatest, Byron. Even Carlyle has tried his hand at it; but none have succeeded in giving the force of the original—the concise, yet exquisitely tender, comprehensiveness of the *Divina Commedia*. This endeavor aims at condensing this translation into as few words as the Italian and yet afford a full development of the sense. Dante was perhaps the most original of all poets, and yet he borrowed from the Bible many ideas which give his verses strength, while others have borrowed from him and lost the force of the original.

[2] Canto V. of DANTE's "*Inferno*" treats of "The Second Circle, or proper commencement of Hell, and Minos, the Infernal Judge, at its entrance. It contains the souls of carnal sinners and their punishment consists in being driven about incessantly, in total darkness, by fierce winds. First among them comes Semiramis the Babylonian queen, Dido, Cleopatra, Helena, Achilles, Paris, and a great multitude of others pass in succession."

"Dante is overcome and bewildered with pity at the sight of them, when his attention is suddenly attracted to Two Spirits that keep together and seem strangely light upon the wind. He is unable to speak for some time, after finding that it is Francesca of Rimini, with her lover Paolo, and falls to the ground, as if dead, when he has heard the painful story. Francesca was the daughter of Guido Vecchio da Polenta, Lord of Ravenna, and was given in marriage to Gianciotto, or Giovanni Sciancato (John the lame, or hipshot), eldest son of Malatesta Vecchio, Lord or Tyrant of Rimini. Paolo, her lover, was a younger son of Malatesta. They were surprised and slain together by the husband, about the year 1288; and buried in the same grave. Guido Novello, the true and generous friend with whom Dante resided at Ravenna, was the son of Francesca's brother, Ostagio da Polenta."

"The facts of Francesca's story are given by Hieronymus Rubens, in his Hist. Ravennat. Venetiis, 1572, fol.; lib.: vi., p. 308–9. The genealogy of the Guidos is given at the end, and completely agrees with and explains all that is said respecting them by Boccaccio, Benvenuto da Imola, and the other early commentators. A later edition (1603) of the same work places the death of Francesca and her lover at the commencement of the year 1289. In the first edition it is placed between 1287 and 1289."—CARLYLE.

³ Ravenna.

⁴ "With sequent streams seeking rest in the sea " [Adriatic].—CAREY.

⁵ Love through the eye; the love of inexperienced youth is something like Mary Stuart's sudden, insane, soon-repented passion for Darnley. There is another instantaneous love, like that Shakspeare depicts in Romeo and Juliet :

"The fire of love in gentle heart is caught,
As virtue in the precious stone."

Or, better :

"The light of love in gentle heart's reflected,
As is the sunlight in a drop of dew."

⁶ Caina.—Cain's place in the lowest circle of Hell, occupied by fratricides, etc. CANTO XXVII.

⁷ By the murderous stroke of Lanciotto, malformed husband of Francesca and brother of Paolo.

⁸ "LANCELOT OF THE LAKE, in the old Romances of the Round Table, is described as "the greatest knight of all the world," and his love for Queen Guenever, or Ginevra, is infinite. Galeotto, Galishant, or Sir Galahad, is he who gives such a detailed declaration of Lancelot's love to the Queen, and is to them, in the romance, what the book and its author are here to Francesca and Paolo."—CARLYLE.

⁹ Any man who has been in love, and as yet uncertain of his fate, if his observation was vivid and his memory tenacious, he must recall the alternating flushes of hope and the pallid ashen of despair, while awaiting the spoken or silent reply of word or act that crowned his hopes or precipitated them into the abyss of despair.

"Il Riso d'Iddio," "The smile of the deity," the dawn of love; the smile never seen but at the very moment of the inception of love, or perhaps the perception of love's living existence, when the lips part with the intensest earnestness of desire to express all that the heart feels and yet cannot, from the very inadequacy of words, while the whole face is irradiated with a glory and a sentiment it has never shown before and is never to know again. This is the smile to which Dante refers, and which no one can recognize but one who has loved in the fullest signification of love.

[10] The "kiss upon the mouth" has inspired some of the finest poetry in every language, heathen, Mahomedan and modern. A few illustrations must suffice, viz.:

QUEEN. "Fain would I tell thee what I feel within.
But Shame and Modesty have ty'd my Tongue!
Yet, I will tell, that thou may'st weep with me.
How dear, how sweet his first Embraces were!
*With what a Zeal he join'd his Lips to mine!*
*And sucked my Breath at every Word I spoke,*
*As if he drew his Inspiration thence:*
*While both our Souls came upward to our Mouths,*
As neighboring Monarchs at their Borders meet:
I thought: Oh, no; 'Tis false: I could not think,
'Twas neither Life nor Death, but both in one."
                              DRYDEN'S *"Spanish Fryar."*

"My heart can kiss no heart but thine,
And if these lips but rarely pine
    In the pale abstinence of sorrow,
It is that nightly I divine,
As I this world-sick soul recline,
    I shall be with thee ere the morrow."

"We had talked long; and then a silence came,
    And in the topmost firs
To her nest the white dove floated like a flame;
    And my lips closed on hers
Who was the only she,
And in one girl all womanhood to me."

MARIAN. "You are a wanton."

ROBIN HOOD. "One I do confess
I *want*-ed till you came; but now I have you
I'll grow to your embraces till two souls,
Distilled into kisses through our lips,
Do make one spirit of love."

"'Sweet Helen, make me immortal with a kiss.'"
Her lips suck forth my soul; see, where it flies
'Oh, let me live forever on those lips!
The nectar of the gods to these is tasteless.'"

In an old Latin religious commentary in my possession, published in 1565, *i. e.* over three hundred years ago, and just about seventy-five years before my people came to this country, the following note occurs on the first words of Solomon's "Song of Songs," I., 2. (Read in this connection verses 2, 3. 10, 11, Chap. IV.; verses 13 and 16, Chap. V.; verse 9, Chap. VII.) : "*Vere amat, qui vere dat osculum.*" I translate the Latin of the original, "He truly loves who [knows how to give a kiss truly, or] truly kisses. For the spirit poured forth our heart finds the ambassador of real love in a kiss. Thus [through such a kiss] we learn the truth and that the love thus expressed is not a feigned passion."

Curious truth to be found in an old monkish Latin commentary upon Solomon's Hebrew idyl, which is said to be the loveliest of the kind ever written. It is lovely if properly read. The description of Spring, in Chapter II., verses 11—13, is not susceptible of improvement. Those who seek for evil everywhere may find much that is suggestive in Solomon, but, rightly taken, there is more that is unmistakenbly pure and sweet.

> "Last night, when some one spoke his name,
> From my swift blood that went and came
> A thousand little shafts of flame,
> Were shiver'd in my narrow frame.
> *O Love, O fire! once he drew
> With one long kiss, my whole soul thro'
> My lips, as sunlight drinketh dew.*
>
> "My whole soul waiting silently,
> All naked, in a sultry sky,
> Droops blinded with his shining eye ;
> I *will* possess him or will die.
> I will grow round him in his place,
> Grow, love, die, looking on his face.
> Die, dying clasp'd in his embrace."
> TENNYSON'S "*Fatima.*"

www.ingramcontent.com/pod-product-compliance
Lightning Source LLC
Chambersburg PA
CBHW031947230426
43672CB00010B/2082